D1109655

DISCUSSIONS OF LITERATURE

429

discussions of **poetry**

FORM AND STRUCTURE

Edited with an Introduction by
FRANCIS MURPHY, Smith College

D. C. HEATH AND COMPANY
BOSTON

Copyright 1964 by D. C. Heath and Company
No part of the material covered by this copyright may be reproduced for any purpose without written permission of the publisher.
Printed in the United States of America

Printed February 1965

Library
I.U.P.
Indiana, Pa.
426 M953
c.2

CONTENTS

INTRODUCTION

The essays in this volume are concerned with form in poetry exclusive of imagery and meter. Together with two other volumes in this series, George Hemphill's *Rhythm and Sound* and a volume in preparation, *Metaphor and Symbol,* these discussions consider four aspects of poetry: rhetorical structure, minor forms (metaphor, symbol, imagery, those forms whose effects partly depend upon their function within the whole), conventional form and sound. These aspects of form are here defined in Kenneth Burke's "The Nature of Form" and explored by Yvor Winters in his essay on "The Experimental School in American Poetry: An Analytical Survey of its Structural Methods Exclusive of Meter."

It is a curious fact that most current formal criticism deals almost exclusively with the pattern of imagery or metaphorical structure. No one would argue with Aristotle's dictum that for a poet "the greatest thing by far is to have a command of metaphor." Yet a poem is not merely an accumulation of words but an accumulation of words in a certain order. A poem has a rhetorical structure as well as a metaphorical one. All poetry is, in this sense, poetry of statement, regardless of whether or not the matter of the poem is presented—as in imagist poetry—in a qualitative or associative rather than logical way.

Mr. Burke and others have distinguished three kinds of rhetorical structure: repetitive, progressive, and syllogistic. Three brief examples may help to make these distinctions clear. The opening lines of Whitman's "Song of Myself" might serve as a familiar example of repetitive structure:

> I celebrate myself and sing myself,
> And what I assume you shall assume,
> For every atom belonging to me as good belongs to you.
>
> I loafe and invite my soul,
> I lean and loafe at my ease observing a spear of grass.

> My tongue, every atom of my blood, form'd from this soil,
> this air,
> Born here of parents born here from parents the same,
> and their parents the same,
> I, now thirty-seven years old in perfect health begin,
> Hoping to cease not till death. . . .

This is a poem of a great singer. The poet argues nothing (he removes the possibility of differences with his reader in the second line), he affirms. His catalogues make the world an infinite chain of relations. The form of this poem might be described as theme and variations. It is cumulative in effect and rhapsodic in tone. In spite of seeming progression, the poem takes us nowhere, its stanzas are interchangeable. In the opening line (composed of two clauses identical in meaning) the poet declares his intention, the remaining lines of the poem expand and explore the implications. Free verse (the adjective is a metaphor expressive of the spirit not the structure of this kind of verse) by depriving the writer of the two most conventional media, meter and rhyme, is apt to throw him back on other structural devices: balance, repetition, parallelism of clauses, the paragraph as a unit of thought. Two essays in this volume, R. G. Moulton's "Parallelism: the Basis of Biblical Verse," and Gay Wilson Allen's "Walt Whitman: the Search for a Democratic Structure," explore devices of repetitive structure. William Empson, in his essay on Sidney's double sestina, "You Gote-heard Gods, that love the grassie mountaines," looks at repetitive structure in a conventional form.

We might describe the poem which follows as narrative or progressive in structure; we share with the writer her attempt to discover a word which will best characterize her peculiarly anxious and cautious progress through life:

> I stepped from Plank to Plank
> A slow and cautious way
> The Stars about my head I felt
> About my Feet the Sea.
>
> I knew not but the next
> Would be my final inch—
> This gave me that precarious Gait
> Some call Experience.

For Emily Dickinson, life is full of inherent dangers. She has experienced too much hurt to proceed through life in anything but a skeptical way. We move from day to day, she tells us, at the mercy of the pirate Fate and we walk the plank never knowing when everything will be void beneath us. The placement of the word "felt" and the repeated "about," the curious near-rhymes, all contribute to our sense of the writer's insecurity. Unlike repetitive structure, narrative structure unfolds step by step. We share in the rightness of the conclusion.

In this way syllogistic structure shares with progressive structure a movement toward resolution. It is the structure of a perfectly conducted argument. In John Donne's "Death Be Not Proud," for example, the first lines set forth the conclusion to be proved: "Death be not proud, though some have called thee/ Mighty and dreadful, for thou art not so. . ." The speaker proceeds to destroy his enemy Death by the reasonableness of his argument: Death is mistaken, Immortality destroys Death; we are not slaves to Death but rather Death is a slave to himself:

> Thou'rt slave to fate, chance, kings and desperate men,
> And dost with poison, war, and sickness dwell . . .

Donne seems to delight in the framework of argument. He is at his wittiest and most sophistical in "The Flea," a poem which intends to shock us by the contrasting nature of its passionate subject (the persuasion to love) and its methodical, syllogistic structure. J. V. Cunningham's essay "Logic and Lyric" explores syllogistic argument in Marvell, Dunbar, and Nashe. His reading of "To His Coy Mistress" is usefully supplemented by Francis Berry's study of that poem's resolution through tense and mood in "The Metaphysicals' Craft of the Verb."

"The way a language constructs its sentences," Josephine Miles has written, "is the way it constructs its poems." Miss Miles's essay "The Sublime Poem" explores the implications of this statement in attempting to characterize the "panoramic" poem of the eighteenth century. Rachel Trickett's essay "The Idiom of Augustan Poetry," printed here for the first time, deals with what she calls the "discoursive structure" of Pope and Johnson. Both of these essays explore rhetorical structure in an effort to define poetic genre.

One essay in this volume may seem to belong more properly in a discussion of rhyme and sound than in a volume on rhetorical structure, William Wimsatt's "One Relation of Rhyme to Reason." I have included it here because it seems to me that Mr. Wimsatt's conclusion that rhyme serves as a greater contribution to poetic structure than mere likeness of sound, that it imposes upon "the logical pattern of expressed argument a kind of fixative counter-pattern of alogical implication," is a unique contribution to the analysis of rhetorical structure.

A word remains to be said about the essays on conventional form which conclude this volume. "Any form," Burke writes, "can become conventional and be sought for itself—whether it be as complex as the Greek tragedy or as compact as the sonnet." In conventional form the "element of categorical expectancy is essential. That is, whereas the anticipations and gratifications of progressive and repetitive form arise *during the process* of reading, the expectation of conventional form may be *anterior* to the reading." The number of fixed forms used by English poets is not large, nor is it a subject that has attracted a great deal of critical attention. Perhaps only the sonnet, the ballad, and the couplet elicit anterior response in English poetry today. The ode, while conventional in various periods in subject (that is, a hymn of praise to an heroic subject in the seventeenth and eighteenth centuries and a hymn to the imagination in the nineteenth), has no conventional stanza form. I have, therefore, made no effort at inclusiveness, but have, rather, selected four essays which seem to me to offer, both in method and content, possibilities for approaching the question of conventional form in lyric poetry: Edward Hubler, in his essay on "Form and Matter," explores, with particular attention to argument, Shakespeare's use of sonnet form; Catherine Ing looks at juxtaposition and parallelism in the song forms of Spenser, Shakespeare and Donne; William Empson's essay on Sidney's double sestina is a study of verbal ambiguity in a complex repetitive form; and Walter Jackson Bate explores Keats's reworking of a conventional form in his essay "Keats's Odes of May, 1819."

FRANCIS MURPHY

a note on the
CONTRIBUTORS

gay wilson allen is the leading authority in America on the work of Walt Whitman. His numerous published works include: *American Prosody* (1935), *Walt Whitman Handbook* (1946), and *The Solitary Singer* (1955). He teaches at New York University.

walter jackson bate is Professor of English and Chairman of the Department at Harvard. His published works include: *The Stylistic Development of Keats* (1945), *From Classic to Romantic* (1946), and *The Achievement of Samuel Johnson* (1955), which received the Christian Gauss award for criticism.

francis berry teaches at Sheffield University, England. He has published several volumes of poetry and in addition to *Poet's Grammar* (1958) is the author of *Poetry and the Physical Voice* (1962).

kenneth burke taught for many years at Bennington College and now lives in New Jersey. He has published both poetry and fiction. His critical works include: *Counter-Statement* (1931), *The Philosophy of Literary Form* (1941), *A Grammar of Motives* (1945), and *A Rhetoric of Motives* (1950).

j. v. cunningham teaches at Brandeis University. In addition to two volumes of critical studies, *Woe or Wonder* (1951) and *Tradition and Poetic Structure* (1960), he has published a volume of poems and epigrams *The Exclusions of a Rhyme* (1960).

william empson's most recent study is *Milton's God* (1961). He is the author of *Seven Types of Ambiguity* (1930), *Some Versions of Pastoral* (1935), and *The Structure of Complex Words* (1951). His *Collected Poems* was published in 1955. He teaches at Sheffield University, England.

edward hubler teaches at Princeton University. In addition to his study *The Sense of Shakespeare's Sonnets* (1952), he has published *The Riddle of Shakespeare's Sonnets* (1962) and *Shakespeare's Songs and Poems* (1959).

catherine ing is Lecturer in English at Lady Margarett Hall and St. Hilda's College, Oxford. She is at present preparing an edition of the works of Thomas Campion. *Elizabethan Lyrics* was published in 1951.

josephine miles published her *Collected Poems* in 1961. Her critical studies include: *The Vocabulary of Poetry* (1946), *The Continuity of English Poetic Language* (1951) and *Eras and Modes in English Poetry* (1957). She teaches at the University of California at Berkeley.

r. g. moulton (1849–1924) taught for many years at the University of Chicago. He was the distinguished editor of *The Modern Reader's Bible* (1896–1906).

rachel trickett is a Fellow of St. Hugh's College, Oxford. In addition to her critical work she has published four novels, the most recent of which, *A Changing Place,* was published in 1962. Her study of Augustan poetry, *The Honest Muse,* will soon be published.

william k. wimsatt, jr. is Professor of English, Yale University. He published *The Prose Style of Samuel Johnson* in 1941 and *The Verbal Icon* in 1954. In 1957, with Cleanth Brooks, he published *Literary Criticism: A Short History.*

yvor winters teaches at Stanford University. His *Collected Poems* received the Bollingen Prize in 1952. His published works include: *Primitivism and Decadence* (1937), *Maule's Curse* (1938), *Anatomy of Nonsense* (1943), *Edwin Arlington Robinson* (1946) and *In Defense of Reason* (1947).

discussions of

poetry

FORM AND STRUCTURE

kenneth burke

THE NATURE OF FORM

(1) *Form* in literature is an arousing and fulfilment of desires. A work has form insofar as one part of it leads a reader to anticipate another part, to be gratified by the sequence. The five aspects of form may be discussed as progressive form (subdivided into syllogistic and qualitative progression), repetitive form, conventional form, and minor or incidental forms.

(2) *Syllogistic progression* is the form of a perfectly conducted argument, advancing step by step. It is the form of a mystery story, where everything falls together, as in a story of ratiocination by Poe. It is the form of a demonstration in Euclid. To go from A to E through stages B, C, and D is to obtain such form. We call it syllogistic because, given certain things, certain things must follow, the premises forcing the conclusion. In so far as the audience, from its acquaintance with the premises, feels the rightness of the conclusion, the work is formal. The arrows of our desires are turned in a certain direction, and the plot follows the direction of the arrows. The peripety, or reversal of the situation, discussed by Aristotle is obviously one of the keenest manifestations of syllogistic progression. In the course of a single scene, the poet reverses the audience's expectations—as in the third act of Julius Caesar, where Brutus' speech before the mob prepares us for his exoneration, but the speech of Antony immediately after prepares us for his downfall.

(3) *Qualitative progression*, the other aspect of progressive form, is subtler. Instead of one incident in the plot preparing us for some other possible incident of plot (as Macbeth's murder of Duncan prepares us for the dying of Macbeth), the presence of one quality prepares us for the introduction of another (the grotesque seriousness of

From *Counter-Statement*, by Kenneth Burke, originally published by Harcourt, Brace and Company, 1931; reprinted 1953 by Hermes Publications, Los Altos, California. This excerpt on The Nature of Form is the opening section of an essay entitled "Lexicon Rhetoricae." The other sections concern: The Individuation of Forms; Patterns of Experience (subject-matter and forms as combined in the Symbol); Ritual; Permanence, Universality, Perfection.

the murder scene preparing us for the grotesque buffoonery of the porter scene). In T. S. Eliot's The Waste Land, the step from "Ta ta. Goonight. Goonight" to "Good night, ladies, good night, sweet ladies" is a qualitative progression. In Malcolm Cowley's sonnet Mine No. 6 there is a similar kind of qualitative progression, as we turn from the octave's description of a dismal landscape ("the blackened stumps, the ulcerated hill") to the sestet's "Beauty, perfection, I have loved you fiercely." Such progressions are qualitative rather than syllogistic as they lack the pronounced anticipatory nature of the syllogistic progression. We are prepared less to demand a certain qualitative progression than to recognize its rightness after the event. We are put into a state of mind which another state of mind can appropriately follow.

(4) *Repetitive form* is the consistent maintaining of a principle under new guises. It is restatement of the same thing in different ways. Thus, in so far as each detail of Gulliver's life among the Lilliputians is a new exemplification of the discrepancy in size between Gulliver and the Lilliputians, Swift is using repetitive form. A succession of images, each of them regiving the same lyric mood; a character repeating his identity, his "number," under changing situations; the sustaining of an attitude, as in satire; the rhythmic regularity of blank verse; the rhyme scheme of *terza rima*—these are all aspects of repetitive form. By a varying number of details, the reader is led to feel more or less consciously the principle underlying them—he then requires that this principle be observed in the giving of further details. Repetitive form, the restatement of a theme by new details, is basic to any work of art, or to any other kind of orientation, for that matter. It is our only method of "talking on the subject."

(5) *Conventional form* involves to some degree the appeal of form *as form.* Progressive, repetitive, and minor forms may be effective even though the reader has no awareness of their formality. But when a form appeals as form, we designate it as conventional form. Any form can become conventional, and be sought for itself—whether it be as complex as the Greek tragedy or as compact as the sonnet. The invocation to the Muses; the theophany in the play of Euripides; the processional and recessional of the Episcopalian choir; the ensemble before the front drop at the close of a burlesque show; the exordium in Greek-Roman oratory; the Sapphic ode; the triolet—these are all examples of conventional forms having varying degrees of validity today. Perhaps even the Jew-and-the-Irishman of the Broadway stage is an instance of repetitive form grown into conventional form. Poets who write beginnings *as beginnings* and endings *as endings* show the appeal of conventional form. Thus, in Milton's Lycidas we start distinctly with the sense of introduction ("Yet

once more, O ye laurels, and once more . . .") and the poem is brought to its dextrous gliding close by the stanza, clearly an ending: "And now the sun had stretched out all the hills, And now was dropped into the western bay. . . ." But Mother Goose, throwing formal appeal into relief through "nonsense," offers us the clearest instance of conventional form, a "pure" beginning and "pure" end:

I'll tell you a story of Jack O'Norey
  And now my story's begun;
I'll tell you another about his brother
  And now my story is done.

We might note, in conventional form, the element of "categorical expectancy." That is, whereas the anticipations and gratifications of progressive and repetitive form arise *during the process* of reading, the expectations of conventional form may be *anterior to* the reading. If one sets out to read a sonnet, regardless of what the sonnet is to say he makes certain formal demands to which the poem must acquiesce. And similarly, the final Beethoven rejoicing of a Beethoven finale becomes a "categorical expectation" of the symphony. The audience "awaits" it before the first bar of the music has been played. And one may, even before opening a novel, look forward to an opening passage which will proclaim itself an opening.

(6) *Minor or incidental forms.* When analyzing a work of any length, we may find it bristling with minor or incidental forms—such as metaphor, paradox, disclosure, reversal, contraction, expansion, bathos, apostrophe, series, chiasmus—which can be discussed as formal events in themselves. Their effect partially depends upon their function in the whole, yet they manifest sufficient evidences of episodic distinctness to bear consideration apart from their context. Thus a paradox, by carrying an argument one step forward, may have its use as progressive form; and by its continuation of a certain theme may have its use as repetitive form—yet it may be so formally complete in itself that the reader will memorize it as an event valid apart from its setting. A monologue by Shakespeare can be detached from its context and recited with enjoyment because, however integrally it contributes to the whole of which it is a part, it is also an independent curve of plot enclosed by its own beginning and end. The incident of Hamlet's offering the pipes to Guildenstern is a perfect instance of minor form. Euripides, when bringing a messenger upon the stage, would write him a speech which, in its obedience to the rhetorical laws of the times, was a separate miniature form. Edmund Burke sought to give each paragraph a structure as a paragraph, making it a growth, yet so confining it to one aspect of his

subject that the closing sentence of the paragraph could serve as the logical complement to the opening one. Frequently, in the novel, an individual chapter is distinguished by its progress as a chapter, and not solely by its function in the whole. The Elizabethan drama generally has a profusion of minor forms.

(7) *Interrelation of forms.* Progressive, repetitive, and conventional and minor forms necessarily overlap. A specific event in the plot will not be exclusively classifiable under one head—as it should not, since in so organic a thing as a work of art we could not expect to find any principle functioning in isolation from the others. Should we call the aphoristic couplet of the age of Pope repetitive form or conventional form? A closing scene may be syllogistic in that its particular events mark the dramatic conclusion of the dramatic premises; qualitative in that it exemplifies some mood made desirable by the preceding matter; repetitive in that the characters once again proclaim their identity; conventional in that it has about it something categorically terminal, as a farewell or death; and minor or incidental in that it contains a speech displaying a structural rise, development, and fall independently of its context. Perhaps the lines in Othello, beginning "Soft you, a word or two before you go," and ending "Seized by the throat the uncircumcised dog and smote him thus (*stabs himself*)" well exemplify the vigorous presence of all five aspects of form, as this suicide is the logical outcome of his predicament (syllogistic progression); it fits the general mood of gloomy forebodings which has fallen upon us (qualitative progression); the speech has about it that impetuosity and picturesqueness we have learned to associate with Othello (repetitive form); it is very decidedly a conclusion (conventional form), and in its development it is a tiny plot in itself (minor form). The close of the Odyssey strongly combines syllogistic and qualitative progression. Ulysses' vengeance upon the suitors is the logical outcome of their conduct during his absence—and by the time it occurs, the reader is so incensed with them that he exults vindictively in their destruction. In most cases, we can find some aspects of form predominant, with others tenuous to the point of imperceptibility. Keats's Ode to a Nightingale is a striking instance of repetitive form; its successive stanzas take up various aspects of the mood, the *status evanescentiae,* almost as schematically as a lawyer's brief; but of syllogistic form there is barely a trace. . . . As, in musical theory, one chord is capable of various analyses, so in literature the appeal of one event may be explained by various principles. The important thing is not to confine the explanation to *one* principle, but to formulate sufficient principles to make an explanation possible. However, though the five aspects of form can merge into one another, or can be present in vary-

ing degrees, no other terms should be required in an analysis of formal functionings.

(8) *Conflict of forms.* If the various formal principles can intermingle, they can also conflict. An artist may create a character which, by the logic of the fiction, should be destroyed; but he may also have made this character so appealing that the audience wholly desires the character's salvation. Here would be a conflict between syllogistic and qualitative progression. Or he may depict a wicked character who, if the plot is to work correctly, must suddenly "reform," thereby violating repetitive form in the interests of syllogistic progression. To give a maximum sense of reality he may, like Stendhal, attempt to make sentences totally imperceptible as sentences, attempt to make the reader slip over them with no other feeling than their continuity (major progression here involving the atrophy of minor forms). Or conventional form may interfere with repetitive form (as when the drama, in developing from feudal to bourgeois subjects, chose "humbler" themes and characters, yet long retained the ceremonial diction of the earlier dignified period); and conversely, if we today were to attempt regaining some of these earlier ceremonial effects, by writing a play entirely in a ceremonial style, we should be using the appeal of repetitive form, but we should risk violating a contemporary canon of conventional form, since the non-ceremonial, the "domestic" dialogue, is now categorically expected.

(9) *Rhythm, Rhyme.* Rhythm and rhyme being formal, their appeal is to be explained within the terms already given. Rhyme usually accentuates the repetitive principle of art (insofar as one rhyme determines our expectation of another, and insofar as the rhyme-scheme in one stanza determines our expectation of its continuance in another). Its appeal is the appeal of progressive form insofar as the poet gets his effects by first establishing, and then altering, a rhyme-scheme. In the ballade, triolet, etc., it can appeal as conventional form.

That verse rhythm can be largely explained as repetitive form is obvious, blank verse for instance being the constant recurrence of iambs with changing vowel and consonantal combinations (it is repetitive form in that it very distinctly sets up and gratifies a constancy of expectations; the reader "comes to rely" upon the rhythmic design after sufficient "co-ordinates of direction" have been received by him; the regularity of the design establishes conditions of response in the body, and the continuance of the design becomes an "obedience" to these same conditions). Rhythm appeals as conventional form insofar as specific awareness of the rhythmic pattern is involved in our enjoyment (as when the Sapphic metre is used in English, or when we turn from a pentameter sonnet in English to a hexameter sonnet in French). It can sometimes be said to appeal by qualitative progression, as when the poet, having established a pronounced rhythmic pattern, introduces a variant. Such a variant appeals as qualitative progression to the extent that it provides a "relief from the monotony" of its regular surroundings, to the extent that its appeal depends upon the previous establishment of the constant out of which it arises. Rhythm can also appeal as minor form; a peculiarity of the rhythm, for instance, may strikingly reinforce an incidental image (as with the use of spondees when the poet is speaking of something heavy).

In the matter of prose rhythms, the nature of the expectancy is much vaguer. In general the rhythmic unit is larger and more complex than the individual metric foot, often being the group of "scrambled" syllables between two caesuras. Though the constants of prose rhythm permit a greater range of metric variation than verse rhythms (that is, though in prose much of the metric variability is felt as belonging to the *constant* rather than to the *variation*), a prose stylist does definitely restrict the rhythmic expectations of the reader, as any one can readily observe by turning from a page of Sir Thomas Browne to a page of Carlyle. However, one must also recall Prof. George Saintsbury's distinction: "As the essence of verse-metre is its identity (at least in equivalence) and recurrence, so the essence of prose-rhythm lies in variety and divergence," or again: "Variety of foot arrangement, without definite equivalence, appears to be as much the secret of prose rhythm as uniformity of value, with equivalence or without it, appears to be that of poetic metre." The only thing that seems lacking in this distinction between verse rhythms and prose rhythms is a statement of some principle by which the *variety* in prose rhythms is guided. Perhaps the principle is a principle of logic. An intellectual factor is more strongly involved in the appreciation of prose rhythm than of verse rhythm, as grammatical and ideational relationships figure prominently in the determination of prose balances (a prose balance being the rhythmic differentiation of units which have an intellectual correspondence, by parallelism or antithesis). Thus, to take from Sir Thomas Browne a typical "prose event" (we choose a very simple example from a writer who could afford us many complex ones): the series "pride, vain-glory, and madding vices" is made up of three units which are intellectually equivalent, but their ideational equality coexists with total syllabic asymmetry (the first a monosyllable, the second an amphibrach, the third dochmiac—or one, three, and five syllables, though it is true that in verse scansion the words "and madding vices" would not ordinarily be considered as constituting a single foot). It is also worth noting, as an example of the "intellectual" rhythms in prose, that the third noun is accompanied by an adjective, the second has an adjective engrafted upon it, and the first stands alone; also, the third differs from the other two in number. To consider a slightly more complex example: "Even Scylla, / that thought himself safe in his urn, / could not prevent revenging tongues, / and stones thrown at his monument." Here many complexities of asymmetric balance may be noted: contrast between long subject and short verb; contrast between short verb and long object; the two grammatical components of the subject (noun and clause) are unequal in value, whereas the two main grammatical components of the object ("tongues" and "stones") are equal in value; the modifier in the subject is a clause, whereas the modifiers of the object are participial adjectives; of these two participial adjectives, one ("revenging") is active, precedes its noun, and is of three syllables, but the other ("thrown") is passive, follows its noun, and is monosyllabic; and whereas "revenging" is an unmodified modifier, "thrown" is accompanied by the phrase "at his monument." We might further note that the interval from the beginning to the first caesura ("Even Scylla") greatly contrasts in length with the interval between the first and second caesura ("that thought himself safe in his urn"). In two notable respects the third and fourth intervals are surely inferior as prose to the first two. Their iambic quality is concealed with difficulty; and there is more than a hint of homoeoteleuton ("prevent"–"monument"), which is only suppressed by our placing the caesura at "tongues" and rigorously avoiding the slightest pause after "prevent." The placing of the caesura after "tongues," however, has the further advantage of putting "tongues" and "stones" in different intervals, thus once more giving us the asymmetrical by rhythmically separating the logically joined. [We do not imply that one consciously notes such a multitude of dissimilar balances, any more than one consciously notes the complexity of muscular tensions involved in walking—but as there is an undeniable complexity of muscular tensions involved in walking, so there is a multitude of dissimilar balances involved in expert prose. And we are trying to indicate that the rhythmic variations of prose are not haphazard, that their "planfulness" (conscious or unconscious) arises from the fact that the differentiations are based upon logical groupings. That is, by logically relating one part of a sentence to another part of the sentence, the prose writer is led to a formal differentiation of the two related parts (or sometimes, which is *au fond* the same thing, he is led to a pronounced parallelism in the treatment of the related parts. The logical grouping of one part with another serves as the guide to the formal treatment of both (as "planful" differentiation can only arise out of a sense of correspondence). The logical groupings upon which the rhythmic differentiations are based will differ with the individual, not only as to the ways in which he conceives a sentence's relationships, but also as to their number—and much of the "individuality" in a particular prose style could be traced to the number and nature of the author's logical groupings. Some writers, who seek "conversational" rather than "written" effects, apparently conceive of the sentence as a totality; they ignore its internal relationships almost entirely, preferring to make each sentence as homogeneous as a piece of string. By such avoidance of logical grouping they do undeniably obtain a simple fluency which, if one can delight in it sufficiently, makes every page of Johnson a mass of absurdities—but their sentences are, as sentences, uneventful.][1] The "written" effects of prose seem to stress the progressive rather than the repetitive principle of form, since one part of the sentence is differentiated on the basis of another part (the formal identity of one part awakens in us a response whereby we can be pleased by a formal alteration in another part). But "conversational" rhythm, which is generally experienced "in the lump," as a pervasive monotone rather than as a group of marked internal structures, is—like verse—more closely allied to the repetitive principle. The "conversational" is thus seen to fall half-way between verse-rhythm and prose-rhythm, sharing something of both but lacking the pronounced characteristics of either.

So much for prose rhythm regardless of its subject-matter. We must also recognize the "secondary" aspect of rhythms whereby they can often be explained "at one remove." Thus, a tumultuous character would constantly restate his identity by the use of tumultuous speech (repetitive form), and the rhythm, insofar as it became tumultuous out of sympathy with its subject, would share the repetitive form of the subject. Similarly, it may be discussed as conventional or minor form (as when the author marshals his more aggressive images to mark an ending, and parallels this with a kindred increase in the aggression of his rhythms). In a remote way, all such rhythmic effects may be described as a kind of "onomatopoetic parallelism," since their rhythmic identity would be explainable by the formal nature of the theme to which they are accommodated.

(10) "*Significant form.*" Though admitting the "onomatopoetic correspondence" between form and theme, we must question a quasi-mystical attempt to explain all formal quality as "onomatopoetic" (that is, as an adaptation of sound and rhythm to the peculiarities of the sense). In most cases we find formal designs or contrivances which impart emphasis regardless of their subject. Whatever the theme may be, they add saliency to this theme, the same design serving to make

1 [The bracketed material above is part of the text and was not inserted by the present editor.—Ed.]

dismalness more dismal or gladness gladder. Thus, if a poet is writing in a quick metre, he may stress one point in his imagery as well as another by the use of spondees; or he may gain emphasis by injecting a burst of tonal saliency, as the aggressive repetition of a certain vowel, into an otherwise harmonious context. In either case the emphasis is gained though there be no discernible onomatopoetic correspondence between the form and the theme (the formal saliency being merely a kind of subtler italics, a mechanism for placing emphasis wherever one chooses, or such "absolute" stressing as comes of pounding the table with one's fist to emphasize either this remark or that). To realize that there is such absolute stressing, one has but to consider the great variety of emotions which can be intensified by climactic arrangement, such arrangement thus being a mere "coefficient of power" which can heighten the saliency of the emotion regardless of what emotion it may be.

As illustration, let us trace one formal contrivance through a set of diverse effects, as it is used in Wilde, Wordsworth, and Racine, and as it appeared by chance in actual life. Beginning with the last, we may recall a conversation between two children, a boy and a girl. The boy's mind was on one subject, the girl's turned to many subjects, with the result that the two of them were talking at cross-purposes. Pointing to a field beyond the road, the boy asked: "Whose field is that?" The girl answered: "That is Mr. Murdock's field"—and went on to tell where Mr. Murdock lived, how many children he had, when she had last seen these children, which of them she preferred, but the boy interrupted: "What does he do with the field?" He usually plants the field in rye, she explained; why, only the other day he drove up with a wagon carrying a plough, one of his sons was with him, they left the wagon at the gate, the two of them unloaded the plough, they hitched the—but the boy interrupted severely: "Does the field go all the way over to the brook?" The conversation continued in this vein, always at cross-purposes, and growing increasingly humorous to eavesdroppers as its formal principle was inexorably continued. Note in Salome, however, this mechanism serving to produce a very different effect:

SALOME: (to Iokanaan) . . . Suffer me to kiss thy mouth.
IOKANAAN: Never! daughter of Babylon! Daughter of Sodom! Never!
SALOME: I will kiss thy mouth, Iokanaan. . . .
THE YOUNG SYRIAN: . . . Look not at this man, look not at him. I cannot endure it. . . . Princess, do not speak these things.
SALOME: I will kiss thy mouth, Iokanaan.

And as the Young Syrian, in despair, slays himself and falls dead at her feet, she continues: "Suffer me to kiss thy mouth, Iokanaan."

Turning now to Wordsworth's We Are Seven:

> "You say that two at Conway dwell,
> And two are gone to sea,
> Yet ye are seven. I pray you tell,
> Sweet maid, how this may be."
>
> Then did the little Maid reply,
> "Seven boys and girls are we;
> Two of us in the churchyard lie,
> Beneath the churchyard tree."

The poet argues with her: there were seven in all, two are now dead --so it follows that there are only five. But when he has made his point,

> "How many are you, then," said I,
> "If they two are in heaven?"
> Quick was the little Maid's reply,
> "O Master! we are seven."

Humour, *sournoiserie,* sentiment—we may now turn to Racine, where we find this talking at cross-purposes employed to produce a very poignant tragic irony. Agamemnon has secretly arranged to sacrifice his daughter, Iphigenia, on the altar; he is telling her so, but haltingly and cryptically, confessing and concealing at once; she does not grasp the meaning of his words but feels their ominousness. She has heard, she says, that Calchas is planning a sacrifice to appease the gods. Agamemnon exclaims: Would that he could turn these gods from their outrageous demands (his words referring to the oracle which requires her death, as the audience knows, but Iphigenia does not). Will the offering take place soon? she asks.—Sooner than Agamemnon wishes.—Will she be allowed to be present?—Alas! says Agamemnon.—You say no more, says Iphigenia.—"You will be there, my daughter"—the conflict in meanings being heightened by the fact that each of Agamemnon's non-sequitur rejoinders rhymes with Iphigenia's question:

> *Iphigénie: Périsse le Troyen auteur de nos alarmes!*
> *Agamemnon: Sa perte à ses vainqueurs coûtera bien des larmes.*
> *Iphigénie: Les dieux deignent surtout prendre soin de vos jours!*
> *Agamemnon: Les dieux depuis un temps me sont cruels et sourds.*
> *Iphigénie: Calchas, dit-on, prépare un pompeux sacrifice?*
> *Agamemnon: Puissé-je auparavant fléchir leur injustice!*
> *Iphigénie: L'offrira-t-on bientôt?*
> *Agamemnon: Plus tôt que je ne veux.*
> *Iphigénie: Me sera-t-il permis de me joindre à vos vœux?*
> *Verra-t-on à l'autel votre heureuse famille?*
> *Agamemnon: Hélas!*

Iphigénie: *Vous vous taisez!*
Agamemnon: *Vous y serez, ma fille.*

Perhaps the line, "Hurry up please, it's time," in the public house scene of The Waste Land, as it is repeated and unanswered, could illustrate the use of this formal contrivance for still another effect.

yvor winters

THE EXPERIMENTAL SCHOOL IN AMERICAN POETRY

An Analytical Survey of Its Structural Methods, Exclusive of Meter

During the second and third decades of the twentieth century, the chief poetic talent of the United States took certain new directions, directions that appear to me in the main regrettable. The writers between Robinson and Frost, on the one hand, and Allen Tate and Howard Baker on the other, who remained relatively traditional in manner were with few exceptions minor or negligible; the more interesting writers, as I shall endeavor to show in these pages, were misguided, and in discussing them I shall have little to say of their talents, their ineliminable virtues, but shall rather take these for granted.

In order that I may evaluate the new structural methods, I shall have first to describe at least briefly the old. Inasmuch as a wider range of construction is possible in the short poem than in any of the longer literary forms, I shall deal with principles that are fundamental to all literary composition, and shall here and there have recourse to illustrations drawn from the novel or perhaps from the drama. The virtues of the traditional modes of construction will be indicated chiefly in connection with my discussion of the defects of the recent experimental modes.

Type I: The Method of Repetition

Kenneth Burke has named and described this method without evaluating it.[1] It is the simplest and most primitive method possible, and is still in common use; if limited to a short lyrical form, it may still be highly effective. It consists in a restatement in successive stanzas

Reprinted from *In Defense of Reason* by Yvor Winters by permission of the publisher, Alan Swallow and Routledge & Kegan Paul, Ltd. Copyright 1937, 1947, 1960 by Yvor Winters.

[1] In *Counterstatement* (Harcourt, Brace and Co., 1932). [See Mr. Burke's essay "The Nature of Form" in this volume.]

of a single theme, the terms, or images, being altered in each restatement. Two of the finest poems in the form are Nashe's poem on the plague (*Adieu! Farewell earth's bliss*) and Raleigh's poem entitled *The Lie.* In such a poem there is no rational necessity for any order of sequence, the order being determined wholly by the author's feeling about the graduation of importance or intensity. Nevertheless, such a poem rests on a formulable logic, however simple; that is, the theme can be paraphrased in general terms. Such a paraphrase, of course, is not the equivalent of a poem: a poem is more than its paraphrasable content. But, as we shall eventually see, many poems cannot be paraphrased and are therefore defective.

The method of repetition is essentially the same today as it has always been, if we confine our attention to the short poem. Of recent years, however, there has been a tendency to extend it into longer forms, with unfortunate results. Such extension is the chief method of Whitman, and results in a form both lax and diffuse. Such extension occurs even in many modern attempts at narrative, both in prose and in verse. To illustrate what I say, I shall venture to summarize the structural defects of the narrative poetry of Robinson Jeffers:

Mr. Jeffers is theologically some kind of monist. He envisages, as did Wordsworth, nature as Deity; but his Nature is the Nature of the text-book in physics and not that of the rambling botanist—Mr. Jeffers seems to have taken the terminology of modern physics more literally than it is meant by its creators. Nature, or God, is thus a kind of self-sufficient mechanism, of which man is a product, but from which man is cut off by his humanity (just what gave rise to this humanity, which is absolutely severed from all communication with God, is left for others to decide): as there is no mode of communication with God or from God, God is praised adequately only by the screaming demons that make up the atom. Man, if he accepts this dilemma as necessary, can choose between two modes of action: he may renounce God and rely upon his humanity, or he may renounce his humanity and rely upon God.

In the narratives preceding *Cawdor*[2] and in most of the lyrics, Mr. Jeffers preaches the second choice. In *Cawdor* and in *Thurso's Landing,*[3] he has attempted a compromise: that is, while the tragic characters recognize that the second choice would be the more reasonable, they make the first in a kind of half-hearted stubbornness. They insist on living, but without knowing why, and without any good to which to look forward save the final extinction in God, when it comes in God's time. Their stubbornness is meaningless.

Life as such is incest, an insidious and destructive evil. So much,

[2] *Cawdor and Other Poems,* by Robinson Jeffers. Horace Liveright, New York, 1928.

[3] *Thurso's Landing,* same. Liveright Inc., New York, 1932.

says Mr. Jeffers by implication, for Greek and Christian ethics. Now the mysticism of such a man as San Juan de la Cruz offers at least the semblance of a spiritual, a human, discipline as a preliminary to union with Divinity; but for Mr. Jeffers a simple and mechanical device lies always ready; namely, suicide, a device to which he has, I believe, never resorted.

In refusing to take this step, however, Mr. Jeffers illustrates one of a very interesting series of romantic compromises. The romantic of the ecstatically pantheistic type denies life yet goes on living;[4] nearly all romantics decry the intellect and philosophy, yet they offer justifications, necessarily incoherent but none the less rational in intention, of their attitude; they are prone to belittle literary technique, yet they write, and too often with small efficiency; they preach, in the main, the doctrine of moral equivalence, yet their every action, whether private or literary, since it rests on a choice, is a denial of the doctrine. Not all romantics are guilty of all these forms of conclusion, but the romantic who is guilty of all is more consistent than is he who is guilty only of some, for all inhere in each from a rational standpoint. And Mr. Jeffers, having decried human life, and having denied the worth of the rules of the game, endeavors to write narrative and dramatic poems, poems, in other words, dealing with people who are playing the game. Jesus, the hero of *Dear Judas*,[5] speaking apparently for Mr. Jeffers, says that the secret reason for the doctrine of forgiveness is that all men are driven to act as they do, by the mechanism-God, that they are entirely helpless; yet he adds in the next breath that this secret must be guarded, for if it were given out, men would run amuck—they would begin acting differently.[6]

The Women at Point Sur[7] is a perfect laboratory of Mr. Jeffers' philosophy and a perfect example of his narrative method. Barclay, an insane divine, preaches Mr. Jeffers' religion, and his disciples, acting upon it, become emotional mechanisms, lewd and twitching conglomerations of plexuses, their humanity annulled. Human experience in these circumstances, having necessarily and according to the doctrine, no meaning, there can be no necessary sequence of events: every act is equivalent to every other; every act is devoid of consequence and occurs in a perfect vacuum; most of the incidents could be shuffled about into

4 Hart Crane, unlike Mr. Jeffers, demonstrated the seriousness of his conviction, but the demonstration did nothing to clarify his concepts.

5 *Dear Judas* (Horace Liveright: 1929).

6 This dilemma is not new in American literature. In the eighteenth century, Jonathan Edwards accomplished a revival in the Puritan Church, that is, induced large numbers of sinners to repent and enter the church, by preaching the doctrine of election and the inability to repent.

7 *The Women at Point Sur* (Boni and Liveright: 1927).

different sequences without violating anything save Mr. Jeffers' sense of their relative intensity.

Since the poem is his, of course, this sense may appear a legitimate criterion; the point is, that this is not a narrative nor a dramatic but is a lyrical criterion. A successful lyrical poem of one hundred and seventy-five pages is unlikely, for the essence of lyrical expression is concentration; but it is at least hypothetically possible. The difficulty here is that the lyric achieves its effect by the generalization of experience (that is, the motivation of the lyric is stated or implied in a summary form, and is ordinarily not given in detailed narrative) and by the concentration of expression; lyrical poetry tends to be expository. Narrative can survive fairly well without distinction of style, provided the narrative logic is complete and compelling, as in the works of Balzac, though this occurs most often in prose. Now Mr. Jeffers, as I have pointed out, has abandoned narrative logic with the theory of ethics, and he has never, in addition, achieved a distinguished style: his writing, line by line, is pretentious trash. There are a few good phrases, but they are very few, and none is first-rate.

Mr. Jeffers has no method of sustaining his lyric, then, other than the employment of an accidental (that is, a non-narrative and repetitious) series of anecdotes (that is, of details that are lyrically impure, details clogged with too much information to be able to function properly as lyrical details); his philosophical doctrine and his artistic dilemma alike decree that these shall be at an hysterical pitch of feeling. By this method, Mr. Jeffers continually *lays claim* to extreme feeling, which has no support whether of structure or of detail and which is therefore simply unmastered and self-inflicted hysteria.

Cawdor contains a plot which in its rough outlines might be sound, and *Cawdor* likewise contains his best poetry: the lines describing the seals at dawn, especially, are very good. But the plot is blurred for lack of style and for lack of moral intelligence on the part of the author. As in *Thurso's Landing,* of which the writing is much worse, the protagonists desire to live as the result of a perfectly unreasoning and meaningless stubbornness, and their actions are correspondingly obscure. Mr. Jeffers will not even admit the comprehensible motive of cowardice. In *The Tower beyond Tragedy,*[8] Mr. Jeffers takes one of the very best of ready-made plots, the Orestes-Clytemnestra situation, the peculiar strength of which lies in the fact that Orestes is forced to choose between two crimes, the murder of his mother and the failure to avenge his father. But at the very last moment, in Mr. Jeffers' version, Orestes is converted to Mr. Jeffers' religion and goes off explaining to Electra (who has just tried to seduce him) that though men may think he is

[8] In the volume called *The Women at Point Sur,* previously mentioned.

fleeing from the furies, he is really doing no more than drift up to the mountains to meditate on the stars. And the preceding action is, of course, rendered meaningless.

Dear Judas is a kind of dilution of *The Women at Point Sur,* with Jesus as Barclay, and with a less detailed background. *The Loving Shepherdess*[9] deals with a girl who knows herself doomed to die at a certain time in child-birth, and who wanders over the countryside caring for a small and diminishing flock of sheep in an anguish of devotion. The events here also are anecdotal and reversible, and the feeling is lyrical or nothing. The heroine is turned cruelly from door to door, and the sheep fall one by one before the reader's eyes, the sheep and the doors constituting the matter of the narrative; until finally the girl dies in a ditch in an impossible effort to give birth to her child.

Type II: The Logical Method

By the logical method of composition, I mean simply explicitly rational progression from one detail to another: the poem has a clearly evident expository structure. Marvell's poem *To His Coy Mistress,* as Mr. T. S. Eliot has said, has something of the structure of a syllogism, if the relationships only of the three paragraphs to each other be considered:[10] within each paragraph the structure is repetitive. The logical method is a late and sophisticated procedure that in Europe is most widespread in the sixteenth and seventeenth centuries, though it appears earlier and continues later. It was exploited, mastered, and frequently debauched by the English Metaphysical School, for example, though it was not invariably employed by them.

Sometimes in the Metaphysical poets, frequently in the dramatists contemporary with them, and far too often in the poetry of the twentieth century, the logical structure becomes a shell empty of logic but exploiting certain elusive types of feeling. The forms of pseudo-logic I shall reserve for treatment under another heading.

By stretching our category a trifle we may include under this heading poems *implicitly* rational, provided the implications of rationality are at all points clear. William Carlos Williams' poem, *By the road to the contagious hospital,* may serve as an example.[11] On the other hand, Rimbaud's *Larme,* a poem which, like that of Dr. Williams, describes a landscape, is unformulable: it is an example of what Kenneth Burke has called qualitative progression, a type of procedure that I shall consider later. The poem by Williams, though its subject is

[9] In the volume entitled *Dear Judas.*

[10] *Selected Essays,* by T. S. Eliot. Harcourt, Brace and Co., New York: 1932.

[11] *Spring and All,* by William Carlos Williams. Contact Editions, Paris. The poem is quoted in full in the essay on *Poetic Convention,* in this book [*In Defense of Reason*].

simple, is a poem of directed meditation; the poem by Rimbaud is one of non-rational and hallucinatory terror.

TYPE III: NARRATIVE

Narrative achieves coherence largely through a feeling that the events of a sequence are necessary parts of a causative chain, or plausible interferences with a natural causative chain. In this it is similar to logic. The hero, being what he is and in a given situation, seems to act naturally or unnaturally; if his action seems natural, and is in addition reasonably interesting and, from an ethical point of view, important, the narrative is in the main successful. To this extent, Mr. Kenneth Burke is wrong, I believe, in censuring nineteenth century fiction for its concern with what he calls the psychology of the hero as opposed to the concern with the psychology of the audience:[12] by the former, he means the plausibility of the portrait; by the latter the concern with those rhetorical devices which please and surprise the reader, devices, for example, of the type of which Fielding was a consummate master. Mr. Burke overlooks the facts that rhetoric cannot exist without a subject matter, and that the subject matter of fiction is narration, that, in short, the author's most important instrument for controlling the attitude of the audience is precisely the psychology of the hero. Mr. Burke is right, however, in that there are other, less important but necessary means of controlling the attitude of the audience, and that most of the standard fiction of the nineteenth century, sometimes for neglecting them, sometimes for utilizing them badly, suffers considerably.

Mr. Burke, in his own compositions, with a precocious security that is discouraging, reverses the Victorian formula: in his novel, *Towards a Better Life*,[13] he concentrates on the sentence, or occasionally on the paragraph, that is, on the incidental. He has attained what appears to be his chief end: he has made himself quotable. His book contains some good aphorisms and many bad; it contains some excellent interludes, such as the fable of the scholar with the face like a vegetable, or the paragraph on Voltaire. Any of these felicities may be removed from their context with perfect impunity, for there really is no context: *Towards a Better Life,* as a whole, is duller than Thackeray. On the other hand, such writers as Jane Austen and Edith Wharton are likely to be wittier than Mr. Burke; but their wit, like that of Molière, is not often separable from their context, since it is primarily a context that they are creating.

Short sketches in prose often deal with the revelation of a situation

[12] In the volume called *Counterstatement,* already mentioned.

[13] *Towards a Better Life,* by Kenneth Burke. Harcourt, Brace and Co.: New York: 1932.

instead of with the development of one. The result is static, but if the prose is skillful and does not run to excessive length, it may be successful: Cunninghame Graham's *At Dalmary*[14] is a fine example. Other things being equal, however (which, of course, they never are), action should lend power. In a short narrative poem it matters little whether the situation be revealed or developed: the force of the poetic language can raise the statement to great impressiveness either way; in fact, the process of revelation itself may take on in a short poem a quality profoundly dramatic.[15] The famous English Ballad, *Edward*, Mr. E. A. Robinson's *Luke Havergal*,[16] *Her Going*[17] by Agnes Lee, are all examples of revelation at a high level of excellence. Mr. Robinson's *Eros Turannos*[16] is a fine example of development within a short form.

The coherence of character may be demonstrated, as in the novels of Henry James, in a closed, or dramatic plot, in which personage acts upon personage, and in which accident and mechanical change play little part; or the personage may prove himself coherent in a struggle with pure accident, as in Defoe, who pits Moll Flanders against the wilderness of London, or as in Melville, who pits Ahab against the complex wilderness of the sea, of brute nature, and of moral evil; or there may be, as in Mrs. Wharton, a merging of the two extremes: in Mrs. Wharton, the impersonal adversary is usually represented by a human being such as Undine Spragg or the elder Raycie, who is morally or intellectually undeveloped, so that the protagonist is unable to cope with him in human terms. The novel is not the drama, and to demand of it dramatic plot appears to me unreasonable. The form permits the treatment of a great deal of material impossible in the drama, and the material, since it is important in human life, ought to be treated. It is certain, however, that narrative requires coherence of character, and coherence necessitates change. Fielding is dull in bulk because his characters do not develop and because his incidents are without meaning except as anecdotal excuses for the exercise of style. Defoe's rhetoric is less agile, but his conception is more solid.

In addition to having greater range, the novel of accident may have advantages over the dramatic novel which are perhaps too seldom considered. The author is less likely to be restricted to the exact contents of the minds of his characters, and so he may have greater opportunity to exhibit, directly or indirectly, his own attitudes, which, in most cases,

[14] *Hope*, by Cunninghame Graham. Duckeworth, London.

[15] It is curious that this procedure if employed in a long form, such as the novel or the play, tends to degenerate into bold melodrama; it is the essential, for example, of detective fiction. On the other hand, it is in a large part the form of *The Ambassadors*, the revelation in this, however, motivating further development.

[16] *Collected Poems*, by E. A. Robinson: Macmillan.

[17] *Faces and Open Doors*, by Agnes Lee. R. F. Seymour, Chicago, 1932.

may be more complex than the attitudes of his characters. Fielding, for example, would have been seriously embarrassed to treat Tom Jones from the point of view of Tom Jones. Melville accomplishes even more with his personal freedom than does Fielding. The superstition that the author should write wholly from within the minds of his characters appears to have grown up largely as a reaction to the degeneration of Fieldingese among the Victorians, notably Thackeray and Dickens, and perhaps Meredith, and perhaps in part as a result of the achievements in the newer mode by Flaubert and by Henry James. Flaubert is misleading, however, in that the perfection and subtlety of his style introduces an important element from without the consciousness of the character in a manner that may be overlooked; and James is misleading not only in this respect but because his characters are usually almost as highly developed as the author himself, so that the two are frequently all but indistinguishable. The superstition is reduced to absurdity in some of Mr. Hemingway's short stories about prize-fighters and bull-fighters, whose views of their own experience are about as valuable as the views of the Sunbonnet Babies or of Little Black Sambo.

Theoretically, that fictional convention should be most desirable which should allow the author to deal with a character from a position formally outside the mind of the character, and which should allow him to analyze, summarize, and arrange material, as author, and without regard to the way in which the character might be supposed to have perceived the material originally. This procedure should permit the greatest possibility of rhetorical range; should permit the direct play of the intelligence of the author, over and above the intelligence and limitations of the character; it should permit the greatest possible attention to what Mr. Kenneth Burke has called the psychology of the audience in so far as it is separable from what he calls the psychology of the hero: Mr. Burke, in fact, in his own novel, *Towards a Better Life,* employs a modified stream-of-consciousness convention, thus limiting the rhetorical range very narrowly, and confining himself to a very narrow aspect of the psychology of the hero, so far as the construction of his work as a whole is concerned, and in a large measure as regards all relationships beyond those within the individual sentence. The convention which I should recommend is that of the first-rate biography or history (Johnson's *Lives,* for example, or Hume, or Macaulay) instead of the various post-Joycean conventions now prevalent. Exposition may be made an art; so may historical summary; in fact, the greatest prose in existence is that of the greatest expository writers. The novel should not forego these sources of strength. If it be argued that the first aim of the novelist is to reach a public from whom the great expositors are isolated by their very virtues, then the novelist is in exactly that measure unworthy of serious discussion. My recommendation is not made wholly in the absence of example, however: allowances made for individual limitations of scope and defects of procedure, Jane Austen, Melville, Hawthorne, Henry James, Fielding, and Defoe may be called to serve; Edith Wharton at her best, in such performances as *Bunner Sisters* and *False Dawn,* as *The Valley of Decision* and *The Age of Innocence,* is nearly the perfect example.

Type IV: Pseudo-Reference

Every line or passage of good poetry, every good poetic phrase, communicates a certain quality of feeling as well as a certain paraphrasable content. It would be possible to write a poem unimpeachable as to rational sequence, yet wholly inconsecutive in feeling or even devoid of feeling. Meredith and Browning often display both defects. Chapman's *Hero and Leander* is a rational continuation of Marlowe's beginning, but the break in feeling is notorious.

Suppose that we imagine the reversal of this formula, retaining in our language coherence of feeling, but as far as possible reducing rational coherence. The reduction may be accomplished in either of two ways: (1) we may retain the syntactic forms and much of the vocabulary of rational coherence, thus aiming to exploit the feeling of rational coherence in its absence or at least in excess of its presence; or (2) we may abandon all pretence of rational coherence. The first of these methods I have called *pseudo-reference* and shall treat in this section. The second I shall reserve for the next section.

Pseudo-reference takes a good many forms. I shall list as many forms as I have observed. My list will probably not be complete, but it will be nearly enough complete to illustrate the principle and to provide a basis of further observation.

1. *Grammatical coherence in excess of, or in the absence of, rational coherence.* This may mean no more than a slight excess of grammatical machinery, a minor redundancy. Thus Miss Moore, in *Black Earth:*

> *I do these*
> *things* which I do, *which please*
> *no one but myself.*[18]

The words which I have set in Roman are redundant. Again, in *Reinforcements,*[18] Miss Moore writes:

> *the future of time is determined by*
> *the power of volition*

[18] *Observations,* by Marianne Moore. The Dial Press: N. Y. 1924.

when she means:

volition determines the future.

Miss Moore is usually ironic when writing thus, but not always; and I confess that it appears to me a somewhat facile and diffuse kind of irony, for the instrument of irony (the poetry) is weakened in the interests of irony. It is an example of what I shall have repeated occasion to refer to as the fallacy of expressive, or imitative, form; the procedure in which the form succumbs to the raw material of the poem. It is as if Dryden had descended to imitating Shadwell's style in his efforts to turn it to ridicule.

Closely related to this procedure, but much more audacious, is the maintenance of grammatical coherence when there is no coherence of thought or very little. Hart Crane, for example, has placed at the beginning of his poem, *For the Marriage of Faustus and Helen,*[19] the following quotation from Ben Jonson's play, *The Alchemist:*

And so we may arrive by Talmud skill
And profane Greek to raise the building up
Of Helen's house against the Ismaelite,
King of Thogarma, and his habergeons
Brimstony, blue and fiery; and the force
Of King Abaddon, and the beast of Cittim;
Which Rabbi David Kimchi; Onkelos,
And Aben Ezra do interpret Rome.[20]

This is one of the numerous passages in the play, in which the characters speak nonsense purporting to contain deep alchemical secrets or to express a feignedly distraught state of mind: this particular passage serves both functions at once. The nonsense is necessary to Jonson's plot; the reader recognizes the necessity and can make no objection, so that he is forced to accept with unalloyed pleasure whatever elusive but apparently real poetic implications there may be in such a passage, since he receives these implications absolutely gratis. The technique of expressive form, to which I have alluded, is here forced upon Jonson in a measure by the dramatic medium, for the characters must be represented in their own persons; this may or may not indicate a defect in the medium itself, as compared to other methods of satire, but at any rate there is no misuse of the medium. Jonson appears, then, to have been wholly aware of this procedure, which is usually regarded as a

[19] *White Buildings*, by Hart Crane. Boni and Liveright: 1926. [From *The Collected Poems of Hart Crane.* By Permission of *Liveright*, Publishers, N. Y. Copyright © ® 1961 by Liveright Publishing Corp. *Black & Gold* Library $4.50.]

[20] Act IV: 3. Regarding this discussion, see Foreword on p. 153 [of *In Defense of Reason*].

Mallarméan or Rimbaudian innovation, and Crane appears to have found at least one of his chief models for this kind of writing in Jonson. Jonson differs from Crane in that he does not employ the method when writing in his own name, but merely employs it to characterize his cozeners.

The two sections in blank verse of *Faustus and Helen* resemble Jonson's nonsense very closely. For example:

> *The mind is brushed by sparrow wings;*
> *Numbers, rebuffed by asphalt, crowd*
> *The margins of the day, accent the curbs,*
> *Conveying divers dawns on every corner*
> *To druggist, barber, and tobacconist,*
> *Until the graduate opacities of evening*
> *Take them away as suddenly to somewhere*
> *Virginal, perhaps, less fragmentary, cool.*

This is perfectly grammatical, and if not examined too carefully may appear more or less comprehensible. But the activities of the numbers, if the entire sentence is surveyed, appear wholly obscure. If one suppose *numbers* to be a synonym for *numbers of persons*, for *crowds*, one or two points are cleared up, but no more. If one suppose the numbers to be the mathematical abstractions of modern life, structural, temporal, financial, and others similar, there is greater clarity; but the first five lines are so precious and indirect as to be somewhat obscure, and the last three lines are perfectly obscure.

There is a pleasanter example of the same kind of writing in a shorter poem by Crane, and from the same volume, the poem called *Sunday Morning Apples:*

> *A boy runs with a dog before the sun, straddling*
> *Spontaneities that form their independent orbits,*
> *Their own perennials of light*
> *In the valley where you live*
> (*called Brandywine*).

The second line, taken in conjunction with the first, conveys the action of the boy, but it does so indirectly and by suggestion. What it says, if we consider rational content alone, is really indecipherable. One can, of course, make a rational paraphrase, but one can do it, not by seeking the rational content of the lines, but by seeking suggestions as to the boy's behavior, and by then making a rational statement regarding it. The line has a certain loveliness and conveys what it sets out to convey: the objection which I should make to it is that it goes through certain motions that are only half effective. A greater poet would have made the rational formula count rationally, at the same time that he was utilizing suggestion; he would thus have achieved a more concentrated poetry.

2. *Transference of Values from one field of experience to another and unrelated field.* I shall illustrate this procedure with passages from Crane's poem, *The Dance.*[21] The poem opens with the description of a journey first by canoe up the Hudson, then on foot into the mountains. As the protagonist, or narrator, proceeds on his way, he appears to proceed likewise into the past, until he arrives at the scene of an Indian dance, at which a chieftain, Maquokeeta, is being burned at the stake. The poem from this point on deals with the death and apotheosis of Maquokeeta, the apotheosis taking the form of a union with Pocahontas, who has been introduced in this poem and in the poem preceding, *The River,* as a kind of mythic deity representing the American soil. The following passage is the climax and the most striking moment in the poem:

O, like the lizard in the furious noon,
That drops his legs and colors in the sun,
—And laughs, pure serpent, Time itself, and moon
Of his own fate, I saw thy change begun!

And saw thee dive to kiss that destiny
Like one white meteor, sacrosanct and blent
At last with all that's consummate and free
There where the first and last gods keep thy tent.

The remainder of the poem develops the same theme and the same mood. The following phrases are typical:

Thy freedom is her largesse, Prince . . .
And are her perfect brows to thine? . . .

The difficulty resides in the meaning of the union. It may be regarded in either of two ways: as the simple annihilation and dissolution in the soil of Maquokeeta, or as the entrance into another and superior mode of life. There is no possible compromise.

If we select the former alternative, the language of mystical and physical union has no relationship to the event: it is language carried over, with all or a good deal of its connotation, from two entirely different realms of experience. The passage is thus parasitic for its effect upon feelings unrelated to its theme. The words *consummate and free,* for example, carry the connotations common to them, but their rational meaning in this context is *terminated and dissipated. Sacrosanct,* simi-

[21] From *The Bridge,* by Hart Crane. Horace Liveright, N. Y.: 1930. [From *The Collected Poems of Hart Crane.* By Permission of *Liveright,* Publishers, N. Y. Copyright © ® 1961 by Liveright Publishing Corp. *Black & Gold* Library $4.50.]

larly, while carrying certain feelings from its religious past, would mean *devoid of human meaning*, or, more concisely, *devoid of meaning*. Similarly, *perfect*, in the last line quoted, carries feelings from love poetry, but it would actually signify *meaningless*. In other words, extinction is beatitude. But this is nonsense: extinction is extinction. If there is a state of beatitude, it is a state; that is, it is not extinction.

If we accept the second alternative and assume that some really mystical experience is implied, there is nothing in the poem or elsewhere in Crane's work to give us a clue to the nature of the experience. The only possible conclusion is that he was confused as to his own feelings and did not bother to find out what he was really talking about. That odd bits of this obscurity can be glossed I am fully aware; but it cannot be cleaned up to an extent even moderately satisfactory. There is a wide margin of obscurity and of meaningless excitement, despite a certain splendor of language which may at times move one to forget, or to try to forget, what the poem lacks.

Further, there seems actually little doubt that Crane did confuse in some way the ideas of extinction and of beatitude, and that he was an enthusiastic pantheistical mystic. The mere fact that beatitude is represented in this poem by the union with Pocahontas, who stands for the soil of America, is evidence in itself; and further evidence may be found in *The River* and in some of the shorter poems. But one does not create a religion and a conception of immortality simply by naming the soil Pocahontas and by then writing love poetry to the Indian girl who bore that name. Crane repeatedly refers to an idea which he cannot define and which probably never had even potential existence.

A similar difficulty occurs in *Atlantis*, the final section of *The Bridge*, the sequence of which *The Dance* and *The River* are central parts. The Brooklyn Bridge is seen in a kind of vision or hallucination as the new Atlantis, the future America. The language is ecstatic; at certain moments and in certain ways it comes near to being the most brilliant language in Crane's work:

Like hails, farewells—up planet-sequined heights
Some trillion whispering hammers glimmer Tyre:
Serenely, sharply up the long anvil cry
Of inchling æons silence rivets Troy . . .

But the only poetic embodiment of the future, the only source of the ecstacy, is a quantitative vision of bigger cities with higher buildings. One can read a certain amount of allegory into this, but in so far as one makes the allegory definite or comprehensible, one will depart from the text; the enthusiasm again is obscure.

Library
I.U.P.
Indiana, Pa.
426 M153
c.2

3. *Reference to a non-existent plot.* This is most easily illustrated by selections from T. S. Eliot. I quote from *Gerontion:*[22]

> *To be eaten, to be divided, to be drunk*
> *Among whispers; by Mr. Silvero*
> *With caressing hands, at Limoges*
> *Who walked all night in the next room;*
> *By Hakagawa, bowing among the Titians;*
> *By Madame de Tornquist, in the dark room*
> *Shifting the candles; Fraülein von Kulp*
> *Who turned in the hall, one hand on the door.*

Each one of these persons is denoted in the performance of an act, and each act, save possibly that of Hakagawa, implies an anterior situation, is a link in a chain of action; even that of Hakagawa implies an interior and unexplained personality. Yet we have no hint of the nature of the history implied. A feeling is claimed by the poet, the motivation, or meaning, of which is withheld, and of which in all likelihood he has no clearer notion than his readers can have. I do not wish to seem to insist that Mr. Eliot should have recounted the past histories in order to perfect this particular poem. Given the convention, the modus operandi, the obscurity is inevitable, and compared to the obscurity which we have just seen in Crane, it is relatively innocent. But obscurity it is: discreetly modulated diffuseness. A more direct and economical convention seems to me preferable.

Mr. Eliot does much the same thing, but less skillfully, elsewhere. The following passage is from *Burbank with a Baedecker; Bleistein with a Cigar.*[23]

> *Burbank crossed a little bridge,*
> *Descending at a small hotel;*
> *Princess Volupine arrived,*
> *They were together, and he fell.*

What is the significance of the facts in the first two lines? They have no real value as perception: the notation is too perfunctory. They must have some value as information, as such details might have value, for example, in a detective story, if they are to have any value at all. Yet they have no bearing on what follows; in fact, most of what follows is obscure in exactly the same way. They are not even necessary to what occurs in the next two lines, for Princess Volupine might just as well have encountered him anywhere else and after any other transit.

[22] *Collected Poems 1909–1935,* by T. S. Eliot, published by Harcourt, Brace and World, Inc.

[23] *Collected Poems 1909–1935,* by T. S. Eliot, published by Harcourt, Brace and World, Inc.

4. *Explicit Reference to a non-existent symbolic value.* The following lines are taken from a poem entitled *Museum*,[24] by Mr. Alan Porter:

> *The day was empty. Very pale with dust,*
> *A chalk road set its finger at the moors.*
> *The drab, damp air so blanketed the town*
> *Never an oak swung leather leaf. The chimneys*
> *Pushed up their pillars at the loose-hung sky;*
> *And through the haze, along the ragstone houses,*
> *Red lichens dulled to a rotten-apple brown.*
>
> . . . . .
>
> *Suddenly turning a byeway corner, a cripple,*
> *Bloodless with age, lumbered along the road.*
> *The motes of dust whirled at his iron-shod crutches*
> *And quickly settled. A dog whined. The old*
> *Cripple looked round, and, seeing no man, gave*
> *A quick, small piping chuckle, swung a pace,*
> *And stopped to look about and laugh again.*
> *"That," said a girl in a flat voice, "is God."*
> *Her mother made no answer; she remembered,*
> *"I knew an old lame beggar who went mad."*
> *He lumbered along the road and turned a corner.*
> *His tapping faded and the day was death.*

This poem is ably written and has an unusually fine texture; in fact, it is the texture of the entire work which provides the effective setting for the factitious comment on the beggar, and the comment is introduced with great skill. The landscape is intense and mysterious, as if with meaning withheld. In such a setting, the likening of the beggar to God appears, for an instant, portentous, but only for an instant, for there is no discernible basis for the likening. The beggar is treated as if he were symbolic of something, whereas he is really symbolic of nothing that one can discover. The introduction of the beggar appears to be a very skillful piece of sleight-of-hand; yet it is not an incidental detail of the description, but is rather the climax of the description, the theme of the poem. We have, in other words, a rather fine poem about nothing.

5. *Implicit Reference to a non-existent symbolic value.* It may be difficult at times to distinguish this type of pseudo-reference from the last or from the type which I have designated under the heading of transferred value. I shall merely endeavor to select examples as obvious as possible.

There is, in the first place, such a thing as implicit reference to a

[24] *Signature of Pain*, by Alan Porter. The John Day Company: New York: 1931.

genuine symbolic value. The second sonnet in Heredia's *Trophées,* the sonnet entitled *Némée,* describes the slaying of the Nemean lion by Hercules. Hercules is the typical hero; the slaying of the lion is the heroic task; the fleeing peasant is the common mortal for whom the task is performed. It is nakedly and obviously allegorical, yet there is no statement within the poem of the allegorical intention: it is our familiarity with the myth and with other similar myths which makes us recognize the poem as allegory. Similarly, there is no statement of allegorical intention within Blake's poem, *The Tiger:* the recognition of the intention is due to Blake's having been fairly explicit in other works.

Further, it is possible to describe an item with no past history in such a way that it will have a significance fairly general. This is the procedure of a handful of the best poems of the Imagist movement; for example, of Dr. Williams' poem, *By the road to the contagious hospital.* Thus Miss Moore describes a parakeet, in the poem entitled *My Apish Cousins:*

the parakeet,
trivial and humdrum on examination,
destroying
bark and portions of the food it could not eat.

There is also the legitimate field of purely descriptive poetry, with no general significance and no claim to any. For examples, one could cite many passages from *The Seasons,* or from Crabbe. There is no attempt in such poetry to communicate any feeling save the author's interest in visible beauties. Such poetry can scarcely rise to the greatest heights, but within its field it is sound, and it can, as in some of Crabbe's descriptions, especially of the sea, achieve surprising power. There is a good deal of this sort of thing scattered through English literature.

Growing out of these two types of poetry (that which refers to a genuine symbolic value, but implicitly, and the purely descriptive), there is a sentimental and more or less spurious variety, a good deal of which was recently fostered by the Imagist movement, but which actually antedates the Imagist movement by more than a century.

This poetry describes landscape or other material, sometimes very ably, but assumes a quality or intensity of feeling of which the source is largely obscure. Thus in Collins' *Ode to Evening* we find a melancholy which at moments, as in the description of the bat, verges on disorder, and which at all times is far too profound to arise from an evening landscape alone. Collins' bat differs from Miss Moore's parakeet in this: that the parakeet is a genuine example of the way in which the exotic may become humdrum with familiarity—there is, in other words, a real perception of the bird involved, which does not exceed the order of experience which the bird may reasonably represent; whereas Collins' bat is not mad nor a sufficient motive for madness, but is used to express a state of mind irrelevant to him. It is as if a man should murder his mother, and then, to express his feelings, write an *Ode to Thunder.* Or rather, it is as if a man should murder his mother with no consciousness of the act, but with all of the consequent suffering, and should then so express himself. A symbol is used to embody a feeling neither relevant to the symbol nor relevant to anything else of which the poet is conscious: the poet expresses his feeling as best he is able without understanding it. Collins in this poem, and in his odes to the disembodied passions, is perhaps the first purely romantic poet and one of the best. He does not, like Gray, retain amid his melancholy any of the classical gift for generalization, and he has provided the language with no familiar quotations. Shelley's *Ode to the West Wind,* and in a measure Keats' *Ode to the Nightingale,* are examples of the same procedure; namely, of expressing a feeling, not as among the traditional poets in terms of its motive, but in terms of something irrelevant or largely so, commonly landscape. No landscape, in itself, is an adequate motive for the feelings expressed in such poems as these; an appropriate landscape merely brings to mind certain feelings and is used as a symbol for their communication. The procedure can be defended on the grounds that the feeling may be universal and that the individual reader is at liberty to supply his own motive; but the procedure nevertheless does not make for so concentrated a poetry as the earlier method, and as an act of moral contemplation the poem is incomplete and may even be misleading and dangerous.

H. D. employs a formula nearly identical with that of Collins in most of her poems. In describing a Greek landscape, she frequently writes as if it had some intrinsic virtue automatically evoked by a perception of its qualities as landscape but more important than these qualities in themselves. It is not Greek history or civilization with which she is concerned, or most often it is not: the material is simple and more or less ideally bucolic. Frequently the ecstasy (the quality of feeling assumed is nearly identical in most of her poems) is evoked merely by rocks, sea, and islands. But it would not be evoked by any rock, sea, or islands: they must be Greek. But why must they be Greek? Because of Athenian civilization? If so, why the to-do about material irrelevant to Athenian civilization? There is some wholly obscure attachment on the poet's part to anything Greek, regardless of its value: the mention of anything Greek is sufficient to release her very intense feeling. But since the relationship between the feeling and the Greek landscape has no comprehensible source and is very strong, one must call it sentimental.

This is not to say that all her poetry is spoiled by it: much of it is spoiled and nearly all is tainted, but the taint is sometimes very slight; and the description, in addition, is sometimes very fine. Exotic landscapes of one kind or another have been employed in exactly this fashion for about a century, and, in America, the American landscape has been so employed by such writers as Whitman, Sandburg, Crane, and Williams.

6. *Explicit Reference to a non-existent or obscure principle of motivation.* This may at times be hard to distinguish from almost any of the types of obscurity which I have described, but there are to be found occasionally passages of pseudo-reference which will fit into scarcely any other category. Bearing in mind the fundamental obscurity of *The Dance,* by Hart Crane, an obscurity which I have already discussed at some length, let us consider these two lines from it:

> *Mythical brows we saw retiring—loth,*
> *Disturbed, and destined, into denser green.*

This passage depends for its effect wholly upon the feeling of motivation.

The mythical has rational content for the believer in myths or for him who can find an idea embodied in the myth. The major Greek divinities exist for us chiefly as allegorical embodiments of more or less Platonic ideas. What myths have we in mind here? None. Or none unless it be the myth of Pocahontas, which, as we have seen, is irreducible to any idea. There is merely a feeling of mythicalness.

Loth, disturbed, destined are words of motivation; that is, each one implies a motive. But the nature of the motive is not given in the poem, nor is it deducible from the poem nor from the body of Crane's work. In fact, it is much easier to read some sort of general meaning into these lines in isolation than in their context, which has already been discussed.

Such terms give, then, a feeling of reasonable motivation unreasonably obscured. The poet speaks as if he had knowledge incommunicable to us, but of which he is able to communicate the resultant feelings. There is a feeling of mystery back of an emotion which the poet endeavors to render with precision. It is a skillful indulgence in irresponsibility. The skill is admirable, but not the irresponsibility. The poetry has a ghostly quality, as if it were only half there.

7. *Reference to a purely private symbolic value.* A poet, sometimes because of the limitations of his education, and sometimes for other reasons, may center his feelings in symbols shared with no one, or perhaps only with a small group. The private symbol may or may not refer

to a clear concept or understanding. If it does so refer and the poetry is otherwise good, readers are likely eventually to familiarize themselves with the symbols; in fact brilliant writing alone will suffiice to this end, as witness the efforts that have been made to clarify the essentially obscure concepts of Blake and of Yeats. A certain amount of this kind of thing, in fact, is probably inevitable in any poet, and sometimes, as in the references to private experience in the sonnets of Shakespeare, the obscurity, as a result of the accidents of history, can never be penetrated.

I have illustrated one extreme type of pseudo-reference with a passage from Ben Jonson; I might have utilized also the "mad songs" of the sixteenth and seventeenth centuries, such as were written by Shakespeare, Fletcher, and Herrick. Samuel Johnson wrote thus in his *Life of Dryden:* "Dryden delighted to tread upon the brink of meaning, where light and darkness mingle. . . . This inclination sometimes produced nonsense, which he knew; and sometimes it issued in absurdity, of which perhaps he was not conscious." The method appears, then, to have been for a long time one of the recognized potentialities of poetic writing, but to have been more or less checked by the widespread command of rational subject matter.

It should naturally have been released, as it appears to have been, by a period of amateur mysticism, of inspiration for its own sake, by a tendency such as that which we have for some years past observed, to an increasingly great preoccupation with the fringe of consciousness, to an increasing emphasis on the concept of continuous experience, a tendency to identify, under the influence, perhaps, of scientific or of romantic monism, subconscious stimuli and reactions with occult inspiration, to confuse the divine and the visceral, and to employ in writing from such attitudes as this confusion might provide, a language previously reserved to the religious mystics. Such a change would involve along its way such indefinable philosophies as Bergsonism[25] and Transcendentalism,[26] such half-metaphorical sciences as psychoanalysis, and especially the popular myths and superstitions which they and the more reputable sciences have engendered. In such an intellectual milieu, semi-automatic writing begins to appear a legitimate and even a superior method.

Emerson, in *Merlin,* for example, gives this account of the bard's activity:

[25] *Le Bergsonisme,* by Julien Benda. Mercure de France: 1926. Also *Flux and Blur in Contemporary Art,* by John Crowe Ransom in the Sewanee Review, July, 1929.

[26] H. B. Parkes on Emerson, in the Hound and Horn, Summer, 1932; included in *The Pragmatic Test,* by H. B. Parkes, The Colt Press, San Francisco, 1942.

He shall not his brain encumber
With the coil of rhythm and number;
But, leaving rule and pale forethought,
He shall aye climb
For his rhyme.
"Pass in, pass in," the angels say
"In to the upper doors,
Nor count compartments of the floors,
But mount to paradise
By the stairway of surprise."

Just how much Emerson meant by this passage it would be hard to say; it is always hard to say just how much Emerson meant, and perhaps would have been hardest for Emerson. Mr. Tate reduces Emerson's Transcendentalism[27] to this formula: ". . . In Emerson, man is greater than any idea, and being the Over-Soul is potentially perfect; there is no struggle because – I state the Emersonian doctrine, which is very slippery, in its extreme terms – because there is no possibility of error. There is no drama in human character, because there is no tragic fault."

To continue with extreme terms–which will give us, if not what Emerson desired, the results which his doctrine and others similar have encouraged–we arrive at these conclusions: If there is no possibility of error, the revision of judgment is meaningless; immediate inspiration is correct; but immediate inspiration amounts to the same thing as unrevised reactions to stimuli; unrevised reactions are mechanical; man in a state of perfection is an automaton; an automatic man is insane. Hence, Emerson's perfect man is a madman.

The important thing about all this is not Emerson's originality, but his complete lack of any: exactly the same conclusions are deducible from the *Essay on Man,* and the convictions which lead to them one meets everywhere in the eighteenth, nineteenth, and twentieth centuries.

Dr. W. C. Williams, for example, who, like Emerson, does not practice unreservedly what he preaches, but who more perhaps than any writer living encourages in his juniors a profound conviction of their natural rightness, a sentimental debauchery of self-indulgence, is able to write as follows: "It is the same thing you'll see in a brigand, a criminal of the grade of Gerald Chapman, some of the major industrial leaders, old-fashioned kings, the Norsemen, drunkards and the best poets. . . . Poetry is imposed on an age by men intent on something else, whose primary cleanliness of mind makes them automatically first-rate."[28]

[27] *New England Culture and Emily Dickinson,* by Allen Tate: The Symposium, April, 1932. Reprinted in a somewhat revised form in *Reactionary Essays on Poetry and Ideas,* by Allen Tate, Scribners, 1936.

[28] *Blues* (published by C. H. Ford, at Columbus, Miss.) for May, 1929.

A few months later Dr. Williams writes of and to his young admirers somewhat querulously:[29] "Instead of that—Lord how serious it sounds—let's play tiddly-winks with the syllables. . . . Experiment we must have, but it seems to me that a number of the younger writers has forgotten that writing doesn't mean just inventing new ways to say 'So's your Old Man.' I swear I myself can't make out for the life of me what many of them are talking about, and I have a will to understand them that they will not find in many another." He demands substance, not realizing that his own teachings have done their very respectable bit toward cutting the young men off from any.

The Emersonian and allied doctrines differ in their moral implications very little from any form of Quietism or even from the more respectable and Catholic forms of mysticism. If we add to the doctrine the belief in pantheism—that is, the belief that the Over-Soul is the Universe, that body and soul are one—we have the basis for the more or less Freudian mysticism of the surrealists and such of their disciples as Eugene Jolas; we have also—probably—a rough notion of Hart Crane's mysticism. There is the danger for the Quietist that the promptings of the Devil or of the viscera may be mistaken for the promptings of God. The pantheistic mystic identifies God, Devil, and viscera as a point of doctrine: he is more interested in the promptings of the "subconscious" mind than of the conscious, in the half-grasped intention, in the fleeting relationship, than in that which is wholly understood. He is interested in getting just as far off in the direction of the uncontrolled, the meaningless, as he can possibly get and still have the pleasure of talking about it. He is frequently more interested in the psychology of sleeping than in the psychology of waking;[30] he would if he could devote himself to exploring that realm of experience which he shares with sea-anemones, cabbages, and onions, in preference to exploring the realm of experience shared specifically with men.

So far as my own perceptions are able to guide me, it appears that the writers employing such methods are writing a little too much as Jonson's alchemists spoke, with a philosophical background insusceptible of definition, despite their apparently careful references to it, but as their own dupes, not to dupe others. They have revised Baudelaire's dictum that the poet should be the hypnotist and somnambulist combined; he should now be the cozener and the cozened. Crane, despite his genius, and the same is true of Mr. James Joyce, appears to answer Ben Jonson's scoundrels across the centuries, and in their own language, but like a somnambulist under their control.

[29] Blues for Autumn of 1930. The reference to the game of tiddly-winks will be clear only to those persons familiar with the imitators of Mr. James Joyce's fourth prose work, exclusive of *Exiles,* entitled *Finnegans Wake.*

[30] Cf. Mr. James Joyce's *Finnegans Wake,* and the voluminous works by Mr. Joyce's apologists and imitators.

This kind of writing is not a "new kind of poetry," as it has been called perennially since Verlaine discovered it in Rimbaud. It is the old kind of poetry with half the meaning removed. Its strangeness comes from its thinness. Indubitable genius has been expended upon poetry of this type, and much of the poetry so written will more than likely have a long life, and quite justly, but the nature of the poetry should be recognized: it can do us no good to be the dupes of men who do not understand themselves.

TYPE V: QUALITATIVE PROGRESSION

The term *qualitative progression* I am borrowing from Mr. Kenneth Burke's volume of criticism, *Counterstatement,* to which I have already had several occasions to refer. This method arises from the same atttitude as the last, and it resembles the last except that it makes no attempt whatever at a rational progression. Mr. Pound's *Cantos*[31] are the perfect example of the form; they make no unfulfilled claims to matter not in the poetry, or at any rate relatively few and slight claims. Mr. Pound proceeds from image to image wholly through the coherence of feeling: his sole principle of unity is mood, carefully established and varied. That is, each statement he makes is reasonable in itself, but the progression from statement to statement is not reasonable: it is the progression either of random conversation or of revery. This kind of progression might be based upon an implicit rationality; in such a case the rationality of the progression becomes clearly evident before the poem has gone very far and is never thereafter lost sight of; in a poem of any length such implicit rationality would have to be supported by explicit exposition. But in Mr. Pound's poem I can find few implicit themes of any great clarity, and fewer still that are explicit.[32]

[31] *A Draft of XXX Cantos,* by Ezra Pound. Hours Press: 15 rue Guénégaud: Paris: 1930. [Reprinted in *The Cantos of Ezra Pound.* Copyright 1934, 1948 by Ezra Pound. New Directions, New York. Reprinted by permission of New Directions.]

[32] Mr. Pound, writing in The New English Weekly, Vol. III, No. 4, of remarks similar to the above which I published in The Hound and Horn for the Spring of 1933, states: "I am convinced that one should not as a general rule reply to critics or defend works in process of being written. On the other hand, if one prints fragments of a work one perhaps owes the benevolent reader enough explanation to prevent his wasting time in unnecessary misunderstanding.

"The nadir of solemn and elaborate imbecility is reached by Mr. Winters in an American publication where he deplores my 'abandonment of logic in the Cantos,' presumably because he has never read my prose criticism and has never heard of the ideographic method, and thinks logic is limited to a few 'forms of logic' which better minds were already finding inadequate to the mental needs of the XIIIth century."

As to the particular defects of scholarship which Mr. Pound attributes to me, he is, alas, mistaken. For the rest, one may only say that civilization rests on the recognition that language possesses both connotative and denotative powers; that the abandonment of one in a poem impoverishes the poem to that extent; and that the abandonment of the denotative, or rational, in particular, and in a pure state, results in one's losing the only means available for checking up on the qualitative or "ideographic" sequences to see if they really are coherent in more than vague feeling. Mr. Pound, in other words, has no way of knowing whether he can think or not.

The principle of selection being less definite, the selection of details is presumably less rigid, though many of the details display a fine quality. The symbolic range is therefore reduced, since the form reduces the importance of selectiveness, or self-directed action. The movement is proportionately slow and wavering—indeed is frequently shuffling and undistinguished—and the range of material handled is limited: I do not mean that the poetry cannot refer to a great many types of actions and persons, but that it can find in them little variety of value—it refers to them all in the same way, that is, casually. Mr. Pound resembles a village loafer who sees much and understands little.

The following passage, however, the opening of the fourth *Canto*, illustrates this kind of poetry at its best:

> *Palace in smoky light,*
> *Troy but a heap of smouldering boundary stones,*
> *ANAXIFORMINGES! Aurunculeia!*
> *Hear me, Cadmus of Golden Prows!*
> *The silver mirrors catch the bright stones and flare,*
> *Dawn, to our waking, drifts in the cool green light;*
> *Dew-haze blurs, in the grass, pale ankles moving.*
> *Beat, beat, whirr, thud, in the soft turf under the apple-trees,*
> *Choros nympharum, goat-foot, with the pale foot alternate;*
> *Crescent of blue-shot waters, green-gold in the shallows,*
> *A black cock crows in the sea-foam;*
> *And by the curved, carved foot of the couch, claw-foot and*
> *lion-head, an old man seated*
> *Speaking in the low drone. . . . :*
> *Ityn*
> *Et ter flebiliter, Ityn, Ityn!*
> *And she went toward the window and cast her down*
> *"And the while, the while swallows crying:*
> *Ityn!*
> *"It is Cabestan's heart in the dish."*
> *"It is Cabestan's heart in the dish?*
> *"No other taste shall change this."*

The loveliness of such poetry appears to me indubitable, but it is merely a blur of revery: its tenuity becomes apparent if one compares it, for example, to the poetry of Paul Valéry, which achieves effects of imagery, particularly of atmospheric imagery, quite as extraordinary, along with precision, depth of meaning, and the power that comes of close and inalterable organization, and, though Mr. Pound's admirers have given him a great name as a metrist, with incomparably finer effects of sound.

Mr. Kenneth Burke defines the qualitative progression[33] by means

[33] *Counterstatement:* page 38 and thereafter.

of a very fine analysis of the preparation for the ghost in *Hamlet* and by reference to the porter scene in *Macbeth,* and then proceeds to the public house scene in *The Waste Land*[34] as if it were equally valid. Actually, the qualitative progression in Shakespeare is peripheral, the central movement of each play being dependent upon what Mr. Burke calls the psychology of the hero, or narrative logic, and so firmly dependent that occasional excursions into the rationally irrelevant can be managed with no loss of force, whereas in *The Waste Land* the qualitative progression is central: it is as if we should have a dislocated series of scenes from *Hamlet* without the prince himself, or with too slight an account of his history for his presence to be helpful. The difference between Mr. Eliot and Mr. Pound is this: that in *The Waste Land,* the prince is briefly introduced in the footnotes, whereas it is to be doubted that Mr. Pound could manage such an introduction were he so inclined. And the allegorical interpretation, or the germ of one, which Mr. Eliot has provided helps very little in the organization of the poem itself. To guess that the rain has a certain allegorical meaning when the rain is so indifferently described, or to guess at the allegorical relationships as a scholar might guess at the connections between a dozen odd pages recovered from a lost folio, is of very small aid to ourselves or to the poet.

If Mr. Eliot and Mr. Pound have employed conventions that can be likened to revery or to random conversation, Rimbaud and Mr. Joyce have gone farther. I quote Rimbaud's *Larme:*

Loin des oiseaux, des troupeaux, des villageoises,
Je buvais accroupi dans quelque bruyère
Entourèe de tendres bois de noisetiers,
Par un brouillard d'après-midi tiède et vert.

Que pouvais-je boire dans cette jeune Oise,
Ormeaux sans voix, gazon sans fleurs, ciel couvert:
Que tirais-je à la gourde de colocase?
Quelque liqueur d'or, fade et qui fait suer.

Tel j'eusse été mauvaise enseigne d'auberge.
Puis l'orage changea le ciel jusqu' au soir.
Ce furent des pays noirs, des lacs, des perches,
Des colonnades sous la nuit bleue, des gares.

L'eau des bois se perdait sur les sables vierges.
Le vent, du ciel, jetait des glaçons aux mares . . .
Or! tel qu'un pêcheur d'or ou de coquillages,
Dire que je n'ai pas eu souci de boire!

[34] *Poems 1909–25,* by T. S. Eliot.

The feelings of this poem are perhaps those attendant upon dream, delirium, or insanity. The coming of night and the storm is an intensification of the mood; the protagonist is suddenly sucked deeper in the direction of complete unconsciousness, and the terror becomes more profound.

In *Finnegans Wake,* by James Joyce, the dream convention is unmistakable. It penetrates the entire texture of the work, not only the syntax but the words themselves, which are broken down and recombined in surprising ways.

This unbalance of the reasonable and the non-reasonable, whether the non-reason be of the type which I am now discussing or of the pseudo-referent type, is a vice wherever it occurs, and in the experimental writers who have worked very far in this direction, it is, along with Laforguian irony, which I shall discuss separately, one of the two most significant vices of style now flourishing. The reasons have already been mentioned here and there, but I shall summarize them.

Since only one aspect of language, the connotative, is being utilized, less can be said in a given number of words than if the denotative aspect were being fully utilized at the same time. The convention thus tends to diffuseness. Further, when the denotative power of language is impaired, the connotative becomes proportionately parasitic upon denotations in previous contexts, for words cannot have associations without meanings; and if the denotative power of language could be wholly eliminated, the connotative would be eliminated by the same stroke, for it is the nature of associations that they are associated with something. This means that non-rational writing, far from requiring greater literary independence than the traditional modes, encourages a quality of writing that is relatively derivative and insecure.

Since one of the means to coherence, or form, is impaired, form itself is enfeebled. In so far as form is enfeebled, precision of detail is enfeebled, for details receive precision from the structure in which they function just as they may be employed to give that structure precision; to say that detail is enfeebled is to say that the power of discrimination is enfeebled. Mr. Joyce's new prose has sensitivity, for Mr. Joyce is a man of genius, but it is the sensitivity of a plasmodium, in which every cell squirms independently though much like every other. This statement is a very slight exaggeration if certain chapters are considered, notably the chapter entitled *Anna Livia Plurabelle,* but for the greater part it is no exaggeration.

The procedure leads to indiscriminateness at very turn. Mr. Joyce endeavors to express disintegration by breaking down his form, by experiencing disintegration before our very eyes, but this destroys much of his power of expression. Of course he controls the extent to which he impairs his form, but this merely means that he is willing to sacrifice just so much power of expression—in an effort to express something—and no more. He is like Whitman trying to express a loose America by writing loose poetry. This fallacy, the fallacy of expressive, or imitative, form, recurs constantly in modern literature.

Anna Livia Plurabelle is in a sense a modern equivalent of Gray's *Elegy*, one in which the form is expressive of the theme to an unfortunate extent; it blurs the values of all experience in the fact of change, and is unable, because of its inability to deal with rational experience, to distinguish between village Cromwells and the real article, between Othello on the one hand and on the other hand Shem and Shaun. It leads to the unlimited subdivision of feelings into sensory details till perception is lost, instead of to the summary and ordering of perception; it leads to disorganization and unintelligence. In Mr. Joyce we may observe the decay of genius. To the form of decay his genius lends a beguiling iridescence, and to his genius the decay lends a quality of novelty, which endanger the literature of our time by rendering decay attractive.

Mr. T. S. Eliot, in his introduction to the *Anabase* of St. Jean Perse,[35] has written: "There is a logic of the imagination as well as a logic of concepts. People who do not appreciate poetry always find it difficult to distinguish between order and chaos in the arrangement of images." Later in the same essay he says: "I believe that this is a piece of writing of the same importance as the later work of Mr. James Joyce, as valuable as *Anna Livia Plurabelle*. And this is a high estimate indeed."

The logic in the arrangement of images of which Mr. Eliot speaks either is formulable, is not formulable, or is formulated. If it is neither formulated nor formulable (and he admits that it is not formulated), the word *logic* is used figuratively, to indicate qualitative progression, and the figure is one which it is hard to pardon a professed classicist for using at the present time. If the logic is formulable, there is no need for an apology and there is no excuse for the reference to *Anna Livia Plurabelle;* and there is reason to wonder why no formulation is given or suggested by the critic. Mr. Eliot has reference obviously, merely to the type of graduated progression of feeling that we have been discussing, and the poem shares the weakness of other works already discussed.

Mr. Eliot's remarks are typical of the evasive dallying practiced by the greater number of even the most lucid and reactionary critics of our time when dealing with a practical problem of criticism. It is well enough to defend Christian morality and to speak of tradition, but

[35] *Anabasis,* a poem by St. Jean Perse, with translation and Preface by T. S. Eliot. Faber and Faber, London: 1930.

forms must be defined and recognized or the darkness remains. A classicist may admire the sensibilities of Joyce and Perse with perfect consistency (though beyond a certain point not with perfect taste), but he cannot with consistency justify the forms which those sensibilities have taken.

If the reader is curious to compare with the *Anabase* a prose work of comparable length and subject in the traditional manner, he will find a specimen of the highest merit in *The Destruction of Tenochtitlan*[36] by William Carlos Williams, which, like the *Anabase*, deals with the military conquest of an exotic nation, but which utilizes not only qualitative progression but every other mode proper to narrative and in a masterly way. The form is exact; the rhetoric is varied and powerful; the details, unlike those of the *Anabase*, are exact both as description and, where symbolic force is intended, as symbols. Displaying fullness and precision of meaning, it is in no wise "strange" and has been ignored. But its heroic prose is superior to the prose of *Anabase* and of *Anna Livia Plurabelle*, is superior in all likelihood to nearly any other prose of our time and to most of the verse.

The so-called stream-of-consciousness convention of the contemporary novel is a form of qualitative progression. It may or may not be used to reveal a plot, but at best the revelation can be fragmentary since the convention excludes certain important functions of prose—summary, whether narrative or expository, being the chief. It approximates the manner of the chain of thought as it might be imagined in the mind of the protagonist: that is, it tends away from the reconsidered, the revised, and tends toward the fallacy of imitative form, which I have remarked in the work of Joyce and of Whitman.[37] It emphasizes, wittingly or not, abject imitation at the expense of art; it is technically naturalism; it emphasizes to the last degree the psychology of the hero, but the least interesting aspect of it, the accidental. Mr. Kenneth Burke, in his novel, *Toward a Better Life*[38] thus falls into the very pit which he has labored most diligently to avoid: he expends his entire rhetorical energy on his sentences, but lets his story run loosely through the mind of his hero. The quality of the detail is expository and aphoristic; the structure is not expository but is qualitative. One feels a discrepancy

[36] *In the American Grain*, by W. C. Williams. A. and C. Boni, New York, 1925.

[37] This law of literary æsthetics has never that I know been stated explicitly. It might be thus formulated: Form is expressive invariably of the state of mind of the author; a state of formlessness is legitimate subject matter for literature, and in fact all subject matter, as such, is relatively formless; but the author must endeavor to give form, or meaning, to the formless—in so far as he endeavors that his own state of mind may imitate or approximate the condition of the matter, he is surrendering to the matter instead of mastering it. Form, in so far as it endeavors to imitate the formless, destroys itself.

[38] Op. cit.

between the detail and the form; the detail appears labored, the form careless and confused.

The convention of reminiscence, a form of the stream-of-consciousness technique, which is employed by Mr. Burke and by others, has a defect peculiar to itself alone. It commonly involves the assumption, at the beginning of a story, of the state of feeling proper to the conclusion; then by means of revelation, detail by detail, the feeling is justified. In other words, the initial situations are befogged by unexplained feeling, and the feeling does not develop in a clean relationship to the events. The result is usually a kind of diffuse lyricism.

Type VI: The Alternation of Method

Two or more methods may be used in formal arrangements. In a play or novel, where there is plenty of room for change, a great many modes of procedure may be employed. In a lyrical poem there will seldom be more than two. In Marvell's *To His Coy Mistress,* for example, the progression from stanza to stanza is logical, but within each stanza the progression is repetitive.

Mallarmé's *L'Après-Midi d'un Faune* illustrates a method toward which various writers have tended; namely to shift out of the logical into the pseudo-referent or qualitative, back into the logical, and so on, but at irregular intervals. The appearance of shifting may be due, of course, to my own inability to follow the argument, but it appears to be a real shifting. The faun recounts his adventure, trying to philosophize concerning it: hence narrative alternates with what should be exposition, but actually both narrative and exposition move in a more or less dreamy fashion at times, so that the cleavage in method does not coincide with the cleavage in subject matter.

Type VII: The Double Mood

A short poem or passage may be composed of alternating passages of two distinct and more or less opposed types of feeling, or of two types of feeling combined and without discernible alternation. A long poem may involve many types of feeling, but where two types alone are involved, one of them is usually ironic: it is with this situation in particular that I am here concerned. Byron, for example, commonly builds up a somewhat grandiloquent effect only to demolish it by ridicule or by ludicrous anticlimax. His effects are crude in the main, the poems being ill-written, but he was the first poet to embody on a pretentious scale, and to popularize, this common modern attitude.

The particular form which his method has taken in modern poetry is closely related to the poetry of Jules Laforgue, though Laforgue is not in every case an influence. I quote Laforgue's *Complainte du Printemps:*

Permettez, ô sirène,
Voici que votre haleine
Embaume la verveine;
C'est le printemps qui s'amène!

—Ce système, en effet, ramène le printemps,
Avec son impudent cortège d'excitants.

Otez donc ces mitaines;
Et n'ayez, inhumaine,
Que mes soupirs pour traine:
Ous'qu'il y a de la gêne . . .

—Ah! yeux bleus méditant sur l'ennui de leur art!
Et vous, jeunes divins, aux soirs crûs de hasard!

Du géant à la naine,
Vois, tout bon sire entraine
Quelque contemporaine,
Prendre l'air, par hygiène . . .

—Mais vous saignez ainsi pour l'amour de l'exil!
Pour l'amour de l'Amour! D'ailleurs, ainsi soit-il . . .

T'ai-je fait de la peine?
Oh! viens vers les fontaines
Où tournent les phalènes
Des nuits Elyséennes!

—Pimbèche aux yeux vaincus, bellâtre aux beaux jarrets,
Donnez votre fumier à la fleur du Regret.

Voilà que son haleine
N'embaum' plus la verveine!
Drôle de phénomène . . .
Hein, à l'année prochaine?

Vierges d'hier, ce soir traineuses de fœtus,
A genoux! voici l'heure où se plaint l'Angélus.

Nous n'irons plus au bois,
Les pins sont éternels,
Les cors ont des appels! . . .
Neiges des pâles mois,
Vous serez mon missel!
—Jusqu'au jour du dégel.

The opposition and cancellation of the two moods is so obvious as to need no particular comment: there is romantic nostalgia (romantic because it has no discernible object, is a form of unmotivated feeling) canceled by an immature irony (immature because it depends upon the obviously but insignificantly ridiculous, as in the third quatrain, or upon a kind of physical detail which is likely to cause pain to the adolescent but which is not likely to interest the mature, as in couplets four and five). The application of the irony, in turn, deepens the nostalgia, as in the fourth quatrain and the conclusion. It is the formula for adolescent disillusionment: the unhappily "cynical" reaction to the loss of a feeling not worth having.

A few years earlier than Laforgue, Tristan Corbière had employed the same procedure in a few poems, most vigorously in *Un Jeune Qui S'en Va,* but from his greatest work (*La Rapsode Foraine* and *Cris d'Aveugle,* two poems which are probably superior to any French verse of the nineteenth century save the best of Baudelaire), it is either absent or has lost itself amid an extremely complex cluster of feelings.

Previously to Corbière, Gautier had written in much the same fashion, but usually of very different subjects. His *Nostalgies des Obélisques* are examples. They consist of two poems, monologues spoken by two Egyptian obelisks, one of which has been transported to Paris and compares the Parisian and Egyptian scenes, lamenting the loss of the latter, the other of which remains behind, only to make the same comparison but to long for Paris. The alternations are almost mathematically balanced, though occasionally both moods will rest on a single image, as when an Egyptian animal performs a grotesquely ludicrous action in magnificent language. There is not, in Gautier, the adolescent mood of Laforgue, for Gautier was a vastly abler rhetorician and was too astute to give way to such a mood, but there is no meaning to his experience, as it appears in such poems, outside of the contrast, and the contrast is painfully precise. Gautier resembles a child fascinated by the task of separating and arranging exactly, blocks of exactly two colors. The moral sense of such a poet is too simple to hold the interest for many readings. Mr. Eliot in his quatrains employed the same formula; in fact several of his most striking lines are translated or imitated from *Emaux et Camées.*[39]

Similar to Laforgue's use of this kind of irony is Mr. Pound's use of it in *Hugh Selwyn Mauberly.*[40] The two attitudes at variance in this sequence are a nostalgic longing of which the visible object is the society of the Pre-Raphaelites and of the related poets of the nineties, and a

[39] Poems 1909–35, by T. S. Eliot: the series of poems in octosyllabic quatrains, of which the most successful is *Sweeney among the Nightingales.*

[40] *Hugh Selwyn Mauberly,* by Ezra Pound. Included in *Personæ,* by Ezra Pound. Boni and Liveright. New York. 1926. [Reprinted in *Personae: The Collected Poems of Ezra Pound.* Copyright 1926, 1954 by Ezra Pound. New Directions, New York. Reprinted by permission of New Directions.]

compensatory irony which admits the mediocrity of that society or which at least ridicules its mediocre aspects. Even in the midst of the most biting comment, the yearning is unabated:

> *The Burne-Jones cartons*
> *Have preserved her eyes;*
> *Still, at the Tate, they teach*
> *Cophetua to rhapsodize;*
>
> *Thin, like brook-water,*
> *With a vacant gaze.*
> *The English Rubaiyat was still-born*
> *In those days.*[41]

And again, to quote an entire poem:

> *Among the pickled foetuses and bottled bones*
> *Engaged in perfecting the catalogue,*
> *I found the last scion of the*
> *Senatorial families of Strassbourg, Monsieur Verog.*
>
> *For two hours he talked of Gallifet;*
> *Of Dowson; Of the Rhymers' Club;*
> *Told me how Johnson (Lionel) died*
> *By falling from a high stool in a pub . . .*
>
> *But showed no trace of alcohol*
> *At the autopsy, privately performed—*
> *Tissues preserved—the pure mind*
> *Arose toward Newman as the whiskey warmed.*
>
> *Dowson found harlots cheaper than hotels;*
> *Headlam for uplift; Image impartially imbued*
> *With raptures for Bacchus, Terpsichore, and the Church*
> *So spoke the author of "The Dorian Mood,"*
>
> *M. Verog, out of step with the decade,*
> *Detached from his contemporaries,*
> *Neglected by the young,*
> *Because of these reveries.*[42]

As so often happens when this kind of irony occurs, the poem is guilty of a certain amount both of doggerel and of verbosity. It is not without virtues, however; and it is not the best poem in the sequence. It is worth noting that the two moods are not precisely separable here, as in

[41] *Yeux, Glaugues,* from *Mauberly.* [Reprinted in *Personae: The Collected Poems of Ezra Pound.* Copyright 1926, 1954 by Ezra Pound. New Directions, New York. Reprinted by permission of New Directions.]

[42] *"Siena Mi Fe': Disfecemi Maremma."* The same. [Reprinted in *Personae: The Collected Poems of Ezra Pound.* Copyright 1926, 1954 by Ezra Pound. New Directions, New York. Reprinted by permission of New Directions.]

so much of Eliot and of Gautier, but are usually coincident. This likewise is true of the irony of Wallace Stevens.

Mr. Stevens' commonest method of ironic comment is to parody his own style, with respect to its slight affectation of elegance; or perhaps it were more accurate to say that this affectation itself is a parody, however slight, of the purity of his style in its best moments. The parody frequently involves an excess of alliteration, as in the opening lines of the poem entitled *Of the Manner of Addressing Clouds:*[43]

Gloomy grammarians in golden gowns,
Meekly you keep the mortal rendezvous. . . .

The same device is more obviously employed in *The Comedian as the Letter C,* in which appears an explicit statement of the source of the irony, his inability to justify the practice of his art, his own lack of respect for what he is doing, and in which the irony frequently descends to the tawdry. In some poems he is entirely free of the quality, as, for examples, in *Sunday Morning, Death of a Soldier, Of Heaven Considered as a Tomb.* In such work, and in those poems such as that last quoted and, to choose a more ambitious example, *Le Monocle de Mon Oncle,* in which the admixture is very slight, he is probably the greatest poet of his generation.

The double mood is not strictly post-romantic, either in English or in French, nor is ironic poetry, but both are perhaps more frequently so, and in pre-romantic poetry neither is employed for the purpose which I have been describing. For instance, in Dryden's *MacFlecknoe,* the combination of the heroic style and the satirical intention constitutes a kind of double mood, but there is no mutual cancellation; the same is true of Pope's *Dunciad,* of *La Pucelle* by Voltaire, and of a good many other poems. Churchill's *Dedication to Warburton,* in its semblance of eulogy actually covering a very bitter attack, employs both irony (as distinct from satire) and something that might be called a double mood. But in all of these examples, the poet is perfectly secure in his own feelings; he is attacking something or someone else from a point of view which he regards as tenable. The essence of romantic irony, on the other hand, is this: that the poet ridicules himself for a kind or degree of feeling which he can neither approve nor control; so that the irony is simply the act of confessing a state of moral insecurity which the poet sees no way to improve.[44]

A twentieth century ironist who resembles the earlier ironists instead

[43] This poem and others by the same author may be found in: *Harmonium,* by Wallace Stevens, Alfred A. Knopf, New York, 1931.

[44] The relationship and partial indebtedness of this technical analysis of romantic irony to Irving Babbitt's more general treatment of the same subject in *Rousseau and Romanticism* will be evident to anyone familiar with the latter.

of her contemporaries is Miss Marianne Moore. If one can trust the evidence of her earlier and shorter poems, she stems from the early Elizabethan epigrammatists. Turberville, a few years before Spenser and Sidney, writes *To One of Little Wit:*

> *I thee advise*
> *If thou be wise*
> *To keep thy wit*
> *Though it be small.*
> *'Tis hard to get*
> *And far to fet—*
> *'Twas ever yet*
> *Dear'st ware of all.*

Miss Moore writes *To an Intramural Rat:*[45]

> *You make me think of many men*
> *Once met, to be forgot again,*
> *Or merely resurrected*
> *In a parenthesis of wit*
> *That found them hastening through it*
> *Too brisk to be inspected.*

In Miss Moore's later work, the same quality is developed through a very elaborate structure, in which the magnificent and the curious are combined with the ironical and the ludicrous: I have in mind in particular such poems as *My Apish Cousins* (later entitled *The Monkeys*), *New York, A Grave,* and *Black Earth.* These poems illustrate perfectly Miss Moore's virtues: unshakable certainty of intention, a diction at once magnificent and ironic (her cat, for example, in *My Apish Cousins,* raises Gautier's formula for fantastic zoölogy into the realm of high art), and the fairly consistent control of an elaborate rhetoric. They suggest her weaknesses, which are more evident in other poems: a tendency to a rhetoric more complex than her matter, a tendency to be led astray by opportunities for description, and a tendency to base her security on a view of manners instead of morals.

The romantic antithesis of moods is the central theme of Joyce's *Ulysses,* which, at the same time, is rendered diffuse by a stream-of-consciousness technique and by the fallacy of imitative form.[46] The book has great virtues, which its admirers have long since fully enumerated, but it lacks final precision both of form and of feeling. It is adolescent as Laforgue is adolescent; it is ironic about feelings which are not worth the irony.

Mr. Kenneth Burke's novel, *Towards a Better Life,* displays the same kind of irony, which adds to the confusion coming from other

[45] *Observations,* by Marianne Moore, The Dial Press, New York, 1924.

[46] *Ulysses,* by James Joyce, Shakespeare and Co., Paris.

sources which I have already mentioned. Mr. Burke, instead of giving us the progression of a narrative, endeavors, as I have said, to give us a progression of pure feeling. Frequently there is not even progression; we have merely a repetitious series of Laforguian antitheses.

Mr. Burke, in his volume of criticism, *Counterstatement,* offers the best defense with which I am familiar, of the attitudes to which I am now objecting.[47] He writes: "The ironist is essentially *impure,* even in the chemical sense of purity, since he is divided. He must deprecate his own enthusiasms, and distrust his own resentments. He will unite waveringly, as the components of his attitude, 'dignity, repugnance, the problematical, and art.' To the slogan-minded, the ralliers about a flag, the marchers who convert a simple idea into a simple action, he is an 'outsider.' Yet he must observe them with nostalgia, he must feel a kind of awe for their fertile assurance, even while remaining on the alert to stifle it with irony each time he discovers it growing in unsuspected quarters within himself."

In admitting no distinction save that between the ironist and the slogan-minded, Mr. Burke himself verges upon a dangerous enthusiasm, perhaps even upon a slogan. The whole issue comes down to the question of how carefully one is willing to scrutinize his feelings and correct them. Miss Rowena Lockett once remarked to me that Laforgue resembles a person who speaks with undue harshness and then apologizes; whereas he should have made the necessary subtractions before speaking. The objection implies an attitude more sceptical and cautious than that of Mr. Burke; instead of irony as the remedy for the unsatisfactory feeling, it recommends the waste-basket and a new beginning. And this recommendation has its basis not only in morality but in æsthetics: the romantic ironists whom I have cited write imperfectly in proportion to their irony; their attitude, which is a corruption of feeling, entails a corruption of style—that is, the irony is an admission of careless feeling, which is to say careless writing, and the stylist is weak in proportion to the grounds for his irony. To see this, one has only to compare the best work of these writers to the best of Churchill, Pope, Gay, Marot, or Voltaire.

Mr. Burke states elsewhere:[48] "The 'sum total of art' relieves the artist of the need of seeing life steadily and seeing it whole. He will presumably desire to be as comprehensive as he can, but what he lacks in adjustability can be supplied by another artist affirming some other pattern with equal conviction."

Except for the likelihood that two opposite excesses may not be equivalent to something intelligent, Mr. Burke's statement may up to a certain point be well enough for Society (whatever the word may mean

[47] In the essay on *Thomas Mann and André Gide,* pages 116 and following.

[48] *Counterstatement:* the chapter called *Lexicon Rhetoricæ:* page 231.

in this connection), but from the standpoint of the individual seeking to train himself, it is not very helpful.

Mr. Burke does give the artist a morality, however: he bases it upon what he believes Society needs: "Alignment of forces. On the side of the practical: efficiency, prosperity, material acquisitions, increased consumption, 'new needs,' expansion, higher standards of living, progressive rather than regressive evolutions, in short, ubiquitous optimism. . . . On the side of the æsthetic (the Bohemian): inefficiency, indolence, dissipation, vacillation, mockery, distrust, 'hypochondria,' non-conformity, bad sportsmanship, in short, negativism." We have here a summary of the basic notion of all of Mr. Burke's writings, the doctrine of balanced excesses. Perhaps they will balance each other, and perhaps not, but suppose a man should desire to be intelligent with regard to himself alone; suppose, in other words, a particular artist should lack entirely the high altruism which Mr. Burke demands of him—of what value will he find Mr. Burke's morality? Mr. Burke's doctrine, in the realms of art and of morality, is really the least sceptical, the most self-confident possible: no point of view is tenable and hence no feeling is adequately motivated; all feeling is thus seen to be excessive, and neither more nor less excessive than any other, for there is no standard of measurement; any excess can be canceled by an opposite excess, which is automatically equal, and careful evaluation, as it is impossible, is likewise unnecessary.

I have stated the matter very badly, but quite fairly. Any artist holding Mr. Burke's views, in so far as he is an artist, will be restrained more or less by his natural feeling for rightness of expression; but as the theory does not, if pushed to its conclusions, admit the existence of rightness, the theory encourages shoddy writing and shoddy living. The hero of Mr. Burke's novel goes mad, for the reason that, the need of judgment having been removed by his (and Mr. Burke's) theories, the power of judgment atrophies; yet Mr. Burke continues to preach the doctrine which brought him to this end.

The perfect embodiment of Mr. Burke's doctrines, whether as an individual man, or as an allegorical representation of Society, is that Shan O'Neale who flourished in Ireland in the sixteenth century, and whose character David Hume has described as follows in his *History of England:* "He was a man equally noted for his pride, his violence, his debaucheries, and his hatred of the English nation. He is said to have put some of his followers to death because they endeavored to introduce the use of bread after the English fashion. Though so violent an enemy to luxury, he was extremely addicted to riot; and was accustomed, after his intemperance had thrown him into a fever, to plunge his body into the mire, that he might allay the flame which he had raised by former excesses."

richard g. moulton

PARALLELISM
THE BASIS OF BIBLICAL VERSE

. . . In Greek and Latin what constitutes verse is a succession of syllables of varying quantity; in Old English it was alliteration, in modern English it is a number of syllables and rhyme that constitute verse. In the Bible, what makes a "verse" is not any particular number or quality of syllables, but the parallelism of two or more clauses:

> *Why do the nations rage?*
> *And the peoples imagine a vain thing?*

The parallelism of which this is the simplest form can be extended to an infinite complexity, the parallelism connecting together not only contiguous lines, but also masses of verse widely separated from one another.

It is to be observed that the word "metre" is used in two different senses. In the broader usage it is almost the equivalent of rhythm in general; in the more particular sense it describes certain kinds of rhythm, especially that depending upon feet and syllables. I use the word in this work in the broad sense, which will include a system founded on parallelism. At the present time it is a subject of discussion among Hebraists whether the Bible in the original has not a metrical system in the other sense; and strophic arrangements of portions of Bible poetry are offered, which will be found to be very different from those in the present work. I allude to this subject only to point out that the results of such discussion cannot affect the arrangement offered here. The other metrical arrangement belongs to the original Hebrew, and has not been followed in the received translations. But parallelism of clauses is independent of particular languages, and appears in any adequate translation. Nor is there anything strange in the idea that the same poetry should admit of more than one metrical system. To illustrate I append a stanza of Spenser's *Fairy Queen.*

Reprinted with permission of the publisher from *The Modern Reader's Bible* by Richard G. Moulton. Copyright 1895, 1896, 1897, 1898, 1899, 1907 by The Macmillan Company. Some references to other pages in the volume have been deleted without ellipsis.

Wrath, jealousy, grief, love, do thus expell:
Wrath is a fire; and jealousy a weed;
Grief is a flood; and love a monster fell;
The fire of sparks, the weed of little seed,
The flood of drops, the monster filth did breed:
But sparks, seed, drops, and filth, do thus delay;
The sparks soon quench, the springing seed outweed,
The drops dry up, and filth wipe clean away:
So shall wrath, jealousy, grief, love, die and decay.

Now this is printed so as to represent the rhyme and metrical feet of the passage, these being the basis of modern English verse. But this particular passage is full of parallelism and antithesis, and it is perfectly possible, disregarding rhyme and syllabic metre, to print the passage on a basis of clause parallelism.

Wrath, jealousy, grief, love, do thus expell:
Wrath is a fire;
And jealousy a weed;
Grief is a flood;
And love a monster fell;
The fire of sparks,
The weed of little seed,
The flood of drops,
The monster filth did breed;
But sparks, seed, drops, and filth, do thus delay;
The sparks soon quench,
The springing seed outweed,
The drops dry up,
And filth wipe clean away:
So shall wrath, jealousy, grief, love, die and decay.

Thus both the metrical system of feet and the metrical system of parallelism apply to the same passage; they are not inconsistent with one another; and either, displayed by printing to the eye, assists the reader to the rhythmic heart of the poetry.

It is necessary to distinguish **Similar and Dissimilar Parallelism.** The first obtains where, in a given sequence, all the lines are parallel with one another.

Yet he commanded the skies above,
And opened the doors of heaven;
And he rained down manna upon them to eat,
And gave them of the corn of heaven.
Man did eat the bread of the mighty:
He sent them meat to the full.

Dissimilar Parallelism implies that particular lines adhere together with a bond that is closer than the bond which unites them all into a sequence. [*abab*]

> *The LORD is my light and my salvation;*
> *Whom shall I fear?*
> *The LORD is the strength of my life;*
> *Of whom shall I be afraid?*

This passage is obviously a single sequence; and yet the third line is closely parallel with the first, the fourth with the second. In the next example it is clear that the first two lines are bound together, and again the last seven:—

> *Is the righteousness ye should speak dumb?*
> *Do ye judge uprightly the sons of men?*
> *Yea, in your heart ye work wickedness;*
> *Ye weigh out the violence of your hands in the earth.*
> *The wicked are estranged from the womb:*
> *They go astray as soon as they be born, speaking lies.*
> *Their poison is like the poison of a serpent:*
> *They are like the deaf adder that stoppeth her ear;*
> *Which hearkeneth not to the voice of charmers, charming never so wisely.*

Yet that the whole makes one sequence is clear from the fact that this same dissimilar parallelism of 2 and 7 is reproduced in the stanza that immediately follows the above (in psalm lviii). [*aabb*]

> *Break their teeth, O God, in their mouth:*
> *Break out the great teeth of the young lions, O LORD.*
> *Let them melt away as water that runneth apace:*
> *When he aimeth his arrows, let them be as though they were cut off.*
> *Let them be as a snail which melteth and passeth away:*
> *Like the untimely birth of a woman, that hath not seen the sun.*
> *Before your pots can feel the thorns,*
> *He shall take them away as a whirlwind,*
> *The green and the burning alike.*

The term **Variation** may be applied to the effect by which, in a series of sequences otherwise parallel, the dissimilar parallelism is differently distributed. Thus the stanzas of psalm cxliii are all quatrains, but three different arrangements of the lines in the stanzas can be traced, viz., *aabb, abab, abba.* Similarly with the sonnet on *Wisdom and Perversity* ["Withhold not good from them to whom it is due . . ."] the two first sections have each six lines in the proportion of 4*a* + 2*b;* but the first runs *abaab,* the other *ababaa.* Such variation is not so mechanical a thing as might at first be thought; it is used for example with great effect in the strophe and antistrophe of *The Two Paths:*

[Hear, O my son, and receive my sayings;
And the years of thy life shall be many.
I have taught thee in the way of wisdom;
I have led thee in paths of uprightness.
When thou goest, thy steps shall not be straitened;
And if thou runnest, thou shalt not stumble.
    Take fast hold of instructions:
    Let her not go:
    Keep her;
    For she is thy life.

Enter not into the Path of the Wicked,
And walk not in the way of evil men.
    Avoid it,
    Pass not by it;
    Turn from it,
    And pass on.
For they sleep not, except they have done mischief;
And their sleep is taken away, unless they cause some to fall,
For they eat the bread of wickedness,
And drink the wine of violence.

But the Path of the Righteous is as the light of dawn,
    That shineth more and more unto the perfect day.
The way of the wicked is as darkness:
    They know not at what they stumble.]

Coming to particular figures of parallelism we may note **three different sources of metrical rhythm** in biblical poetry, which have contributed three different **metrical units.** (1) The Traditional poetry preserved in the historical books is for the most part in "Antique Rhythm," which seems to be based upon a unit that may be called a **strain.** This consists of a couplet, either line of which may be strengthened by an additional line, but not both.

Strive thou, O LORD, with them that strive with me:
Fight thou against them that fight against me.

Take hold of shield and buckler and stand up for mine help:
Draw out also the spear and stop the way against them that pursue me:
    Say unto my soul, I am thy salvation.

Let destruction come upon him at unawares;
    And let his net that he hath hid catch himself;
    Into that very destruction let him fall.

All three are "strains": the first is a simple couplet; the second is a couplet with the first line strengthened; the third has the second line strengthened. The elasticity of the strain has a special fitness for extemporisation, which figures largely in Traditional poetry. It is very important for the appreciation of biblical lyrics to accustom the mind to this idea of an elastic unit. When once this idea is grasped it becomes easy to see, for example, that the two divisions of psalm iii are perfectly symmetrical, although one contains eight lines, the other nine:

[NIGHT

Lord, how are mine adversaries increased!
  Many are they that rise up against me.
Many there be which say of my soul,
  There is no help for him in God.
But thou, O Lord, art a shield about me;
  My glory, and the lifter up of mine head.
I cry unto the Lord with my voice,
  And he answereth me out of his holy hill.

MORNING

I laid me down and slept;
  I awaked; for the Lord sustaineth me.
I will not be afraid of ten thousands of the people,
  That have set themselves against me round about.
Arise, O Lord; save me, O my God:
  For thou hast smitten all mine enemies upon the cheek bone;
  Thou hast broken the teeth of the wicked.
Salvation belongeth unto the Lord:
  Thy blessing be upon thy people.]

[I]t is obvious to the eye that each portion is made up of four strains. Similarly in the more elaborate rhythm of psalm vii the first and third sections are symmetrical, though one has four, the other six lines: each contains just two of these "strains."

(2) Wisdom literature is founded on the proverb, which is a couplet (rarely a triplet) of parallel lines: this contributes as a unit the **couplet**, and aggregates couplets into **stanzas.**

(3) Dancing with musical accompaniment is a leading feature in primitive poetry: the intricate involutions of the dance reflect themselves in similar involutions of metre, especially by means of antiphony (different singers answering one another), and antistrophic effect (portions of a poem answering one another apart from difference of performers). A glance at *Deborah's Song*[1] will show to what minuteness these effects can be carried. Thus from the dance we get the single line (*i.e.* half a parallel) as a unit, and the aggregation of lines into **strophes.** All these divisions of poetry exercise an influence upon one another: in

[1] [pp. 223–225.]

the psalms all three units obtain—the strain, the couplet, and the single line.

Three main types of structure may be distinguished. The first is **Stanza Structure.** Stanzas founded upon the strain as a unit may be illustrated from psalms vi, xxii, lxxvii: the first has three stanzas of three strains, the second has three of eleven strains; the third has seven stanzas of three strains. Stanzas founded on the couplet unit are very common; especally the Quatrain (xii, xiii, xxviii, xxxii, xxxvii, lxi, lxiv, cxx, cxxi, cxxii, cxxiii, cxxix, cxliii). Psalm xiv (= liii) is in triplets. Sextets are found in psalms xlviii, lxxvi, lxxxvii, cxlii. A longer stanza of eight couplets distinguishes the acrostic psalm cxix. Psalm cxlv is in acrostic couplets.

A great rhythmic effect is produced by Mixed Stanzas. The companion psalms ciii, civ[2] are cast in a common mould of stanzas of four and five (couplets or strains). The first has stanzas of five at the beginning and end, changing to stanzas of four where the topic of the frailty of man comes in; similarly, the general view of nature in civ is expressed by stanzas of five, which change to stanzas of four to express the dependence of all nature on God: the first form is renewed for the final burst of glory in nature. The elaborate Anthem of Judgment, made by psalms ix-x, is in quatrains, which change to sextets at the two places where the tone of complaint comes in. In the companion psalms cxi, cxii, a sextet is used for the conclusion, the rest of the poem being in quatrains. The dramatic change from trouble to deliverance which distinguishes so many psalms is in psalm xxxi twice repeated: to vary this repetition triplets are substituted for quatrains. In lxxxiii the change from octets to sextets seems to mark an intensification. Other examples of mixed stanzas are psalms lx, lxxi, cviii, cxxxv.

The effect of **Duplication** is common in Wisdom poetry. A fine example is the Sonnet on the *Strange Woman*[3]: besides the introduction and conclusion this has four octet stanzas with the second of them duplicated. It will be seen that this duplication does not merely imply that the second stanza consists of sixteen lines instead of eight, but further that its dissimilar parallelism is one of 4 + 12, thus exactly duplicating the dissimilar parallelism of the other stanzas, which in each case is 2 + 6. This effect will be found to play a great part in the metrical scheme of *Job*.

Augmenting is distinct from Duplication, as implying a gradual increase of number of lines in successive stanzas. In the great monologue of Wisdom[4], as the thought crescendoes the stanzas augment from

[2] [pp. 831–834.]
[3] [pp. 908–909.]
[4] [pp. 913–914.]

four to five, six, seven lines. . . . It is interesting to note the contrasted effect of **Diminution** in psalm xliv ["We have heard with our ears, O God . . ."]

The Stanza Structure admits of **introductions** and **conclusions** outside the rhythmic form of the stanzas themselves. Compare psalms xxvi, cxvi, cxxxviii. Sometimes the conclusions may be postscripts adapting the song to other uses (xiv, li, cxxviii, cxxx, cxxxi). From these may be distinguished the **leads**: a couplet or triplet leading off a theme which is then developed in stanzas: psalms xc, xciv, and the two portions of cxxxii are good examples of this effect. Other leads may be found in lxxxv, ci, cxxxiii, cxliv; or the monologue on pages 911–4.

To Stanza Structure naturally belongs the **Refrain**: though occasionally (compare psalms lvii and xl) it is found in connection with antistrophic arrangement. The Refrain is a verse, or portion of a verse, which recurs in two or more successive stanzas. Typical examples are psalms xlvi and lxvii, though in each case the refrain has been omitted by ordinary versions in one of the places where it ought to occur. Psalm cxxxvi has a continuous refrain—

For his mercy endureth for ever—

after every line. In lxii, cxl we have initial refrains. Fine effects are produced by **Double Refrains** in psalms xcix and cvii. In the first case, each stanza is a sextet: the first and third consist each of five lines, completed by the short refrain—

Holy is He—

(this has been dropped by ordinary versions in the third stanza); the second and fourth have only three lines, brought to a proper length by the longer refrain—

Exalt ye the LORD our God,
And worship at his footstool:
Holy is He.

In the main body of psalm cvii each stanza brings forward a different type of sufferer: one refrain—

Then they cried unto the LORD in their trouble,
And he delivered them out of their distresses—

with a sequel verse represents the cry for help; the burst of thanksgiving is conveyed by the refrain—

O that men would praise the LORD for his goodness,
And for his wonderful works to the children of men—

which also has a sequel verse. This stanza structure is four times repeated. In some cases the refrain is varied (*e.g.* psalms xlix, lxxx, cxvi, cxliv). In the lament made by psalms xlii-iii the words of the refrain are unchanged, but its recurrence at the end of the changing stanzas seems to give the effect of hope gradually becoming firmer and firmer.

In **Antistrophic Structure**, the second of the three main types, the stanzas run in pairs, strophe and antistrophe: the second of the pair "answers" its strophe, the answering effect implying both rhythmic symmetry and (in biblical, though not in Greek lyrics) a certain degree of correspondence of thought. This antistrophic effect is familiar to most readers in Greek poetry, and was there an effect of dance origin: the Chorus worked their way in a strophe from the centre to the end of the orchestra, and in the antistrophe worked back to the starting point, reversing all movements. In Greek the relation of strophe and antistrophe is only rhythmic; in biblical Wisdom a relation of thought goes with the rhythmic relation: such Antistrophic may also be called Rhetoric structure. The structure admits of "introductions" and "conclusions" of different rhythm.

This type of structure is most marked where the unit is the single line, and Dissimilar Parallelism comes in. A good example is psalm 1:

[A VISION OF JUDGMENT

The God of gods, the Lord, hath spoken,
    And called the earth from the rising of the sun unto the
        going down thereof.
Out of Zion, the perfection of beauty, God hath shined forth.
    Our God cometh, and shall not keep silence:
A fire devoureth before him,
    And it is very tempestuous round about him.
He calleth to the heavens above,
    And to the earth, that he may judge his people:
"Gather my saints together unto me;
    Those that have made a covenant with me by sacrifice":
And the heavens declare his righteousness;
    For God is judge himself.]

[GOD

Hear, O my people, and I will speak;
O Israel, and I will testify unto thee:
I am God, even thy God.
    I will not reprove thee for thy sacrifices;
    And thy burnt offerings are continually before me.
    I will take no bullock out of thy house,
    Nor he-goats out of thy folds.
    For every beast of the forest is mine,

And the cattle upon a thousand hills.
I know all the fowls of the mountains:
And the wild beasts of the field are mine.
If I were hungry, I would not tell thee:
For the world is mine, and the fulness thereof.
Will I eat the flesh of bulls,
Or drink the blood of goats?
Offer unto God the sacrifice of thanksgiving;
And pay thy vows unto the Most High:
And call upon me in the day of trouble;
I will deliver thee, and thou shalt glorify me.

But unto the wicked God saith,
What hast thou to do to declare my statutes,
And that thou hast taken my covenant in thy mouth?
Seeing thou hatest instruction,
And castest my words behind thee.
When thou sawest a thief, thou consentedst with him,
And hast been partaker with adulterers.
Thou givest thy mouth to evil,
And thy tongue frameth deceit.

Thou sittest and speakest against thy brother;
Thou slanderest thine own mother's son.
These things hast thou done, and I kept silence;
Thou thoughtest that I was altogether such an one as thyself
But I will reprove thee,
And set them in order before thine eyes.
Now consider this, ye that forget God,
Lest I tear you in pieces, and there be none to deliver:
Whoso offereth the sacrifice of thanksgiving glorifieth me;
And to him that ordereth his conversation aright will I shew the salvation of God.]

After an introduction, presenting the visionary surroundings of the judgment that is to be pronounced, the Divine address to the "saints" makes a strophe, the address to the "wicked" an antistrophe. It is easy to see that the two strophes correspond, not only in the number of their lines (nineteen), but also in the distribution of the dissimilar parallelism: there is first (three lines) an invocation, then (twelve lines) an argument, then (four lines) a solemn decree. Psalm xlix has an introduction and strophes of eighteen lines, each with a refrain and a parenthesis (though, by "variation," the parenthesis appears at different points of the two sequences): the difference in the refrains shows that the strophe and antistrophe are successive stages in the solution of a mystery.—For other examples compare psalms xxxvi, lviii.

Simpler examples of antistrophic structure are (on units of strains) iii, xvi, xxiv, xxxviii, xlv, lxvi, lxxii, lxxv, lxxxii, xci, xcvii, cxxiv, cxxxix. Founded on the couplet unit are the following: xxi, lvii, lxii, lxxxi, xcii, xciii, cxxvi.

Where the antistrophic structure runs to more than a single strophe and antistrophe, certain elaborations come in. **Antistrophic Alternation** implies a succession in which each strophe is immediately followed by its antistrophe (the form *aa′*, *bb′*, *cc′*). Examples are psalms xxx (which has the form *6, 6; 3, 3; 4, 4*), and cxxxvii (the lines of which run *aabaa* for the first pair, *aabbb* for the second pair); psalms ii, xxxiv, xxxix, xl. The last has the form *6, 6; 4, 4; 5, 5;* with parenthetic enlargement in the second pair, and refrains for the third pair.

A second elaboration of antistrophic structure is **Interlacing**: a strophe is followed by a strophe of a different rhythm, then come the antistrophes to each. (The form is thus *ab, a′b′*.) A clear example is psalm cx: an oracle (in triplets) is followed by its glorious fulfilment (quatrains of longer lines): again an oracle, and a glorious fulfilment in corresponding rhythm:

> The Lord saith unto my lord,
> "Sit thou at my right hand,
> Until I make thine enemies thy footstool."

The Lord shall stretch forth the rod of thy strength out of Zion:
Rule thou in the midst of thine enemies.
Thy people offer themselves willingly in the day of thy power;
On the mountains of holiness, from the womb of the morning, thy youth are to thee as the dew.

> The Lord hath sworn, and will not repent,
> "Thou art a priest for ever
> After the order of Melchizedek."

The Lord at thy right hand shall strike through kings in the day of his wrath.
He shall judge among the nations—the places are full of dead bodies—
He shall strike through the head over a wide land:
He shall drink of the brook in the way, therefore shall he lift up the head.]

Compare also v, xix, lix, xcix. Psalm vii is compound: its first part has interlacing strophes (*2, 3; 2, 3* in strains), its second part alternation (*3, 3*).

Another elaboration is **Inversion** (or **Introversion**). Here a strophe is followed by a different strophe, but the antistrophe to the second precedes the antistrophe to the first strophe. (The form thus becomes *ab, b′a′*). A fine example is psalm cxiv. Here all the strophes are quatrains, the difference is made by the attitude of thought in the four, which may be thus conveyed to the eye:

A new conception of Deity!
All nature convulsed!
Why all nature convulsed?
At the new conception of Deity!

Other examples are lxxix (in strains *4, 3; 3, 4*), cxxvii (in lines *4, 3; 3, 4*). The structure of psalm lxxiii is interesting: a trial of faith is developed in a strophe made up of three sextets, with a final quatrain as the faith almost gives way; for antistrophe the turn of thought opens with a quatrain, and the resulting triumph makes three sextets. Two compound psalms may be noted. The elaborate processional hymn of lxviii has first a single pair of strophes, each made up of four quatrains; then inversion obtains, and we have the form (in lines) *10, 9; 9, 10.* Psalm lxxiv has inversion first (*5, 6; 6, 5* in lines), and then a single pair of sextets. For a remarkable example of inversion in Wisdom poetry see *The House of Wisdom and the House of Folly* ["Wisdom hath builded her house . . ."].

From antistrophic must be distinguished the third type, or **Strophic Structure:** here the strophes have no correspondence of rhythmic form, but are merely divisions resting upon the thought of the poem, like the paragraphs of prose. Examples of this structure are psalms i, iv, xviii, xx, xli, liv, lvi, cxviii, cxxv, cxxxiv. It is the natural form for liturgies, in which each strophe represents a different mood of devotion (psalms xxv, lxv, lxxxvi). Psalm cxxxvi gives an example of **Augmenting:** the stanzas increase from four to five, six, seven couplets, returning in the conclusion to four. This is a Hymn of National Rejoicing: it should be read with the converse Hymn of National Depression (psalm xliv), where (the rhythm being antistrophic) there is a diminution from strophes of five to strophes of four, three, two couplets.

To **Strophic Structure** belongs the **Pendulum Rhythm** so characteristic of biblical literature, by which successive strophes alternate between one and another of two thoughts. This rhythm distinguishes two kindred psalms lxxviii and cvi: also the latter part of psalm cvii. It belongs also to the elaborate hymns and anthems which alternate between ejaculations of praise and development of matter for thanksgiving: the form may be traced by the eye through psalms xlvii, xcv-vi, xcviii, c, cxxxv, cxlvi-cl.

In Wisdom poetry it is antistrophic structure that is usually found in connection with the pendulum effect so common in biblical literature, by which a discourse swings successively between one and the other of two related topics. A simple example is [the following]:

[My son, if sinners entice thee,
Consent thou not.

If they say, Come with us,
Let us lay wait for blood,
Let us lurk privily for the innocent without cause;
Let us swallow them up alive as Sheol,
And whole, as those that go down into the pit;
We shall find all precious substance,
We shall fill our houses with spoil;
Thou shalt cast thy lot among us;
We will all have one purse:
    My son, walk not thou in the way with them;
    Refrain thy foot from their path:
    For their feet run to evil,
    And they make haste to shed blood.
    For in vain the net is spread in the sight of any bird:
    And these lay wait for their own blood,
    They lurk privily for their own lives.
    So are the ways of every one that is greedy of gain;
    It taketh away the life of the owners thereof.]

The first strophe (of a single line) puts temptation, its antistrophe resistance; the next strophe (of nine lines) elaborates the idea of temptation, its antistrophe that of resistance. The structure may be expressed as *1, 1;* 9, 9. A fine example is the middle part of ["Wisdom's Cry of Warning":]

    [Because I have called, and ye refused;
    I have stretched out my hand,
    And no man regarded;
    But ye have set at nought all my counsel,
    And would none of my reproof:
I also will laugh in the day of your calamity;
I will mock when your fear cometh;
When your fear cometh as a storm,
And your calamity cometh on as a whirlwind;
When distress and anguish come upon you.
    Then shall they call upon me,
But I will not answer;
    They shall seek me diligently,
But they shall not find me.
    For that they hated knowledge,
    And did not choose the fear of the Lord:
    They would none of my counsel;
    They despised all my reproof:
Therefore shall they eat of the fruit of their own way,
And be filled with their own devices.
For the backsliding of the simple shall slay them,
And the prosperity of fools shall destroy them.]

Here the thought swings between the obstinate sinners (in the strophes, indented to the right), and the avenging Wisdom (in the antistrophes, indented to the left). The formula would be *5, 5; 1, 1; 1, 1; 4, 4*.—The pendulum constantly recurs in *Job*.

The main types of structure in biblical poetry, with their elaborations, have been described. Two other elements of biblical parallelism may be mentioned.

An interesting figure of parallelism is the **Envelope**: the opening line or lines of the sequence are repeated at the close, all that intervenes being read in the light of this common "envelopment." A perfect example is the eighth psalm . . . Similarly the recurrence of the ejaculation—

Bless the LORD, O my soul—

at the beginning and end of psalms ciii and civ turns both these into examples of envelope structure.

More frequently a modified form of the Envelope Structure is found, by which the opening and closing lines unite in a single thought of which the intermediate parts are an expansion. Thus in psalm xv, the opening lines of question,

LORD, who shall sojourn in thy tabernacle?
Who shall dwell in thy holy hill?

receive an answer in the final line,

He that doeth these things shall never be moved:

while the intermediate parallels contain the "these things." Compare psalm xxvi. A fine example is the great psalm cxxxix: here the opening protest,

O LORD, thou hast searched me, etc.,

concludes as a prayer:

Search me, O LORD:

while the whole antistrophic movement of the psalm is occupied with effecting the transition from the one mood to the other. Psalms xxiii and xxxiii are also examples of modified envelopment; the whole device of antistrophic inversion, and the type of psalm described as Dramatic Anthems, are akin to envelopment.

Interruption plays a leading part in the lyric structure of the psalms. First, we have stanzas interrupted by antistrophic structure. A typical example is psalm lv: here sextets of despairing complaint are broken by a strophe and antistrophe (*8, 8* in couplets) of strong execration: there is a return to the sextet form (varied) with the final stage of trust in God. In psalm lxxxix, the covenantal promises to David developed in a long succession of quatrains make the main topic: when this has been barely opened there is an outburst (strophe in seven quatrains) of adoration; when the main topic is completed an antistrophe puts plaintively the disappointment of all these hopes. A very marked example is psalm lxix. Stanzas of four strains are conveying complaint: before the sixth of these stanzas is quite completed there breaks in an interruption of execration in seven couplets: this is seen to be a strophe when presently, after the broken stanza is completed, there comes an antistrophe of seven couplets celebrating the deliverance that ends the whole trouble. Interruption proceeds a stage further in psalms lxxx and lxxxiv. In the first, stanzas of elegy (two strains and refrain) are interrupted by strophe and antistrophe (four couplets each) developing the image of the Vine and its uprooting: but the refrain of the stanza sections breaks in (with a modification) upon this antistrophic portion: thus the interruption is mutual. A still more striking example of mutual interruption is afforded by psalm lxxxiv: triplet stanzas of longing for the house of God are interrupted by antistrophic description of the pilgrimages (strophe) and the pilgrims' hymn (antistrophe): this last is broken by a parenthetic triplet of longing, and then resumes and concludes.

Or, stanzas are interrupted by stanzas of different rhythm. I have already pointed out this effect in regard to psalms ciii and civ (above, Mixed Stanzas). In psalm cii personal depression expressed in a succession of stanzas of three strains each is interrupted by a succession of stanzas of four couplets each, which rise to the plane of national trouble and its relief: there is then a return to the first rhythm and the first tone.

An effect akin to this Interruption may more properly be called **Suspension.** In psalm xi a stanza expressive of trust in Jehovah is interrupted by a strophe (2, 5) reciting hostile threats and its antistrophe of answering faith. But from the place at which the interruption occurs, viz. the end of a single line of a quatrain, the other three lines following after the interruption is concluded, it is better to regard the single stanza as "suspended" until the antistrophic effect has been elaborated:

[In the Lord put I my trust—

How say ye to my soul,
"Flee as a bird to your mountain?
For, lo, the wicked bend the bow,
They make ready their arrow upon the string,
That they may shoot in darkness at the upright in heart.
If the foundations be destroyed,
What can the righteous do?"

The Lord is in his holy temple,
The Lord, his throne is in heaven;
His eyes behold, his eyelids try, the children of men.
The Lord trieth the righteous:
But the wicked and him that loveth violence his soul hateth.
Upon the wicked he shall rain snares;
Fire and brimstone and burning wind shall be the portion of their cup.—

For the Lord is righteous;
He loveth righteousness:
The upright shall behold his face.]

Exactly similar is xciii: a sextet of confidence in the firmness of Jehovah's rule is broken by antistrophic interruption of an image that suggests assailing power driven back, and the suspended sextet is then concluded.

gay wilson allen

WALT WHITMAN: THE SEARCH FOR A "DEMOCRATIC" STRUCTURE

In so far as the expanding ego psychology results in an enumerative style, the cataloging of a representative and symbolical succession of images, conveying the sensation of pantheistic unity and endless becoming, it is itself a literary technique. But though this psychology may be called the background or basic method of Whitman's poetic technique, the catalog itself was not chronologically the first stylistic device which he adopted. It emerged only after he had found a verse structure appropriate for expressing his cosmic inspiration and democratic sentiment. Nowhere in the universe does he recognize caste or subordination. Everything is equally perfect and equally divine. He admits no supremes, or rather insists that "There can be any number of supremes."[1]

The expression of such doctrines demands a form in which units are co-ordinate, distinctions eliminated, all flowing together in a synonymous or "democratic" structure. He needed a grammatical and rhetorical structure which would be cumulative in effect rather than logical or progressive.

Possibly, as many critics have believed, he found such a structure in the primitive rhythms of the King James Bible, though some of the resemblances may be accidental. The structure of Hebraic poetry, even in English translation, is almost lacking in subordination. The original language of the Old Testament was extremely deficient in connectives, as the numerous "ands" of the King James translation bear witness.[2] It was a language for direct assertion and the expression of emotion rather than abstract thought or intellectual subtleties. Tied to such a lan-

Reprinted from *Walt Whitman Handbook* (New York, Hendricks House), pages 387–409, by permission of the author and the publisher. Copyright 1962 by Hendricks House.

1 *By Blue Ontario's Shore,* sec. 3.

2 See A. S. Cook, "The 'Authorized Version' and Its Influence," *Cambridge History of English Literature* (New York and London: G. P. Putnam's Sons, 1910), IV, 29–58.

guage, the Hebraic poet developed a rhythm of thought, repeating and balancing ideas and sentences (or independent clauses) instead of syllables or accents. He may have had other prosodic conventions also, no longer understood or easily discernible; but at least in the English translation this rhythm of thought or parallelism characterizes Biblical versification.[3]

That Walt Whitman fully understood the nature of these Biblical rhythms is doubtful, and certainly his own language did not tie him down to such a verse system. Despite the fact that he was thoroughly familiar with the Bible and was undoubtedly influenced by the scriptures in many ways, it may, therefore, have been a coincidence that in searching for a medium to express his pantheism he naturally (we might almost say atavistically) stumbled upon parallelism as his basic structure. Furthermore, parallelism is found in primitive poetry other than the Biblical; in fact, seems to be typically primitive,[4] and it is perhaps not surprising that in the attempt to get rid of conventional techniques Whitman should have rediscovered a primitive one.

But whatever the sources of Whitman's verse techniques, the style of the King James Version is generally agreed to provide convenient analogies for the prosodic analysis of *Leaves of Grass*.[5]

"The principles which governed Hebrew verse," says Gardiner, "can be recovered only in part, but fortunately the one principle which really affects the form of the English has been clearly made out, the principle of parallel structure: in the Hebrew poetry the line was the unit, and the second line balanced the first, completing or supplementing its meaning."[6]

Even the scholars of the Middle ages were aware of the parallelism of Biblical verse (*Verdoppelten Ausdruck* or "double expression,"[7] they called it) but it was first fully explained by Bishop Lowth in a Latin speech given at Oxford in 1753. Since his scheme demonstrates the single line as the unit, let us examine it.

[3] See S. R. Driver, *Introduction to the Literature of the Old Testament* (New York, Scribner's Sons, 1910), 361 ff. Also E. Kautzsch, *Die Poesie und die poetischen Bücher des Alten Testaments* (Tübingen und Leipzig, 1902), 2. Bishop Lowth first pointed out the metrical principles of parallelism in the Bible in *De sacra poesi Hebraeorum praelectiones academiae Oxoni habitae*, 1753—see Driver, *op. cit.*, 362. In the main the Lowth system is the basis for R. G. Moulton's arrangement of Biblical poetry in his *Modern Reader's Bible* (New York: Macmillan, 1922). See also note 5 below.

[4] *E.g.*, in American Indian rhythms—Cf. Mary Austin's *The American Rhythm* (New York: Harcourt Brace, 1913).

[5] Observed by many critics and biographers, but first elaborated by Gay Wilson Allen, "Biblical Analogies for Walt Whitman's Prosody," *Revue Anglo-Américaine*, X, 490–507 (August, 1933)—basis for same author's chapter on Whitman in *American Prosody* (New York: American Book Co., 1935), 217–243.

[6] J. H. Gardiner, *The Bible as English Literature* (New York: Scribner's Sons, 1906), 107.

[7] Kautzsch, *op. cit.*, 2.

1. *Synonymous* parallelism: This is the most frequent kind of thought rhythm in Biblical poetry. "The second line enforces the thought of the first by repeating, and, as it were, *echoing* it in a varied form, producing an effect at once grateful to the ear and satisfying to the mind."[8]

> How shall I curse, whom God hath not cursed?
> And how shall I defy, whom the Lord hath not defied?
> —*Nu.* 23:8.

The second line, however, does not have to be identical in thought with the first. It may be merely similar or parallel to it.

> Sun, stand thou still upon Gibeon;
> And thou, Moon, upon the valley of Aijalon.
> —*Josh.* 10:12.

2. *Antithetic* parallelism: The second line denies or contrasts with the first:

> A wise son maketh a glad father,
> But a foolish son is the heaviness of his mother.
> —*Prov.* 10:1.

> For the Lord knoweth the way of the righteous;
> But the way of the wicked shall perish.
> —*Ps.* 1:6.

3. *Synthetic* or *constructive* parallelism: Here the second line (sometimes several consecutive lines) supplements or completes the first. (Although all Biblical poetry tends more toward the "end-stopped" than the "run-on" line, it will be noticed that synthetic parallelism does often have a certain degree of *enjambement*.)

> Better is a dinner of herbs where love is,
> Than a stalled ox and hatred therewith.
> —*Pr.* 15:17.

> Answer not a fool according to his folly,
> Lest thou also be like unto him.
> —*Pr.* 26:4.

> As a bird that wandereth from her nest,
> So is a man that wandereth from his place.
> —*Pr.* 27:8.

"A comparison, a reason, a consequence, a motive, often constitutes one of the lines in a synthetic parallelism."[9]

[8] Driver, *op. cit.*, 340.
[9] *Ibid.*

4. To Lowth's three kinds of parallelism Driver adds a fourth, which for convenience we may include here. It is called *climactic* parallelism—or sometimes "ascending rhythm." "Here the first line is itself incomplete, and the second line takes up words from it and completes them."[10]

> Give unto the Lord, O ye sons of the mighty,
> Give unto the Lord *glory and strength.*
> —*Ps.* 29:1.
>
> The voice of the Lord shaketh the wilderness;
> The Lord shaketh the wilderness *of Kadesh.*
> —*Ps.* 29:8.
>
> Till thy people pass over, O Lord,
> Till the people pass over *which thou hast purchased.*
> —*Ex.* 15:16.

It will be noticed in these examples that parallelism is sometimes a repetition of grammatical constructions and often of words, but the main principle is the balancing of thoughts alongside or against each other. And this produces not only a rhythmical thought-pattern, but also, and consequently, a speech rhythm which we will consider later. This brief summary presents only the most elementary aspects of Biblical rhythm, but it is sufficient to establish the fact that in parallelism, or in the "rhythm of thought," *the single line must by necessity be the stylistic unit.* Before taking up other aspects of parallelism let us see if this fundamental principle is found in Whitman's poetry.

Many critics have recognized parallelism as a rhythmical principle in *Leaves of Grass.* Perry even suggested that *The Lily and the Bee,* by Samuel Warren, published in England in 1851 and promptly reprinted in America by Harpers, may have given Whitman the model for his versification;[11] though Carpenter has pointed out that Whitman's new style had already been formed by 1851.[12] Perry's conjecture is important, however, because parallelism is unquestionably the stylistic principle of *The Lily and the Bee,* and in making the conjecture he is rightly calling attention to this principle of Whitman's style.

But if parallelism is the foundation of the rhythmical styles of *Leaves of Grass,* then, as we have already seen in the summary of the Lowth system, the verse must be the unit. Any reader can observe that this is true in *Leaves of Grass,* and many critics have pointed it out. De Selincourt says:

[10] *Ibid.*

[11] Bliss Perry, *Walt Whitman* (Boston: Houghton Mifflin, 1906), 92.

[12] George Rice Carpenter, *Walt Whitman* (New York: Macmillan, 1924), 42.

> The constitution of a line in *Leaves of Grass* is such that, taken in its context, the poetic idea to be conveyed by the words is only perfectly derived from them when they are related to the line as a unit; and the equivalence of the lines is their equivalent appeal to our attention as contributors to the developing expression of the poetic idea of the whole.[13]

And Ross adds, more concretely:

> Whitman's verse—with the exception that it is not metered—is farther removed from prose than is traditional verse itself, for the reason that the traditional verse is, like prose, composed in sentences, whereas Whitman's verse is composed in lines . . . A run-on line is rare in Whitman—so rare that it may be considered a "slip." The law of his structure is that *the unit of sense is the measure of the line.* The lines, in sense, are end-stopped. Whitman employed everywhere a system of punctuation to indicate his structure. Look down any page of *Leaves of Grass,* and you will find almost every line ending in a comma; you will find a period at the end of a group of lines or a whole poem. Syntactically, there may be many sentences in the groups of the whole poem, there may be two or three sentences in one line. But Whitman was composing by lines, not by sentences, and he punctuated accordingly.[14]

Whitman's Parallelism

It was only after a decade or more of experimentation that Whitman definitely adopted parallelism as his basic verse structure. In a poem of 1850, *Blood-Money,*[15] he was already fumbling for this technique, but here he was paraphrasing both the thought and the prose rhythm of the New Testament (*Matthew* 26–27):

> Of the olden time, when it came to pass
> That the beautiful god, Jesus, should finish his work on earth,
> Then went Judas, and sold the divine youth,
> And took pay for his body.

The run-on lines show how far the poet still is from the characteristic style of *Leaves of Grass.* He is experimenting with phrasal or clausal units; not yet "thought rhythm." But his arrangement of the verse is a step in that direction.

In *Europe,* another poem of 1850, we also see the new form slowly

[13] De Selincourt, *op. cit.,* 103–104. [Basil De Selincourt, *Walt Whitman: A Critical Study* (London: Martin Secker, 1914).]

[14] E. C. Ross, "Whitman's Verse," *Modern Language Notes,* XLV, 363–364 (June, 1930). Autrey Nell Wiley demonstrates this view in "Reiterative Devices in 'Leaves of Grass'," *American Literature,* I, 161–170 (May, 1929). She says: "In more than 10,500 lines in *Leaves of Grass,* there are, by my count, only twenty run-on lines," p. 161.

[15] Whitman himself misdated this poem 1843. It was published in *The Tribune,* Supplement, March 22, 1850, and the occasion of the satire was Webster's speech on March 7, 1850, regarding the Fugitive Slave Law.

evolving. It begins with long lines that at first glance look like the typical verse of the later poems, but on closer observation we see that they are not.

> Suddenly, out of the stale and drowsy lair, the lair of slaves,
> Like lightning it le'pt forth....half startled at itself,
> Its feet upon the ashes and the rags....Its hands tight to the throat of kings.

The disregard for grammatical structure suggests the poet's mature style —the antecedent of *it* is merely implied and the predicate is entirely lacking—, but the lines are only vaguely synonymous.

We see the next stage of this evolving style in the 1855 Preface, which, significantly, is arranged as prose, but the thought-units are often separated by three periods, indicating that the author is striving for a rhythmical effect which conventional prose punctuation can not achieve.

> He sees eternity less like a play with a prologue and a denouement. . . he sees eternity in men and women. . . he does not see men and women as dreams or dots. Faith is the antiseptic of the soul. . . it pervades the common people and preserves them. . . they never give up believing and expecting and trusting.
>
> . . . .
>
> The greatest poet forms the consistence of what is to be from what has been and is. He drags the dead out of their coffins and stands them again on their feet. . . he says to the past, Rise and walk before me that I may realize you. He learns the lesson. . . he places himself where the future becomes present. The greatest poet does not only dazzle his rays over character and scenes and passions. . . he finally ascends and finishes all. . . he exhibits the pinnacles that no man can tell what they are for or what is beyond. . . . He glows a moment on the extremest verge. He is most wonderful in his last half-hidden smile or frown. . .[16]

Notice that the parallelism asserts without qualifications. The poet is chanting convictions about which there is to be no argument, no discussion. He develops or elaborates the theme by enumeration, eliminating so far as possible transitional and connective words. The form is rhapsodic, the tone that of inspired utterance.

In this Preface the third person is used, but the rhetorical form is that of the expanding ego, as clearly revealed in this catalog:

> On him rise solid growths that offset the growths of pine and cedar and hemlock and liveoak and locust and chestnut and cypress and hickory and limetree and cottonwood and tuliptree and cactus and wildvine and tamarind and persimmon. . . and tangles as tangled as any canebrake or swamp. . .

[16] Inclusive Edition, *op. cit.*, 492–495. [Emory Holloway, ed., *Inclusive Edition of Leaves of Grass* (New York: Doubleday, Doran & Co., 1931).]

> and forests coated with transparent ice and icicles hanging from the boughs and crackling in the wind. . . and sides and peaks of mountains....[17]

The "ands" are evidently an attempt to convey the effect of endless continuity in an eternal present—the cosmic unity which the poet incarnates as he sweeps over the continent. Here in this rhapsodic Preface, both in the ideas and the manner in which they are expressed, we see the kind of literary form and style which Whitman has adopted as analogous to his "purports and facts."

And in ten of the twelve poems of the 1855 edition of *Leaves of Grass* parallelism is the structural device, chiefly the *synonymous* variety, though the others are found also, especially the *cumulative* and *climactic*. As a matter of fact, it is often difficult to separate these three, for as Whitman asserts or repeats the same idea in different ways—like a musician playing variations on a theme—he tends to build up to an emotional, if not logical, climax. The opening lines of *Song of Myself* are obviously cumulative in effect:

> I celebrate myself, [and sing myself],[18]
> And what I assume you shall assume,
> For every atom belonging to me as good belongs to you.

The following lines are synonymous in thought, though there is a cumulation and building up of the emotion:

> I loafe and invite my soul,
> I lean and loafe at my ease . . . . observing a spear of summer grass.

(No doubt much of this effect is due to the pronounced caesura—which we will consider later.)

In this poem, as in the following ones, the parallelism has three functions. First of all it provides the basic structure for the lines. Each line makes an independent statement, either a complete or an elliptical sentence. In the second place, this repetition of thought (with variations) produces a loose rhythmical chanting or rhapsodic style. And, finally, the parallelism binds the lines together, forming a unit something like a stanza in conventional versification.

> This grass is very dark to be from the white heads of old mothers,
> Darker than the colorless beards of old men,
> Dark to come from under the faint red roofs of mouths.
>
> O I perceive after all so many uttering tongues!
> And I perceive they do not come from the roofs of mouths for nothing.

[17] *Ibid.*, 490.
[18] [Bracketed words represent additions to the 1855 edition.—Ed.]

I wish I could translate the hints about the dead young men and women,
And the hints about old men and mothers, and the offspring taken soon out of their laps.

What do you think has become of the young and old men?
And what do you think has become of the women and children?

They are alive and well somewhere;
The smallest sprout shows there is really no death,
And if ever there was it led forward life, and does not wait at the end to arrest it,
And ceased the moment life appeared.

All goes onward and outward. . . . and nothing collapses,
And to die is different from what any one supposed, and luckier.[19]

Here Whitman's characteristic structure and rhythm is completely developed and he handles it with ease and assurance. But that he does not yet completely trust it is perhaps indicated by the occasional use of a semicolon (as in next to last stanza or strophe above) and four periods to emphasize a caesura. In his later verse (including revisions of this poem) he depended upon commas in both places.

In the above extract from *Song of Myself* the similarity of the parallelism to that of Biblical poetry is probably closer than in more typical passages of Whitman's longer poems, for the couplet, triplet, and quatrain are found more often in the Bible than in *Leaves of Grass;* and the Bible does not have either long passages of synonymous parallelism or extended catalogs. The Biblical poets were not, like Whitman, attempting to inventory the universe in order to symbolize its fluxional unity. They found unity in their monotheism, not (or seldom) in a pantheism. But when Whitman's poetic vision sweeps over the occupations of the land, as in section 15 of *Song of Myself,* he enumerates dozens of examples in more or less synonymous parallelistic form. And he repeats the performance in section 33 in a kind of omnipresent world-panorama of scenes, activities, and pictures of life, in a strophe (or sentence) of 82 lines.

Another poem in the first edition, later known as *There Was a Child Went Forth,* further amplifies both the psychology of the poet's identification of his consciousness with all forms of being and his expression of it through enumeration and parallelism:

There was a child went forth every day,
And the first object he looked upon and received with wonder or pity or love or dread, that object he became,
And that object became part of him for the day or a certain part of the day. . . . or for many years or stretching cycles of years.

[19] *Song of Myself,* sec. 6.

Then comes the list—early lilacs, grass, morning glories, March-born lambs, persons, streets, oceans, etc.—a veritable photomontage. The catalog and parallelism techniques arise from the same psychological impulse and achieve the same general effects of poetic identification.

The catalog, however, is most typical of the 1855–56 poems, when Whitman's cosmic inspiration found its most spontaneous and unrestrained expression. But even here we find a number of strophes arranged or organized as "envelopes" of parallelism, a device which the poet found especially useful in the shorter and more orderly poems of *Calamus*, *Drum-Taps*, and the old-age lyrics. It is essentially a stanzaic form, something like the quatrain of the Italian sonnet. The first line advances a thought or image, succeeding lines amplify or illustrate it by synonymous parallelism, and the final line completes the whole by reiterating the original line or concluding the thought. For example, in section 21 of *Song of Myself:*

> Smile O voluptuous coolbreathed earth!
> Earth of the slumbering and liquid trees!
> Earth of departed sunset! Earth of the mountains misty-topt!
> Earth of the vitreous pour of the full moon just tinged with blue!
> Earth of shine and dark mottling the tide of the river!
> Earth of the limpid gray clouds brighter and clearer for my sake!
> Far-swooping elbowed earth! Rich apple-blossomed earth!
> Smile, for your lover comes!

Far more common, however, is the incomplete envelope, the conclusion being omitted, as in the 1860 *Song at Sunset:*

> Good in all,
> In the satisfaction and aplomb of animals
> In the annual return of the seasons,
> In the hilarity of youth
> In the strength and flush of manhood,
> In the grandeur and exquisiteness of old age,
> In the superb vistas of death.

But of course an "incomplete envelope" is not an envelope at all. Without a conclusion it is not a container. And it is characteristic of Whitman, especially in 1855–56, that he more often preferred not to finish his comparisons, analogies, representative examples of reality, but let them trail off into infinity. In his later poems, however, the envelope often provides a structure and unity for the whole composition, as in *Joy, Shipmate, Joy!:*

Joy, shipmate, joy!
(Pleas'd to my soul at death I cry)
Our life is closed, our life begins,
The long, long anchorage we leave,
The ship is clear at last, she leaps!
She swiftly courses from the shore,
Joy, shipmate, joy!

Other Reiterative Devices

In the above discussion parallelism was referred to as both a *structure* and a *rhythm* in Whitman's verse technique. Since rhythm means orderly or schematic repetition, a poem can have several kinds of rhythms, sometimes so coördinated in the total effect that it is difficult to isolate and evaluate the separate function of each. Thus Whitman's parallelism can give esthetic pleasure as a recognizable pattern of thought, which is to say that it is the basis of the structure of the composition. This does not necessarily result in a repetition or rhythm of sounds, cadences, music, etc. But since thoughts are expressed by means of spoken sounds (or symbols that represent spoken sounds), it is possible for the *thought rhythm* to produce, or to be accompanied by, *phonic rhythm*. The latter need not be a rhythm of accents or stressed syllables (though it often is in *Leaves of Grass* as will be demonstrated later). Rime, or repetition of similar sounds according to a definite pattern, is another kind of phonic rhythm, and may serve several purposes, such as pleasing the ear (which has been conditioned to anticipate certain sounds at regular intervals) or grouping the lines and thereby (in many subtle ways) emphasizing the thought.

Whitman's parallelism, or thought rhythm, is so often accompanied and reinforced by parallel wording and sounds that the two techniques are often almost identical. An easy way to collect examples of his "thought rhythm" is to glance down the left-hand margin and notice the lines beginning with the same word, and usually the same grammatical construction: "I will... I will... I will..." or "Where...Where... Where..." or "When...When...When," etc.[20]

These repetitions of words or phrases are often found in modern conventional meters. Tennyson, for example,[21] repeats consecutively the same word or phrase throughout many passages; and the refrain and repetend in Poe's versification is the same device in a somewhat different manner. In conventional meters these reiterations may even set up a rhythm of their own, either syncopating or completely distorting the

[20] Cf. *Song of Myself*, sec. 33 or *Salut au Monde!*

[21] Cf. Emile Lauvriere, *Repetition and Parallelism in Tennyson* (London: Oxford University Press, 1901).

regular metrical pattern. But there is this very important difference between reiteration in rime and meter and reiteration in *Leaves of Grass:* in the former the poem has a set pattern of accents (iambic, trochaic, anapestic, etc.), whereas in Whitman's verse the pattern of sounds and musical effects is entirely dependent upon the thought and structure of the separate lines.

In every emotionally and intellectually pleasing poem in *Leaves of Grass* these reiterations do set up a recognizable pattern of sounds.[22] Since the line is not bound by a specific number of syllables, or terminated by conventional rime, the sound patterns may seem to the untrained reader entirely free and lawless. It was part of Whitman's "organic" style to make his rhythms freer than those of classical and conventional versification, but they are no freer than those of the best musical compositions of opera and symphony. They can, of course, be too free to recognize, in which case Whitman failed as a poet—and like almost all major poets, he has many failures to his name. But in the best poems of *Leaves of Grass*—such as *Out of the Cradle Endlessly Rocking, When Lilacs Last in the Dooryard Bloom'd,* or *Passage to India,* —the combined thought and sound patterns are as definite and organized as in *Lycidas* or *Samson Agonistes.*

Several names have been given Whitman's reiterative devices in addition to the ones used here (phonic reiteration, etc.) Miss Autrey Nell Wiley, who has made the most thorough study of this subject, uses the rhetorical terms *epanaphora* and *epanalepsis.*[23] The nineteenth-century Italian scholar, Jannaccone,[24] calls these reiterations *rima psichica iniziale e terminale* (initial and terminal psychic rime) and *rima psichica media e terminale.* "Psychic rime"[25] is a suggestive term, but it probably overemphasizes the analogy with conventional rime—though it is important to notice the initial, medial, and terminal positions of Whitman's reiterations. The initial is most common, as in the "Cradle" poem:

> *Out of the* cradle endlessly rocking,
> *Out of the* mocking bird's throat, the musical shuttle,
> *Out of the* Ninth-month midnight.

Although this reiteration might be regarded as "psychic rime," its most significant function is the setting up of a cadence to dominate the whole line, as the "Give me" reiteration does in *Give Me the Splendid*

[22] Here again Emerson's theory preceded Whitman's practice. In the section on "Melody, Rhyme, and Form" in his essay on *Poetry and Imagination* Emerson wrote: "Another form of rhyme is iterations of phrases . . ."

[23] See note 14, above.

[24] P. Jannaccone, *La Poesia di Walt Whitman e L'Evoluzione delle Forme Ritmiche* (Torino, Italy, 1898), 64 ff.

[25] Cf. note 22, above.

Silent Sun, or the "What," "I hear," "I see," etc. in *Salut au Monde!* though scarcely any poem in *Leaves of Grass* is without the combined use of parallelism and reiteration. Often a short poem is a single "envelope" of parallelism with initial reiteration, as in *I Sit and Look Out:*

> I sit and look out upon all the sorrows of the world, and upon all oppression
> and shame,
> I hear secret convulsive sobs from young men at anguish with themselves,
> remorseful after deeds done,
> I see in low life the mother misused by her children, dying, neglected,
> gaunt, desperate,
> I see the wife misused by her husband, I see the treacherous seducer of
> young women,
> I mark the ranklings of jealousy and unrequited love attempted to be hid,
> I see these sights on the earth,
> I see the workings of battle, pestilence, tyranny, I see martyrs and prisoners,
> I observe a famine at sea, I observe the sailors casting lots who shall be
> kill'd to preserve the lives of the rest,
> I observe the slights and degradations cast by arrogant persons upon laborers, the poor, and upon negroes, and the like;
> All these—all the meanness and agony without end I sitting look out upon,
> See, hear, and am silent.

Initial reiteration, as in the above passage, occurs oftener in *Leaves of Grass* than either medial or final. Miss Wiley has estimated that 41 percent of the more than 10,500 lines in the *Leaves* contain epanalepsis, or initial reiteration.[26] But words and phrases are frequently repeated in other positions. *When Lilacs Last in the Dooryard Bloom'd* contains an effective example of a word from the first line repeated and interwoven throughout succeeding lines:

> Over the breast of the spring, the land, *amid* cities,
> *Amid* lanes and through old woods, where lately the violets peep'd from
> the ground, spotting the gray debris,
> *Amid* the grass in the fields each side of the lanes, *passing* the endless grass,
> *Passing* the yellow-spear'd wheat, every grain from its shroud in the dark-
> brown fields uprisen,
> *Passing* the apple-tree blows of white and pink in the orchards,
> Carrying a corpse to where it shall rest in the grave,
> Night and day journeys a coffin.

Here the reiterations have little to do with cadences but aid greatly in the effect of ceaseless motion—and even of *enjambment,* so rare in *Leaves of Grass*—as the body of the assassinated president is carried "night and day" from Washington to the plains of Illinois.

[26] Wiley, *op. cit.,* 161–162.

Final reiteration is found, though Whitman used it sparingly, perhaps because it too closely resembles refrains and repetends in conventional versification, and also because he had little use for the kind of melody and singing lyricism which these devices produce. When he does use final reiteration, it is more for rhetorical emphasis than music, as in sec. 24 of *Song of Myself:*

> Root of wash'd sweet-flag! timorous pond-snipe! nest of guarded duplicate
> eggs! *it shall be you!*
> Mix'd tussled hay of head, beard, brawn, *it shall be you!*
> Trickling sap of maple, fibre of manly wheat, *it shall be you!*
> Sun so generous *it shall be you!*

and so on throughout sixteen lines.

Sometimes Whitman uses reiteration through the entire line, as in *By Blue Ontario's Shore:*

> I will know if I am to be less than they,
> I will see if I am not as majestic as they,
> I will see if I am not as subtle and real as they,
> I will see if I am to be less generous than they, . . .

C. Alphonso Smith in his study of repetitions in English and American poetry (he does not mention Whitman, however) has defined the difference between reiterations in prose and poetry:

> In prose, a word or group of words is repeated for emphasis; whereas in verse, repetition is chiefly employed not for emphasis (compare the use of the refrain), but for melody of rhythm, for continuousness or sonorousness of effect, for unity of impression, for banding lines or stanzas, and for the more indefinable though not less important purposes of suggestiveness.[27]

Of course Smith is thinking of conventional versification, but continuousness of effect, unity of impression, joining of lines and stanzas, and suggestiveness all apply to Whitman's use of reiteration.

Although Whitman's reiteration is not musical in the sense that Poe's is (*i.e.*, for melody and harmony), it is musical in a larger sense. Many critics have developed the analogy of music in Whitman's technique, but De Selincourt's comments are especially pertinent here. "The progress of Whitman's verse," he says, "has much in common with that of musical composition. For we are carrying the sense of past effects along with us more closely and depending more intimately upon them than is possible in normal verse."[28] And he observes that:

[27] C. Alphonso Smith, *Repetition and Parallelism in English Verse* (New York, 1894), 9.

[28] De Selincourt, *op. cit.*, 104.

> repetition, which the artist in language scrupulously avoids, is the foundation and substance of musical expression. Now Whitman . . . uses words and phrases more as if they were notes of music than any other writer . . . it was to him part of the virtue and essence of life that its forms and processes were endlessly reduplicated; and poetry, which was delight in life, must somehow, he thought, mirror this elemental abundance.[29]

Of course Whitman's repetition concerns not only words and phrases (Jannaccone's "psychic rime") but thought patterns as well. In fact, his favorite method of organizing a long poem like *The Sleepers*, *Proud Music of the Storm*, *Mystic Trumpeter*, or even *Song of the Red-Wood Tree* is, as remarked elsewhere, symphonic. He likes to advance a theme, develop it by enumeration and representative symbols, advance other themes and develop them in similar manners, then repeat, summarize, and emphasize. Thus Whitman's repetition of thought, of words, of cadences,—playing variations on each out of exuberance and unrestrained joy both in the thought and form—, all combine to give him the satisfaction and conviction that he has "expressed" himself, not logically or even coherently, but by suggestion and by sharing his own emotions with the reader. This is true even though the background of nearly every poem in *Leaves of Grass* is "Ideas" rather than simple lyric emotion; but Whitman develops these ideas like a poet-musician, not like a philosopher or a polemical writer.

Another kind of reiteration which Whitman uses both for the thought and the musical effect is what Jannaccone calls "grammatical" and "logical rime"[30]—though *grammatical rhythm* might be a more convenient and appropriate term. Instead of repeating the same identical word or phrase, he repeats a part of speech or grammatical construction at certain places in the line. This has nearly the same effect on the rhythm and cadence as the reiteration of the same word or phrase, especially when "grammatical rime" is initial. For example, parallel verbs:

> *Flow* on, river! *flow* with the flood-tide, and *ebb* with the ebb-tide!
> *Frolic* on, crested and scallop-edg'd waves!
> Gorgeous clouds of the sunset! *drench* with your splendor me or
> the men and women generations after me!
> *Cross* from shore to shore, countless crowds of passengers!
> *Stand* up, tall masts of Mannahatta,

The following Jannaccone calls "logical rime":[31]

29 *Ibid.*, 108.

30 Jannaccone, *op. cit.*, 67 ff.

31 *Ibid.*, 73.

> Long and long has the *grass* been *growing,*
> Long and long has the *rain* been *falling,*
> Long has the *globe* been rolling *round.*

Not only are *growing, falling,* and *rolling* grammatically parallel, but they are also the natural (and logical) things for the *grass,* the *rain,* and the *globe* to be doing.

Sometimes Whitman reiterates cognates:

> The *song* is to the *singer,* and comes back most to him,
> The *teaching* is to the *teacher,* and comes back most to him,
> The *murder* is to the *murderer,* and comes back most to him, etc.

In all these examples the various kinds of reiterations produce also a pattern of accents which can be scanned like conventional verse.

> Lóng and lóng has the gráss been grówing, . . .

Parallelism gives these lines a *thought* rhythm, but this is reinforced by the phonic recurrences, giving additional rhythm which depends upon *sounds* for its effect. Of course these examples are unusually regular (or simple), whereas the same principles in other passages give a much greater variety and complexity of phonic stress. But the combined reiterations always (at least when successful) produce a composite musical pattern—a pattern more plastic than any to be found in conventional versification, but one which the ear can be trained to appreciate no less than patterns of rime and meter.

william empson

SIDNEY'S DOUBLE SESTINA

. . . I have mentioned Spenser, whom no discussion of rhythm can ignore. To show the scale of his rhythm, it may be enough to list some of the ways in which he gave movement to the stanza of the *Faerie Queene;* it is by the delicacy of this movement that he shows his attitude towards his sentences, rather than by devices of implication in the sentences themselves. At the same time, one such an attitude has been fixed, it is more easily described in terms of the meaning of the words than in terms of the meaning of the rhythm; in the next example, from Sidney, I shall use this other mode of approach.

Spenser concentrates the reader's attention on to the movement of his stanza, by the use of archaic words and constructions, so that one is at a safe distance from the exercise of an immediate judgment, by the steady untroubled flow of similar lines, by making no rapid change of sense or feeling, by sustained alliteration, parallel adjectives, and full statement of the accessories of a thought, and by the dreamy repetition of the great stanza perpetually pausing at its close. *Ababbcbcc* is a unit which may be broken up into a variety of metrical forms, and the ways in which it is successively broken up are fitted into enormous patterns. The first quatrain usually gratifies the ear directly and without surprise, and the stanzas may then be classified by the grammatical connections of the crucial fifth line, which must give a soft bump to the dying fall of the first quatrain, keep it in the air, and prevent it from falling apart from the rest of the stanza.

It may complete the sense of the quatrain, for instance, with a couplet, and the stanza will then begin with a larger, more narrative unit, *ababb,* and wander garrulously down a perspective to the alexandrine. Or it may add to the quatrain as by an afterthought, as if with a childish earnestness it made sure of its point without regard to the metre, and one is relieved to find that the metre recovers itself after all. For more energetic or serious statements it will start a new quatrain at

From *Seven Types of Ambiguity.* Copyright 1930, 1947 by William Empson. Reprinted by permission of New Directions, Publishers. Title supplied by the present editor.

the fifth line, with a new sentence; there are then two smaller and tighter, repeatedly didactic, or logically opposed, or historically advancing, units, whose common rhyme serves to insist upon their contrast, which are summed up and reconciled in the final solemnity of the alexandrine. In times of excitement the fifth line will be connected both ways, so as to ignore the two quatrains, and, by flowing straight on down the stanza with an insistence on its unity, show the accumulated energy of some enormous climax; and again, by being connected with neither, it will make the stanza into an unstressed conversational device without overtones of rhythm, picking up stray threads of the story with almost the relief of prose. It would be interesting to take one of the vast famous passages of the work and show how these devices are fitted together into larger units of rhythm, but having said that every use of the stanza includes all these uses in the reader's apprehension of it I may have said enough to show the sort of methods Spenser had under his control; why it was not necessary for him to concentrate on the lightning flashes of ambiguity.

The size, the possible variety, and the fixity of this unit give something of the blankness that comes from fixing your eyes on a bright spot; you have to yield yourself to it very completely to take in the variety of its movement, and, at the same time, there is no need to concentrate the elements of the situation into a judgment as if for action. As a result of this, when there are ambiguities of idea, it is whole civilisations rather than details of the moment which are their elements; he can pour into the even dreamwork of his fairyland Christian, classical, and chivalrous materials with an air, not of ignoring their differences, but of holding all their systems of values floating as if at a distance, so as not to interfere with one another, in the prolonged and diffused energies of his mind.

Nowhere in English literature can this use of diffuseness as an alternative to, or peculiar branch of, ambiguity be seen more clearly than in those lovely sestinas of Sidney, which are so curiously foreign to the normal modes or later developments of the language. This time I must do some serious quotation.

STREPHON. KLAIUS.

STREPHON. You Gote-heard Gods, that love the grassie mountaines,
You nimphes that haunt the springs in pleasant vallies,
You Satyrs joyd with free and quiet forrests,
Vouchsafe your silent eares to playning musique,
Which to my woes gives still an early morning:
And draws the dolor on till wery evening.

KLAIUS. O Mercurie, foregoer to the evening,
O heavenlie huntresse of the savage mountaines,
O lovelie starre, entitled of the morning,
While that my voice doth fill the woeful vallies
Vouchsafe your silent eares to playning musique,
Which oft hath *Echo* tir'd in secrete forrests.

STREPHON. I that was once free-burgess of the forrests
Where shade from Sunne, and sports I sought at evening,
I that was once esteemed for pleasant musique,
Am banisht now amongest the monstrous mountaines
Of huge despaire, and foul afflictions vallies,
Am growne a skrich-owle to myself each morning.

KLAIUS. I that was once delighted every morning,
Hunting the wild inhabiters of forrests,
I that was once the musique of these vallies,
So darkened am, that all my day is evening,
Hart-broken so, that mole-hills seem high mountaines,
And fill the vales with cries in stead of musique.

STREPHON. Long since alas, my deadly Swannish musique
Hath made itself a crier of the morning,
And hath with wailing strength climbed highest mountaines:
Long since my thoughts more desert be than forrests:
Long since my thoughts chase me like beasts in forrests,
And state throwen down to over-troden vallies.

KLAIUS. Long since the happie dwellers of these vallies,
Have praide me leave my strange exclaiming musique,
Which troubles their dayes worke, and joyes of evening:
Long since I hate the night, more hate the morning:
Long since my thoughts chase me like beasts in forrests,
And make me wish myself laid under mountaines.

STREPHON. Me seemes I see the high and stately mountaines,
Transforme themselves to lowe dejected vallies:
Me seemes I heare in these ill-changed forrests,
The nightingales doo learne of Owles their musique:
Me seemes I feele the comfort of the morning
Turnde to the mortal serene of an evening.

KLAIUS. Me seemes I see a filthie cloudie evening,
As soone as Sunne begins to climbe the mountaines:
Me seemes I feel a noisome scent, the morning
When I do smell the flowers of these vallies:
Me seemes I heare, when I doo heare sweet musique,
The dreadful cries of murdered men in forrests.

STREPHON. I wish to fire the trees of all these forrests;
I give the Sunne a last farewell each evening;
I curse the fiddling finders out of musique:
With envy doo I hate the lofty mountaines;
And with despite despise the humble vallies:
I doo detest night, evening, day, and morning.

KLAIUS. Curse to myself my prayer is, the morning:
My fire is more, than can be made with forrests;
My state more base, than are the basest vallies:
I wish no evenings more to see, each evening;
Shamed I have myself in sight of mountaines,
And stoppe mine eares, lest I go mad with musique.

STREPHON. For she, whose parts maintained a perfect musique,
Whose beauty shin'de more than the blushing morning,
Who much did pass in state the stately mountaines,
In straightness past the Cedars of the forrests,
Hath cast me wretch into eternal evening,
By taking her two Sunnes from these dark vallies.

KLAIUS. For she, to whom compared, the Alps are vallies,
She, whose lest word brings from the spheares their musique
At whose approach the Sunne rose in the evening,
Who, where she went, bare in her forehead morning,
Is gone, is gone from these our spoiled forrests,
Turning to deserts our best pastur'de mountaines.

STREPHON. These mountaines witness shall, so shall these vallies,
KLAIUS These forrests eke, made wretched by our musique,
STREPHON. Our morning hymn is this,
KLAIUS. and song at evening.

This form has no direction or momentum; it beats, however rich its orchestration, with a wailing and immovable monotony, for ever upon the same doors in vain. *Mountaines, vallies; forrests; musique, evening, morning;* it is at these words only that Klaius and Strephon pause in their cries; these words circumscribe their world; these are the bones of their situation; and in tracing their lovelorn pastoral tedium through thirteen repetitions, with something of the aimless multitudinous beating of the sea on a rock, we seem to extract all the meaning possible from these notions; we are at last, therefore, in possession of all that might have been implied by them (if we had understood them) in a single sentence; of all, in fact, that is implied by them, in the last sentence of the poem. I must glance, to show this, at the twelve other occasions on which each word is used.

Mountaines are haunts of Pan for lust and Diana for chastity, to both of these the lovers appeal; they suggest being shut in, or banishment; impossibility and impotence, or difficulty and achievement; greatness that may be envied or may be felt as your own (so as to make you feel helpless, or feel powerful); they give you the peace, or the despair, of the grave; they are the distant things behind which the sun rises and sets, the too near things which shut in your valley; deserted wastes, and the ample pastures to which you drive up the cattle for the summer.

Vallies hold nymphs to which you may appeal, and yet are the normal places where you live; are your whole world, and yet limited so that your voice can affect the whole of them; are opposed to *mountaines,* either as places of shelter and comfort, or as places of humility and affliction; are rich with flowers and warmth, or are dark hollows between the hills.

Forests, though valuable and accustomed, are desolate and hold danger; there are both nightingales and owls in them; their beasts, though savage, give the strong pleasures of hunting; their burning is either useful or destructive; though they produce wildness and lack of cultivation, you find there freedom for contemplation, and their straight trunks are symbols of your pride.

Music may express joy or sorrow; is at once more and less direct than talking, and so is connected with one's permanent feeling about the characters of pastoral that they are at once very rustic and rather over-civilised; it may please or distress the bystanders; and while belonging to despair and to the deaths of swans, it may share the living beauty of this very lady, and be an inmate of the celestial spheres.

Morning brings hope, light and labour, *evening* rest, play and despair; they are the variety of Nature, or the tedious repetition of a day; their patrons Venus, whom one dare not name, and Mercury, who will bring no news of her. *Morning,* too, has often attached to it a meaning which, by an intelligent and illuminating misprint, is insisted upon in the eleventh (and subsequent) editions:—

> At whose approach the sun rose in the evening,
> Who where she went bore in her forehead *mourning,*
> Is gone, is gone, from these our spoiled forrests,
> Turning to deserts our best *pastor'd* mountaines.

The form takes its effect by concentrating on these words and slowly building up our interest in them; all their latent implications are brought out by the repetitions; and each in turn so used to build up some simple conceit. So that when the static conception of the complaint has been finally brought into light (I do not mean by this to depreciate the sustained magnificence of its crescendo, but to praise the singleness of its idea), a whole succession of feelings about the local scenery, the whole way in which it is taken for granted, has been enlisted into sorrow and beats as a single passion of the mind.

I have put this poem at the end of a discussion ostensibly about rhythm, and shall mention its rhythm only to remark that it is magnificent; my point is that one can best illustrate its rhythm by showing the cumulative way it uses its words. But more generally, one may say, the poem is a sort of monument to the first type of ambiguity;[1] it is seldom that the meaning of a poet's words is built up so patiently and steadily in the course of using them. And limited as this form may be, the capacity to accept a limitation so unflinchingly, the capacity even to conceive so large a form as a unit of sustained feeling, is one that has been lost since that age.

1 [i.e. "when a word, a syntax, or a grammatical structure, while making only one statement, is effective in several ways at once."—Ed.]

j. v. cunningham

LOGIC AND LYRIC: MARVELL, DUNBAR, AND NASHE

The discussion in the previous chapter raises the question, May the principal structure of a poem be of a logical rather than an alogical sort? For example, to confine ourselves to the Old Logic, May a lyric be solely or predominantly the exposition of a syllogism? and may the propositions of the lyric, one by one, be of the sort to be found in a logical syllogism?

The incautious romantic will deny the possibility, and with a repugnance of feeling that would preclude any further discussion. For logic and lyric are generally regarded as opposites, if not as contradictory terms. "It is a commonplace," says a recent writer on logic, "that poetry and logic have nothing to do with each other, that they are even opposed to one another."[1] You will find this explicitly stated, sometimes with the substitution of 'science' for 'logic,' in most of the school handbooks on the study of literature, in most of the introductions to poetry. "The peculiar quality of poetry," we read in one of these:

> can be distinguished from that of prose if one thinks of the creative mind as normally expressing itself in a variety of literary forms ranged along a graduated scale between the two contrasted extremes of scientific exposition and lyrical verse.

And, a little later:

> [Poetry] strives for a conviction begotten of the emotions rather than of reason.

Consequently, we are told:

> The approach of poetry is indirect. It proceeds by means of suggestion, implication, reflection. Its method is largely symbolical. It is more interested in connotations than in denotations.[2]

Reprinted from *Tradition and Poetic Structure* by J. V. Cunningham by permission of the publisher, Alan Swallow. Copyright 1960 by J. V. Cunningham.

[1] Richard von Mises, *Positivism* (Cambridge, Mass., 1951), p. 289.

[2] Harold R. Walley and J. Harold Wilson, *The Anatomy of Literature* (New York, 1934), pp. 143 and 144.

This is common doctrine. Poetry is in some way concerned with emotion rather than reason, and its method is imaginative, indirect, implicit rather than explicit, symbolical rather than discursive, concerned with what its terms suggest rather than with what they state. The kind of poetry which most fully possesses and exhibits these concerns, methods, and qualities is generally thought to be the lyric, and hence it, of all poetry, is regarded as the most antithetical to reason, logic, and science.

This was not always the case. In the eighth century, for example, a scholiast of the school of Alcuin regarded not only grammar and rhetoric but dialectic or logic also as the disciplines that nourish and form a poet. In the medieval and renaissance traditions of commentary on Aristotle's logic, poetic is sometimes regarded as a part, a sub-division, of logic—as, indeed, I consider it myself. So late as the eighteenth century David Hume writes in an essay *Of the Standard of Taste:*

> Besides, every kind of composition, even the most poetical, is nothing but a chain of propositions and reasonings; not always indeed the justest and most exact, but still plausible and specious, however disguised by the coloring of the imagination.

And even today the writer on logic whom I quoted earlier asserts, in denial of the commonplace: "Every poem, except in rare extreme cases, contains judgments and implicit propositions, and thus becomes subject to logical analysis."[3]

But may the chain of propositions and reasonings be not merely plausible and specious but even sufficiently just and exact? May the poem be not merely subject to logical analysis but logical in form? May, to return to our point, the subject and structure of a poem be conceived and expressed syllogistically? Anyone at all acquainted with modern criticism and the poems that are currently in fashion will think in this connection of Marvell's *To His Coy Mistress.* The apparent structure of that poem is an argumentative syllogism, explicitly stated. "Had we but world enough and time," the poet says,

> This coyness, lady, were no crime . . .
>
> But at my back I always hear
> Time's winged chariot hurrying near . . .
>
> Now, therefore . . .
> . . . let us sport us while we may . . .

If we had all the time and space in the world we could delay consummation. But we do not. Therefore. The structure is formal. The poet

[3] Scholiast cited in Otto Bird, "The Seven Liberal Arts" in Joseph T. Shipley, ed., *Dictionary of World Literature* (New York, 1943), p. 55; J. E. Spingarn, *A History of Literary Criticism in the Renaissance* (2nd ed.: New York, 1908), pp. 24–7; David Hume, *Philosophical Works* (Boston and Edinburgh, 1854), III, 264; von Mises, *loc. cit.*

offers to the lady a practical syllogism, and if she assents to it the appropriate consequence, he hopes, will follow:

Had we but world enough, and time,
This coyness, Lady, were no crime;
We would sit down and think which way
To walk and pass our long love's day.
Thou by the Indian Ganges side
Shouldst rubies find: I by the tide
Of Humber would complain. I would
Love you ten years before the Flood,
And you should, if you please, refuse
Till the conversion of the Jews.
My vegetable love should grow
Vaster than empires, and more slow;
An hundred years should go to praise
Thine eyes and on thy forehead gaze;
Two hundred to adore each breast;
But thirty thousand to the rest;
An age at least to every part,
And the last age should show your heart;
For, Lady, you deserve this state,
Nor would I love at lower rate.

But at my back I always hear
Time's winged chariot hurrying near;
And yonder all before us lie
Deserts of vast eternity.
Thy beauty shall no more be found,
Nor in thy marble vault shall sound
My echoing song: then worms shall try
That long preserved virginity,
And your quaint honor turn to dust,
And into ashes all my lust:
The grave's a fine and private place,
But none, I think, do there embrace.

Now, therefore, while the youthful hue
Sits on thy skin like morning lew.[4]
And while thy willing soul transpires
At every pore with instant fires,
Now let us sport us while we may,
And now, like amorous birds of prey,
Rather at once our time devour
Than languish in his slow-chapt power.
Let us roll all our strength and all

[4] [Warmth. This text is from] H. M. MargoulIouth, ed., *The Poems and Letters* (Oxford, 1927), II.

> Our sweetness up into one ball,
> And tear our pleasures with rough strife
> Thorough the iron gates of life:
> Thus, though we cannot make our sun
> Stand still, yet we will make him run.

The logical nature of the argument here has been generally recognised, though often with a certain timidity. Mr. Eliot hazards: "the three strophes of Marvell's poem have something like a syllogistic relation to each other." And in a recent scholarly work we read: "The dialectic of the poem lies not only or chiefly in the formal demonstration explicit in its three stanzas, but in all the contrasts evoked by its images and in the play between the immediately sensed and the intellectually apprehended."[5] That is, the logic is recognised, but minimized, and our attention is quickly distracted to something more reputable in a poem, the images or the characteristic tension of metaphysical poetry. For Mr. Eliot the more important element in this case is a principle of order common in modern poetry and often employed in his own poems. He points out that the theme of Marvell's poem is "one of the great traditional commonplaces of European literature . . . the theme of . . . *Gather ye rosebuds*, of *Go, lovely rose*." "Where the wit of Marvell," he continues, "renews the theme is in the variety and order of the images." The dominant principle of order in the poem, then, is an implicit one rather than the explicit principle of the syllogism, and implicit in the succession of images.

Mr. Eliot explains the implicit principle of order in this fashion:

> In the first of the three paragraphs Marvell plays with a fancy that begins by pleasing and leads to astonishment. . . We notice the high speed, the succession of concentrated images, each magnifying the original fancy. When this process has been carried to the end and summed up, the poem turns suddenly with that surprise which has been one of the most important means of poetic effect since Homer:
>
> But at my back I always hear
> Time's winged chariot hurrying near,
> And yonder all before us lie
> Deserts of vast eternity.
>
> A whole civilization resides in these lines:
>
> Pallida Mors aequo pulsat pede pauperum tabernas
> Regumque turres . . .

[5] T. S. Eliot, *Selected Essays* (new ed., New York, 1950), p. 254; Helen C. White, Ruth C. Wallerstein, and Ricardo Quintana, edd., *Seventeenth Century Verse and Prose* (New York, 1951), I, 454.

> A modern poet, had he reached the height, would very likely have closed on this moral reflection.

What is meant by this last observation becomes clear a little later where it is said that the wit of the poem "forms the crescendo and diminuendo of a scale of great imaginative power." The structure of the poem, then, is this: it consists of a succession of images increasing in imaginative power to the sudden turn and surprise of the image of time, and then decreasing to the conclusion. But is there any sudden turn and surprise in the image of time? and does the poem consist of a succession of images?

This talk of images is a little odd since there seem to be relatively few in the poem if one means by image what people usually do—a descriptive phrase that invites the reader to project a sensory construction. The looming imminence of Time's winged chariot is, no doubt, an image, though not a full-blown one since there is nothing in the phrasing that properly invites any elaboration of sensory detail. But when Mr. Eliot refers to "successive images" and cites "my *vegetable* love," with *vegetable* italicised, and "Till the conversion of the Jews," one suspects that he is provoking images where they do not textually exist. There is about as much of an image in "Till the conversion of the Jews" as there would be in "till the cows come home," and it would be a psychiatrically sensitive reader who would immediately visualize the lowing herd winding slowly o'er the lea. But "my *vegetable* love" will make the point. I have no doubt that Mr. Eliot and subsequent readers do find an image here. They envisage some monstrous and expanding cabbage, but they do so in mere ignorance. *Vegetable* is no vegetable but an abstract and philosophical term, known as such to every educated man of Marvell's day. Its context is the doctrine of the three souls: the rational, which in man subsumes the other two; the sensitive, which men and animals have in common and which is the principle of motion and perception; and, finally, the lowest of the three, the vegetable soul, which is the only one that plants possess, and which is the principle of generation and corruption, of augmentation and decay. Marvell says, then, my love, denied the exercise of sense, but possessing the power of augmentation, will increase "Vaster than empires." It is an intellectual image, and hence no image at all but a conceit. For if one calls any sort of particularity or detail in a poem an image, the use of the wrong word will invite the reader to misconstrue his experience in terms of images, to invent sensory constructions and to project them on the poem.

A conceit is not an image. It is a piece of wit. It is in the tradition in which Marvell was writing, among other possibilities, the discovery of a proposition referring to one field of experience in terms of an intellectual structure derived from another field, and often enough a field of learning, as is the case in "my vegetable love." This tradition, though it goes back to the poetry of John Donne, and years before that, was current in Marvell's day. The fashionable poetry at the time he was writing this poem, the poetry comparable to that of Eliot or of Auden in the past two decades, was the poetry of John Cleveland, and the fashionable manner was generally known as Clevelandising. It consisted in the invention of a series of witty hyperbolical conceits, sometimes interspersed with images, and containing a certain amount of roughage in the form of conventional erotic statements:

> Thy beauty shall no more be found,
> Nor in thy marble vault shall sound
> My echoing song . . .

It was commonly expressed in the octosyllabic couplet. Cleveland, for example, writes *Upon Phillis Walking in a Morning before Sun-rising:*

> The trees, like yeomen of the guard,
> Serving her more for pomp than ward . . .

The comparison here does not invite visualization. It would be inappropriate to summon up the colors and serried ranks of the guard. The comparison is made solely with respect to the idea: the trees like the guard serve more for pomp than ward. Again:

> The flowers, called out of their beds,
> Start and raise up their drowsy heads,
> And he that for their color seeks
> May see it vaulting to her cheeks,
> Where roses mix—no civil war
> Divides her York and Lancaster.[6]

One does not here picture in panorama the Wars of the Roses. One sees rather the aptness and the wit of York and Lancaster, the white rose and the red, reconciled in her cheeks, or one rejects it as forced and far-fetched. This is a matter of taste.

But if the poem is not a succession of images, does it exhibit that other principle which Mr. Eliot ascribes to it, the turn and surprise which he finds in the abrupt introduction of time's chariot and which forms a sort of fulcrum on which the poem turns. Subsequent critics have certainly felt that it has. In a current textbook we read:

> The poem begins as a conventional love poem in which the lover tries to persuade his mistress to give in to his entreaties. But with the introduction

[6] John M. Berdan, ed., *The Poems* (New Haven, 1911), pp. 80–1.

of the image of the chariot in l. 21, the poet becomes obsessed by the terrible onrush of time, and the love theme becomes scarcely more than an illustration of the effect which time has upon human life.

And the leading scholar in the field, a man who is generally quite unhappy with Mr. Eliot's criticism, nevertheless says:

the poet sees the whole world of space and time as the setting for two lovers. But wit cannot sustain the pretence that youth and beauty and love are immortal, and with a quick change of tone—like Catullus' *nobis cum semel occidit brevis lux* or Horace's *sed Timor et Minae*—the theme of time and death is developed with serious and soaring directness . . .[7]

These, I believe, are not so much accounts of the poem as accounts of Mr. Eliot's reading of the poem. Let us question the fact. Does the idea of time and death come as any surprise in this context? The poem began, "Had we but world enough and time." That is, it began with an explicit condition contrary to fact, which by all grammatical rules amounts to the assertion that we do not have world enough and time. There is no surprise whatever when the proposition is explicitly made in line 21. It would rather have been surprising if it had not been made. Indeed, the only question we have in this respect, after we have read the first line, is, How many couplets will the poet expend on the ornamental re-iteration of the initial proposition before he comes to the expected *but*. The only turn in the poem is the turn which the structure of the syllogism had led us to await.

Mr. Eliot compares the turn and surprise which he finds in this poem to a similar turn in an ode of Horace's, and the scholars seem to corroborate the comparison. This is the fourth ode of the first book:

Solvitur acris hiems grata vice veris et Favoni,
trahuntque siccas machinae carinas . . .

The poem begins with a picture of spring and proceeds by a succession of images, images of the external world and mythological images:

Sharp winter relaxes with the welcome change to Spring and the west wind, and the cables haul the dry keels of ships. The herd no longer takes pleasure in its stalls or the farmer in his fire, and the pastures no longer whiten with hoar frost. Cytherean Venus leads her dancers beneath the overhanging moon, and the beautiful graces and nymphs strike the ground with alternate foot, while blazing Vulcan visits the grim forges of the Cyclops. Now is the time to wind your bright hair with green myrtle or with the flowers that the thawed earth yields. Now is the time to sacrifice to Faunus in the shadowed woods, whether it be a lamb he asks or a kid:

[7] Wright Thomas and Stuart Gerry Brown, edd., *Reading Poems* (New York, 1941), p. 702; Douglas Bush, *English Literature in the Earlier Seventeenth Century* (Oxford, 1945), p. 163.

Pallida mors aequo pulsat pede pauperum tabernas regumque turres.

Pallid death with indifferent foot strikes the poor man's hut and the palaces of kings. Now, fortunate Sestius, the brief sum of life forbids our opening a long account with hope. Night will soon hem you in, and the fabled ghosts, and Pluto's meagre house.[8]

Death occurs in this poem with that suddenness and lack of preparation with which it sometimes occurs in life. The structure of the poem is an imitation of the structure of such experiences in life. And as we draw from such experiences often a generalization, so Horace from the sudden realization of the abruptness and impartiality of death, reflects

vitae summa brevis spem nos vetat incohare longam.

The brief sum of life forbids our opening a long account with hope.

But the proposition is subsequent to the experience; it does not rule and direct the poem from the outset. And the experience in Horace *is* surprising and furnishes the fulcrum on which the poem turns. It has, in fact, the characteristics which are ascribed to Marvell's poem but which Marvell's poem does not have. The two are two distinct kinds of poetry, located in distinct and almost antithetical traditions; both are valuable and valid methods, but one is not to be construed in terms of the other.

In brief, the general structure of Marvell's poem is syllogistic, and it is located in the Renaissance tradition of formal logic and of rhetoric. The structure exists in its own right and as a kind of expandable filing system. It is a way of disposing of, of making a place for, elements of a different order: in this case, Clevelandising conceits and erotic propositions in the tradition of Jonson and Herrick. These re-iterate the propositions of the syllogism. They do not develop the syllogism, and they are not required by the syllogism; they are free and extra. There could be more or less of them since there is nothing in the structure that determines the number of interpolated couplets. It is a matter of tact, and a matter of the appetite of the writer and the reader.

The notion of a structure as a kind of expandable filing system may deserve a few sentences. The narrative structure of a Shakespearean play can be regarded as a structure of this order. It exists in its own right, of course, but it is also a method for disposing various kinds of material of other orders, a set speech or passion here, an interpolated comic routine in another place. The structure offers a series of hooks upon which different things can be hung. Whether the totality will then form a whole, a unity, is a question of interpretation and a question of

[8] My translation, except for "the brief sum of life forbids our opening a long account with hope," which is Gildersleeve's; see Paul Shorey, ed., Shorey and Gordon J. Lang, *Odes and Epodes* (rev. ed., Chicago, 1910), *ad loc.*

value. It is a question, for example, of what sort of unity is demanded, and whether there are various sorts.

In Marvell's poem, only the general structure is syllogistic; the detail and development are of another order, and critics have been diligent in assigning the poetic quality of the whole to the non-syllogistic elements. Is it possible, then, to write a lyric that will be wholly or almost wholly syllogistic? It is. There is such a lyric in the *Oxford Book of English Verse,* a lyric of somewhat lesser repute than Marvell's, but still universally praised and universally conceded to possess the true lyrical power. It is Dunbar's *Lament for the Makaris.*

The structure of Dunbar's poem is the structure of the traditional syllogism with which everyone is acquainted: *All men are mortal, I am a man;* together with a concluding practical syllogism, *What must be, must be accepted, but I must die.* The syllogism is developed in two ways, both characteristic methods in the logical tradition of the later Middle Ages. It begins with the immediate induction from experience of the leading principle, the major premise:

> I that in heill wes and gladnes,
> Am trublit now with gret seiknes,
> And feblit with infermite;
> *Timor mortis conturbat me.*

The experience, then, is the sudden alteration from health to illness, and this yields the generalization:

> Our plesance heir is all vane glory,
> This fals warld is bot transitory,
> The flesche is brukle, the Fend is sle:
> *Timor mortis conturbat me.*

The premise, then, is: this false world is but transitory; and it is presently expressed in more restricted terms:

> The stait of man dois change and vary,
> Now sound, now seik, now blith, now sary,
> Now dansand mery, now like to dee:
> *Timor mortis conturbat me.*

The syllogism is now developed by another form of induction, and this development accounts for the remainder of the poem, except for the last stanza. It is developed through induction by simple enumeration in support and explication of the major premise, but with this special feature, that the induction proceeds by a hierarchical method. Nothing could be more characteristic of medieval logic. The argument is: if everything sublunary changes and varies, is mortal, then every estate of man is mortal, and the poet enumerates the estates:

On to the ded gois all Estatis,
Princis, Prelotis, and Potestatis,
Baith riche and pur of al degre:
Timor mortis conturbat me . . .

He takis the campion in the stour,
The capitane closit in the tour,
The lady in bour full of bewte:
Timor mortis conturbat me.

He sparis no lord for his piscence,
Na clerk for his intelligence;
His awfull strak may no man fle:
Timor mortis conturbat me.

Art, magicianis, and astrologgis,
Rhetoris, logicianis, and theologgis,
Thame helpis no conclusionis sle:
Timor mortis conturbat me.

In medicyne the most practicianis,
Lechis, surrigianis, and phisicianis,
Thame self fra ded may not supple:
Timor mortis conturbat me.

If all estates must die, then poets too must die. And now Dunbar proceeds by a simple enumeration, a roll-call, of poets.

He has done petuously devour
The noble Chaucer, of makaris flour,
The Monk of Bery, and Gower, all thre:
Timor mortis conturbat me.

The gude Syr Hew of Eglintoun,
And eik Heryot, and Wyntoun,
He has tane out of this cuntre:
Timor mortis conturbat me.

He continues to enumerate poet after poet whom death has taken, until he comes finally to his friendly enemy, the poet, Kennedy, and to himself:

Gud Maister Walter Kennedy
In point of dede lyis veraly,
Gret reuth it were that so suld be:
Timor mortis conturbat me.

Sen he has all my brether tane,
He wil nocht lat me lif alane,
Of forse I man his nyxt pray be:
Timor mortis conturbat me.

Therefore, I must die, concludes the syllogism. And now follows the practical syllogism, the act of resignation:

> Sen for the deid remeid is none,
> Best is that we for dede dispone,
> Eftir our deid that lif may we.
> *Timor mortis conturbat me.*[9]

Almost every proposition in the poem is strictly controlled by the syllogistic structure. The exceptions are the refrain and a certain number of affective phrases and affective sentences: "He has done petuously devour / The noble Chaucer" and "Gret reuth it wer that so suld be." These direct the feeling of the poem. Yet though the poem is so completely determined by logical method and logical structure it has seemed, and justly, to generations of readers to be a moving poem and properly poetical.

I shall conclude with another poem of the same sort, a lyric of even greater renown in modern criticism. This is the song from *Summer's Last Will and Testament* by Thomas Nashe, "Adieu, farewell, earth's bliss." It too has a refrain, though in English, a response from the Litany of Saints, which was customarily recited through the streets of London in time of plague. The poem, like Dunbar's, consists of a series of discrete, self-enclosed stanzas, in which each line is end-stopped. The structure of the poem is, like Dunbar's and Marvell's, a practical syllogism explicitly propounded, though not quite so formally as in the preceding poem. It opens with the rejection of earthly happiness. The argument is, to begin with the suppressed premise: true happiness is certain, but the world is uncertain; therefore worldly happiness is not true happiness. The world is uncertain since it is subject to the certainty of death and change. Nor can the goods of this world buy continued life, nor the art of medicine procure it: the plague increases. What is best in this life—and here we have the structure of the next three stanzas —beauty, prowess, and wit, all fade:

> Haste therefore each degree
> To welcome destiny . . .

For the world after death is certain, and its happiness true happiness:

> Adieu, farewell, earth's bliss!
> This world uncertain is:
> Fond are life's lustful joys,
> Death proves them all but toys.
> None from his darts can fly;
> I am sick, I must die—
> Lord, have mercy on us.

[9] W. Mackay Mackenzie, ed., *The Poems* (Edinburgh, 1932), pp. 20–3.

Rich men, trust not in wealth,
Gold cannot buy you health;
Physic himself must fade;
All things to end are made;
The plague full swift goes by;
I am sick, I must die–
  Lord, have mercy on us.

Beauty is but a flower
Which wrinkles will devour;
Brightness falls from the air;
Queens have died young and fair;
Dust hath closed Helen's eye;
I am sick, I must die–
  Lord, have mercy on us.

Strength stoops unto the grave,
Worms feed on Hector brave;
Swords may not fight with fate;
Earth still holds ope her gate;
Come, come! the bells do cry–
I am sick, I must die–
  Lord, have mercy on us.

Wit with his wantonness
Tasteth death's bitterness;
Hell's excutioner
Hath no ears for to hear
What vain art can reply;
I am sick, I must die–
  Lord, have mercy on us.

Haste therefore each degree
To welcome destiny;
Heaven is our heritage;
Earth but a player's stage;
Mount we unto the sky;
I am sick, I must die–
  Lord, have mercy on us.[10]

The poem is a series of fairly literal propositions, some exactly in logical form: *This world uncertain is. All things to end are made, Queens have died young and fair, Haste therefore each degree.* They are such propositions as might have been translated from the *Summa Contra Gentiles* of Thomas Aquinas, and they are located in that general tradition. Thomas, for instance, discusses the following questions: That human happiness does not consist in carnal pleasures; that man's happi-

[10] Ronald B. McKerrow, ed., *Works* (London, 1904–10), III, 283.

ness does not consist in glory; that man's happiness does not consist in wealth; that happiness does not consist in worldly power; that happiness does not consist in the practice of art; that man's ultimate happiness is not in this life, "for if there is ultimate happiness in this life, it will certainly be lost, at least by death."[11] But these are the propositions of Nashe's lyric, some literally, some more figuratively put.

Of the propositions in the poem perhaps the most figurative is *Strength stoops unto the grave,* which yet is fairly literal, as we see the suggestion of an aged figure bent over more and more until he is almost prone. And there are, of course, affective elements in the poem, as in *death's bitterness* and *Hell's executioner.* But the special distinction of the poem and the source of an unusual quality of feeling perhaps lies in the meter as much as in anything else. The six-syllable line glides from a regular iambic pattern into a triple movement—accented, unaccented, accented—and back again as if both were its mode of being and neither had precedence over the other:

> Beauty is but a flower
> Which wrinkles will devour;
> Brightness falls from the air;
> Queens have died young and fair . . .

The poem in this respect belongs to a curious episode in the history of English meter; for this phenomenon appears only to my knowledge in the songs written within a fairly short period, of perhaps ten or twenty years, in the 1590's, and early 1600's. Of a similar sort is Shakespeare's:

> Come away, come away, death,
>   And in sad cypress let me be laid;
> Fly away, fly away, breath;
>   I am slain by a fair cruel maid.

But the special distinction of the poem has usually been found in the line, *Brightness falls from the air.* This is certainly a proposition of a different order from those we have discussed, and one that has excited the sensibilities of inumerable modern readers. It is a line in the symbolist tradition. One remembers how Stephen Dedalus in the *Portrait of the Artist as a Young Man* recalls the line, though at first in an altered form:

> She had passed through the dusk. And therefore the air was silent save for one soft hiss that fell. And therefore the tongues about him had ceased their babble. Darkness was falling.
>
> *Darkness falls from the air.*

[11] *Contra Gentiles,* 3.27, 29–31, 36, 48, in *Opera Omnia* (Rome, 1882–1948), XIV; Anton C. Pegis, ed., *Basic Writings of Saint Thomas Aquinas* (New York, 1945), II.

A trembling joy, lambent as a faint light, played like a fairy host around him. But why? Her passage through the darkening air or the verse with its black vowels and its opening sound, rich and lutelike?

He walked away slowly towards the deeper shadows at the end of the colonnade, beating the stone softly with his stick to hide his revery from the students whom he had left: and allowed his mind to summon back to itself the age of Dowland and Byrd and Nashe.

Eyes, opening from the darkness of desire, eyes that dimmed the breaking east. What was their languid grace but the softness of chambering? And what was their shimmer but the shimmer of the scum that mantled the cesspool of the court of a slobbering Stuart. And he tasted in the language of memory ambered vines, dying failings of sweet airs, the proud pavan . . .

The images he had summoned gave him no pleasure. They were secret and enflaming but her image was not entangled by them . . .

Yes; and it was not darkness that fell from the air. It was brightness.

Brightness falls from the air.

He had not even remembered rightly Nashe's line. All the images it had awakened were false.[12]

But all the images it had awakened were false for still another reason. The line as Joyce quotes it is certainly an evocative line, a line in the symbolist tradition, and hence apt and fitted to entangle itself in revery. But it seems out of place in the poem. It is so much a line in the symbolist tradition that the historical scholar grows wary and suspicious. He turns to the text. He looks in the great modern edition of Nashe, the edition of McKerrow, and he finds that the editor records with a sigh: "It is to be hoped that Nashe meant 'ayre,' but I cannot help strongly suspecting that the true reading is 'hayre,' which gives a more obvious, but far inferior, sense."[13] So we have the alternatives: *Brightness falls from the air* or *Brightness falls from the hair.* But the latter is a literal account of the effect of age and death. The proposition so read is of the same order as all the other propositions in the poem, of the same order as *Queens have died young and fair.* There is no doubt, then, as to the correct reading. In fact, the symbolist line, however good, is a bad line in context since it is out of keeping. And so the poem loses its last claim to modernity. It becomes a Renaissance poem. It returns to the park of logic from the forest of revery. The experience of the poem is the experience of syllogistic thinking with its

[12] James Joyce, *A Portrait of the Artist as a Young Man* ("Modern Library": New York, 1928), pp. 273–5. [Reprinted by permission of Viking Press, Inc.]

[13] McKerrow, IV, 440.

consequences for feeling, attitude, and action. It is a mode of experience that the Renaissance practiced and cherished, and expressed with power, dignity, and precision. It is a poetical experience and a logical, and it is both at once.[14]

[14] This essay has been refuted by Frank Towne, "Logic, Lyric, and Drama," *Modern Philology,* LI (1953–4), pp. 265–8.

francis berry

THE METAPHYSICALS' CRAFT OF THE VERB

1 Preliminary

The plays of Fletcher beginning with a 'let us suppose . . . this,' or 'assuming that . . . ,' arouse a curiosity whose satisfaction is delayed as long as possible. When the satisfaction comes it is seen to be even less related to what we recognize as actuality than was the initial curiosity. Fletcher's plays are contained by the Subjunctive[1] and the manœuvring that takes place is a manœuvring of tenses within that Mood. In contrast to this art of Fletcher, many of the most admired, yet elaborate *lyrics,* of his own generation, or of the generation following, depend for their success on a studied interplay between Moods. Dual-moded, they achieve whatever they do achieve from a strategy, even sportiveness, of mind which starting with a 'let us suppose,' a subjunctive posture, then takes a jump to find an end, or solution, in the Indicative. Thus their Verb-machinery works counter to that of Shakespeare in his last plays. More important, the Verb-machinery of the more admired metaphysical poems works oppositely to the Verb-machinery of poems of the nineteenth century. The admiration bestowed by the 1930's on the metaphysicals was—so far as Poetic Grammar is concerned—promoted by the, perhaps largely unconscious, discovery that these poets had begun with the Subjunctive to end with the Indicative instead of *vice versa.*

We will illustrate this by reference to two famous and, in their way, excellent poems. Doing this, we should remember that we are not

Reprinted from *Poets' Grammar* (London: Routledge & Kegan Paul Ltd.) pages 104–118, with permission of the author and publisher. Copyright 1958 by Francis Berry.

1 [Mr. Berry remarks earlier: "By 'the Future' I mean the Grammatical Tense, but 'the future' refers to 'time to come'; by 'Subjunctive' the specific Grammatical Mood is intended, but a phrase such as 'subjunctive hopes' alludes to the mood (or state of being) which seems to require the Subjunctive Mood for its verbal expression. This principle has been observed with some consistency, but I am aware that 'time' and 'Time', 'Tense' and 'tense', and even 'verb' and 'Verb', variously occur according to the degree of emphasis, or the shade of meaning, needed by the context."—Ed.]

concerned with any mere grammatical quibble nor with any sort of ingenuity for its own sake. Rather, we should remember that the formal division of an English verb's conjugation into Moods reflects a profound division of being as schematized by the human mind but known to the soul.[2]

To instance this, let us take the verb that all people are—or should be—most concerned with: to love. We insert the qualification as a reminder that many transfer their interest, when a stage of life is reached from *to love* to *to have* or *to get:* acquisitiveness supplanting lust. Now on one side of the conjugation of the verb to love is the Indicative. And the Indicative expresses facts or actualities occurring in Time which are conveyed by Tense. Thus, for example: I love; thou wilt love; he was loving *or* used to love; we loved *or* we have loved; you will have loved; they had loved. Hence, if one is sure of the facts, one is also sure of instruments for expressing them—whether the love exists, once certainly existed, or did so in a still remoter past, or whether it will exist in a time to come. Yet as literature—if not our own lives—reveals, actual accomplishments in this verb's indicative do not suffice or contain desire, and the excess—whether of wish or regret—requires, for its expression, that other Mood of the Subjunctive. The door of desire is hinged and has another side to the one we see when enclosed in our room. Or to move from the image of the leaf of the door to the leaves of books: in our Grammar books there is the page either facing the Indicative, or on the other side of the same leaf on which the Indicative is printed, which orders into Tenses not the facts of, but the possibilities of, desire. Now the life of desire in this realm of the Subjunctive is unacted and unsatisfied (turn the leaves as we may), and yet this life is as real as the life in the indicative world of actuality, an equality of status suggested by the Continental grammarians' term: (not *Sub-* but) *Con*junctive Mood. But not only is there perpetual conflict between the life of fact and the life of desire, but within the subjunctive realm itself there can be continual and great tension. For the subjunctive world of wish, or desire, is also the world of moral oughts. Whereas the indicative world is the concern of the scientist, the subjunctive realm is the concern of the poet and the moralist, and within this realm the claims of poet and moralist customarily conflict.

The two poems we are about to consider must be apprehended as poems recognizing the existence of opposed Moods. It is from a study of the Verb Forms in the poems that an appreciation of their meaning is best secured and, in each case, the meaning determines their structure.

[2] I am aware that what is known as the Subjunctive Mood in Latin is the result of a conflation of *two* yet older Moods: an old Subjunctive expressing will (and futurity) and an old Optative expressing desire (and futurity).

2 'To His Coy Mistress': Argument by Mood

A total of forty-six lines, in three paragraphs, go to make up Marvell's *To his Coy Mistress.* Of these forty-six lines the first paragraph claims as many as twenty. (The second has twelve, the third fourteen.) Now it should be understood that the whole of this first paragraph—with the exception of the nineteenth line, which states a fact, namely:

For Lady you deserve this State;[3]

—is a deliberate exercise within the limits of the subjunctive. Within the limits? But that is a paradox, because in the subjunctive realms, unlike the indicative world which is inexorably limited by dimensions of time and space, there are no limits. This indeed is what the poem says.

The poem begins:

Had we but World enough, and Time . . .

'Supposing we were freed from the laws of time and space. . . .' It is 'supposing' for, of course, Marvell knows very well—only too well—that he and his mistress are not free. Starting with the Conditional "Had we" (and we notice that by the simple exchange of the natural-sounding order—'we had'—for one requiring a strong emphasis on the first element, a final difference is effected between a statement of a past *fact* and a desired situation which can *never* be arrived at), there is an extended disporting in the Subjunctive—the impossible possible. Yet Marvell is not doing as Romantic poets, lovers and lunatics do: deluding himself that subjunctive *is* indicative. Remembering the stress on his first word, Marvell is playing a game, and knows that he is playing a game. He knows, and we know, that this play at 'choosing within the subjunctive' is to be *set against* a knowledge of unalterable indicatives, even though a statement of that knowledge is to be deliberately withheld until the opening of the second paragraph with its famous shock:

But at my back I alwaies hear
Times winged Charriot . . .

followed by a series of notes on the checks to will imposed by death and the laws of space. Marvell is not going to assert subjunctive truth as did Shakespeare in his Final Plays; rather he is going to expose the folly of dwelling in hope and the consequent need for immediate action.

But to watch him at his game. Granting the initial premise, then what *would* 'we' do? he asks. Yet it is not quite that, for there is no

[3] Quotations are from the edition of H. M. Margoliouth.

'we'—no wit-ness[4]—so long as coyness puts space between them; there is no 'we' until their two strengths and sweetnesses are in "one Ball"; rather it is a question of what "I would" and "you should" do:

> Thou by the *Indian Ganges* side
> Should'st Rubies find: I by the Tide
> Of *Humber* would complain. I would
> Love you ten years before the Flood:
> And you should if you please refuse
> Till the Conversion of the *Jews*.

So it is at the beginning of their pretended enfranchisement from the laws of time and space. But the pretended situation develops. He has a lover's duties ('should's' or 'ought's') as well as a lover's desires ('would's'), and he ought to pay the tribute, in measure of time, that her beauty deserves:

> An hundred years should go to praise
> Thine Eyes, and on thy Forehead Gaze.
> Two hundred to adore each Breast:
> But thirty thousand to the rest.

(Here, it will be noticed, that as his gaze travels down her naked length, the tribute owed to her parts, and expressed by measures of time, naturally increases!)

Thus, supposing what is impossible to be possible, Marvell plays within the one Mood that does allow freedom of play. The lover has a persistency of desire (he 'would') where the will is free; his mistress has persistency of choice (she 'should—if she pleases'). It might seem that the paragraph is a product of fancy which, as Coleridge tells us:

> . . . is indeed no other than a mode of memory emancipated from the order of time and space; while it is blended with, and modified by that empirical phenomenon of the will, which we express by the word Choice.[5]

But I do not here imply—though Coleridge does—any inferiority of fancy with respect to any other power. The fancy of the first paragraph of *To his Coy Mistress* is necessary to the structure of argument of the whole poem.

Desiring and choosing are both subjunctive activities and, being independent of the indicative laws of space, partake of heaven—with this difference: in heaven (who knows!) the desiring and choosing of one solitary will attains satisfaction, and so end; but, on earth, two wills

[4] For 'wit'-ness, see p. 88 [of *Poets' Grammar*. Mr. Berry writes that a thousand years before Donne the old dual Pronoun of 'we-two'-ness, 'wit,' conveyed "The particular will of lovers when one spoke in the assurance that he spoke for both."—Ed.]

[5] *Biographia Literaria*, chapter XIII.

are necessary; two choices must coincide: the lover's *and* his mistress's. Here, on earth, within the freedom of the subjunctive, he is prepared to await, for as long as *she* chooses, the time (desire demanding satisfaction, even the Subjunctive has its, albeit ghostly, Future[6]) when he and she will be in "one Ball." But:

> . . . at my back I alwaies hear
> Times winged Charriot hurrying near:
> And yonder all before us lye
> Desarts of vast *Eternity*.

Though in the first paragraph Marvell had played the fancy of pretended freedom from the laws of time and space, *supposing* himself and his mistress to have an eternity in which to dally, yet he reminds her and us that they will have "desarts" of that soon. That "vast Eternity" is an indicative certainty and the second paragraph is one of indicative reminders. Indicatively we are bound by time and space for a few years. After that death. And, whatever death is, it will certainly not bring one thing: the opportunity for their bodies to get into "one Ball." But that opportunity certainly exists *now*—in the Indicative. It will, with equal certainty, not exist—even the most orthodox will be constrained to admit this—in the "Desarts of vast Eternity," or at most—if we can allow the indicative and temporal into the context—not until the Resurrection, and then dubitably. And, even if indubitably, then differently because the bodies will be of a different kind.

Thus, placed in the Indicative, the second paragraph is properly a catalogue of reminders of the conditions on the recognition of which the conjugation of the Indicative Mood is precisely constructed. The conditions are of time and space:

> Thy Beauty shall no more be found;
> Nor, in thy marble Vault, shall sound
> My ecchoing Song: then Worms shall try. . . .

The insistency of the auxiliary 'shall' tells us that though the whole of the second paragraph is cast into one Mood—*contra* that Mood of the first paragraph—yet the focus is, in fact, narrower still than that. Except for the generally true statements of its last two lines, it is cast into a single Tense of that Mood—the Future. *Future* facts or certainties are stated. In the context of their paragraph they have their powerful effect,

[6] See pp. 7, 8 [in *Poets' Grammar*. Mr. Berry writes: ". . . the Subjunctive is the Mood of that which lies outside time. . . . the 'time' of the Subjunctive is an unreal time. In our own actual lives we are so time-bound that we transpose our experience of Tense into the categories of the Subjunctive where it does not exist . . . Thus when we say 'We might have done so and so,' the past *time* of the deed denoted by this tense is unreal since the deed, in fact, never took place. . ."—Ed.]

less in themselves than because they occur in a paragraph that is of verbial purity. The facts derive their power from the paragraph and the paragraph derives its power because, engineered all in one Tense and Mood, it follows the first paragraph which is engineered purely in another Mood. Yet it is not so much that the two paragraphs conflict, as that they contrast. For, in seeking *to enjoy* (an activity, demanding a verb) his Mistress, Marvell discovers two prospects to her: one pretending to offer gratification in the end—but this is known to be illusory; the other of a state, soon to be reached, where there can be no enjoyment of anything. Each prospect is governed by a Verb Form; the first by a form where Time is evaded, the other by a form where Time determines. One prospect is unreal, the other real and barren. Neither offers a course of action within the terms of the verb *to enjoy*. This reduces the hope of action to one Tense—the Present.

As the subjunctive 'would's' and 'should's' ruled the first paragraph; and as the auxiliary 'shall,' denoting future certainty, ruled the second paragraph; so does the adverb of time 'now' followed by a First Person plural 'let us' (for *to enjoy* love, the choice must be mutual) of the Imperative Mood, rule the last paragraph:

> Now therefore, while the youthful hew
> . . . .
> Now let us sport us while we may:
> And now, like am'rous birds of prey,
> Rather at once our Time devour,
> Than languish in his slow-chapt pow'r.
> Let us roll. . . .

In a frame of the Imperative, the Mood not of present enjoyment but of invitation to present enjoyment, the present action unreally exists. Unreally, for if the poet's "strength" and his mistress's "sweetness" were actually rolled up "into one Ball" there would be no need to plead for that state or action. The meaning of the Verb, and not the word for it, would be a present experienced. Nor—then—would any of the poem be necessary. The point of arguing this is that the last two lines of the paragraph (which like its predecessors is in a different tense from the rest of the unit which it concludes) *suggest* that a translation from the Imperative to the Present Indicative had been made. In fact, of course, the poet is anticipating.

We have said enough, I think, to show that the structure of *To his Coy Mistress* is rigorously determined by its Verb Forms. It is a poem in three sections in three contrasting Tenses and Moods, each section, having adopted its chosen Tense or Mood, remaining pure in its choice. It is this dominance of the Verbs, and Marvell's respect for the laws of time and space—the Personal Pronouns being at the mercy of the nouns of which they are the subject or complement—and with the freedom of choice restricted to freedom within these laws—which this dominance implies, that makes the poem so severely classical and gives it that "tough reasonableness" of which Mr. Eliot speaks.

As for the Pronouns. Like Donne's *Songs and Sonets, To his Coy Mistress* is an 'I' to 'thou' poem. The aim of the poem is that 'I' and 'thou' should become a 'we,' that the 'thou' should consent to the 'I's' pleading so that this comes about. But Marvell is not, as Donne was, consistent. The Mistress is variously addressed as 'thou' or 'you.' No clear principle seems to govern the use of the two forms, beyond the nonce effect to be gained by one in place of the other. But it is apparent, of course, that the identity of Marvell's Coy Mistress is not apprehended as unique in the way that the identity of the woman Donne addresses is apprehended as unique in her 'thou-ness.'

We have said the poem is 'classical.' It is so also because its philosophy is pagan. In *To his Coy Mistress,* no more than in Catullus' "*Vivamus, mea Lesbia, atque amemus,*" is it recognized that the doctrines of Christianity imply a modification of the conjugations; that its doctrines and beliefs, notably those of personal immortality and the resurrection of the body, altered previous conceptions of time, and of future time in particular. Moreover, Shakespeare, with or without the aid of those doctrines and beliefs, had altered the conjugation of the Future, and of other tenses, in his Final Plays. Yet that Christianity had intervened between Catullus and himself is ignored in Marvell's poem. *To his Coy Mistress* has the same view of the future as "*Vivamus, mea Lesbia, atque amemus,*" and hence in its final paragraph makes the same entreaty as Catullus' poem as a whole. Yet, a generation or two earlier, Jonson had set his translation of Catullus' poem within the Christian terms of *Volpone,* as a lure certainly, but as a lure whose falsity was immediately to be perceived.

But that a stringent respect for Verbs as the basis of composition, and a deliberate manipulation of their Moods, is a mark of seventeenth-century metaphysical poetry—independent of whether the philosophy of the poet is pagan or Christian—is a claim which our next section will endeavour to support further.

3 'The Exequy': Resolution Through Tense

A structural dialogue between opposed, and yet complementary, Moods provides the dynamic of the chief most obviously Christian love poem of the period no less surely than it does of its chief most obviously pagan love poem.

It rested with Mr. Eliot to discover to us Henry King's *The Exequy* as a *great* poem. In *The Oxford Book of English Verse* it had appeared in a 'cut' version. That should hardly be possible now, for the adjective 'great' implies the indispensability of parts.

And we are right to consider it alongside *To his Coy Mistress*. Not only are they both love poems—of love, whose enjoyment is lost or unsatisfied—but they are both Time poems. Both writers find the life of love—that is, the positive expression of love—subject to Time and problematic. Therefore the solution of the problem in poetry is also to be achieved through first a contemplation and then a manipulation of Tense. And of Mood. Rejecting the timeless Mood, Marvell's poem proposes the solution as lying in the Present Tense. King's, rejecting hope in the Present and Future Indicative Tenses, proposes the solution as lying in the timeless. Yet the dialectic *method* is the same in both cases.

The tensal outline of *The Exequy* is wonderfully bold.

The first half of the poem, sixty out of a hundred and twenty lines, is a backward-looking action. King is spending his present time contemplating his past time. This is the verbial mechanism of regret. In his *now* he is engaged in the action of regret, which can be as firmly formularized by the sign ← as the opposite action of hope is expressed thus: →.[7] Yet meditate on the life of the past as he may, this is not life because it will not bring his wife back to life. In fact this ← looking of the mind is, in its way, an abuse of his indicative 'is-ness' and, as such, is as much a subjunctive activity as hope—more so: hope may be realized whereas regret cannot bring back, or redeem; not in this case, at least. Not that there need be "wonder," he says:

> if my time go thus
> Backward and most preposterous.[8]

But for all the great pathos of the excuse:

> . . . thy set
> This eve of blackness did beget,
> Who wast my day,

he knows he is looking the wrong way in looking ←, and this is 'backward.' Moreover, in looking the wrong way, he is advancing in time 'arsy-versy,' i.e. arse-foremost. For, to King, if not for us, 'preposterous' was no simple equivalent for 'outrageous' but carried the literal meaning of the Latin which he applies metaphorically. If King is being con-

[7] These signs seem natural to me; but perhaps to those born into the Hebrew or Arabic, besides other, languages, and to left-handed Englishmen, they might seem more natural in reverse.

[8] *The Caroline Poets*, Vol. III, edited by George Saintsbury, p. 195.

sciously funny (a more accurate word than 'witty' in this circumstance), then by this funniness he reminds us that he is in control in that he *knows* that being simply regretful is to look in the wrong direction, a perverse way of dealing with 'time,' which therefore "lazily creeps about." Indeed, that this "preposterous" spending of time in the subjunctive of the gone past is to refuse to live, he admits when he says:

> For thee (lov'd clay)
> I languish out, not live, the day.

Yet in this state of regret he does more than merely look backward and proceed arsy-versy.[9] He subjunctively tampers with the past by playing games with—or in—a false future as in the next paragraph:

> I could allow thee, for a time,
> To darken me and my sad clime,
> Were it a month, a year, or ten,
> I would thy exile live till then;
> And all that space my mirth adjourn,
> So thou wouldst promise to return;
> And putting off thy ashy shroud,
> At length disperse this sorrow's cloud.

As in Marvell's first paragraph this is a deliberate Subjunctive 'let's pretend.' But the two poems agree on this: both will repudiate their opening Moods. Marvell's fantastic wishes to override the laws of time and King's equally fantastic reclamatory wishes (he is to call them "these empty hopes") are alike to be rejected as unreal.

For King acknowledges:

> 'twixt me and my soul's dear wish
> The earth now interposed is,

and that is indicative enough. Spade-fulls of earth now form (in time and space) a ponderable block between a real past, which is now but a retrospective subjunctive of desire, and his present is-ness of deprivation.

The straight realization of this fact, cutting across the pretence that his wife has gone away on a holiday, compels at length the modal change —from the comforting but deluding Subjunctive to the Indicative. There is first the Present:

> the longest date
> Too narrow is to calculate
> These empty hopes.

[9] *The Exequy* is a very beautiful and very moving poem. To avoid misunderstandings it should be said that I am not blaming King even when he blames himself. It is a beautiful and moving poem because King confesses to behaving as a human being in a situation—that of the survivor of a marriage—which the majority of people must experience. No-one can do more than behave as a human being; the sin is in doing less than is expected of a human being.

And this realization leads to another, and in another tense, in the Future:

> never shall I
> Be so much blest as to descry
> A glimpse of thee, till that day come,
> Which shall the earth to cinders doom,
> And a fierce fever must calcine
> The body of this world, like thine,
> My Little World! That fit of fire
> Once off, our bodies shall aspire
> To our souls' bliss . . .

—lines which state not the "empty hopes" of the Subjunctive but real and dreadful future facts. As Mr. Eliot has said, this is a poem which could have been written in no period other than its own. The doctrines of Christianity, including that of a Last Day and a Bodily Resurrection of the dead, are 'for King' facts and as such require the unequivocal firmness of the Indicative. It is not a matter of subjunctive hope but of indicative truth that the bodies of his wife and himself will rise to invest their souls so that they will see each other in the flesh:

> . . . we shall rise,
> And view ourselves with clearer eyes
> In that calm region, where no night
> Can hide us from each other's sight.

This *will* come about in time, on which tense is constructed but, having come to pass, there will be no more tense.

It should also be noted that up to this point, the poem has been a lament of an 'I' for a lost 'thou.' It has been an 'I' to 'thou' or 'thee' poem, like—in this respect—Marvell's *To his Coy Mistress*. The 'I' and the 'thou' of King's poem have been, or are, separated by time and space. With this consummation of longing and desire—for which the annihilation of time and space, confidently foreseen, is the condition—the Pronoun of the First Person plural, the 'we' and 'us' of the quotation, make their first and only appearance. This reveals the nature of the poem. King's inability to use the Pronoun 'we' with Present Indicative truth is the *raison d'être* of the lament. The point at which he realizes that he will be able to use the word in the future—though only at a position in the future when the word 'future' ceases to have meaning (the timeless Subjunctive of desire gained, but gained in Indicative actuality) is the turning-point of the poem. With his sights laid on this 'we' he ceases to lament and instead becomes "content" that "Heaven's will" has divided them for the duration of all time; becomes ready, even, to make an elaborate and excellent joke:

> Meantime, thou hast her, Earth; much good
> May my harm do thee . . .

—yet the Earth had better look out! what she has is "lent" not given, and each "grain and atom" of his wife's "dust" must be yielded back when she (and the poet with her) is re-assembled in the flesh at the Resurrection. Thus he arrives at the stage of contemplation when she is not merely not dead but sleeping, yet sleeping in a special kind of bed:

> So close the ground, and 'bout her shade
> Black curtains draw;—my Bride is laid.
>
> Sleep on, my Love, in thy cold bed,
> Never to be disquieted!

Hence, in the poem, King is not spending his time 'preposterously' or 'arsy-versy.' His gaze is directed forward: he is 'looking forward,' as the idiom has it, into the Future Indicative, to the occasion when time will

> Marry my body to that dust
> It so much loves; and fill the room
> My heart keeps empty in thy tomb.

Moreover, in 'looking forward' he becomes warm in the anticipation, and though he cannot finish the journey ("Through which to *Thee* I swiftly glide") soon enough, yet the pace of the verse quickens as the ardour of his imagination intensifies:

> But heark! My pulse, like a soft drum,
> Beats my approach, tells *Thee* I come;
> And slow howe'er my marches be,
> I shall at last sit down by *Thee.*

He is spending his time reversely to the way he began. He is now living and living *for* a dissolution which will precede a reunion in the flesh.

4 Reflections

To his Coy Mistress and *The Exequy* are both fine poems and, though having much in common, are yet complementary to each other. Both are long enough to permit changes of Tense and transitions of Mood. But the problem confronting Marvell and King—how to overcome impediments imposed by time and space so as to enjoy union with a loved person—compels just such changes and transitions in the attempt ta find its solution; for no *lasting* solution to any problem can be reached within the terms of one Tense or even one Mood. Both their external length and their internal structure, which are created by these Tense-changes and Mood-transitions, absolutely prevent these poems being considered as lyrics. A lyric, e.g. King's "Tell me no more how fair she is," is not only a short poem meant to be sung but it is a poem cast in one Mood and Tense, and though it may pose a problem it does not attempt to solve it.

Moreover, because of their attempt to solve a problem, Marvell's *Coy Mistress* and King's *Exequy* are not 'strophic' but 'paragraph' poems. The unevenness in the lengths of their paragraphs—more marked in King's case than in Marvell's for the reason that the former's poem is more original and more personally felt by the author while Marvell's plea *'carpe diem'* follows a traditional formula of argument over whose stages, in the course of the ages, a semi-strophic regularity has been imposed—follows from this tensal and modal gear-changing.

Marvell's poem is, then, the more impersonal. Though it is not necessarily the worse for that, it explains the apparent haphazardness in his use of 'thou' and 'you,' to which we have referred above. Mr. F. W. Bateson who privately reports to me that he had once attempted to see whether Marvell, in this poem, was guided by any principle confesses that it seemed that Marvell considered the words as mere synonyms. To Marvell it was the mutual enjoyment he had with the girl, not her identity, that mattered. But King, who consistently uses 'thou,' certainly sensed the unique 'thou'-ness of his wife. And his poem was possibly written earlier than Marvell's. In thought and structure of sensibility it is in some respect a more conservative poem than Marvell's.

Judging by the verbial changes which structure these poems, we see that the breath-unit of the indicative is comparatively short. We say the truth and end, but we hope or regret in larger spirals.

Marvell and King attempt to solve their problem with the aid of traditional philosophies. Marvell's philosophy is the more venerable. While King's had a mere thirteen hundred years' or so history, Marvell's was respectable in the sun-battened yards of the tenements of Rome centuries before Augustine of Canterbury was born. What is remarkable, however, is Marvell's well-nigh[10] total exclusion of Christianity from his poem and from the reader's mind while he is actually reading the poem. So to render us momentarily unaware that Christian philosophy had ever intervened in time between himself and the Rome of Catullus is an extraordinary success of art. But while both poets attempt to reach a solution to a problem through the aid of a philosophy, it must be admitted that while King found a solution—the only solution—satisfactory, at least, to himself, Marvell's solution depends, even at his

[10] For there is a reference to the conversion of the Jews!

poem's conclusion, on the consent of the girl's will to his Imperative invitation.

Nevertheless, both poems exercise the same mechanics of the Verb. In effecting a transition from an initial Subjunctive to an Indicative they illustrate a procedure of the seventeenth-century mind. It is this procedure, more than anything else, which distinguishes the Metaphysicals from the Romantics. In Keats or Shelley the procedure is the opposite one of a movement from a hated Indicative to a Subjunctive and the discovery that it is this Subjunctive which is only 'real.' Instead of the articles of common belief being prescriptive of hope, the substance of individual hope becomes accessible to belief.

rachel trickett

THE IDIOM OF AUGUSTAN POETRY

"No true work of genius dares want its appropriate form." With this statement Coleridge, in the lectures on Shakespeare, introduces his distinction between the two kinds of form, mechanic and organic; the first "not necessarily arising out of the properties of the material," the second innate—"it shapes as it develops itself from within, and the fulness of its development is one and the same with the perfection of its outward form. Such as the life is, such is the form." To Coleridge this organic form is one of the sure signs of a true work of genius, and modern criticism has followed him in looking for it in poetry, by means particularly of a thorough investigation of the imagery. Coleridge himself recognized the importance of the image to his theory of poetry. The celebrated definition of the secondary imagination in the *Biographia Literaria* presents it as a power of making metaphor, of shaping images and bringing things continually into a fresh relationship with each other. It is a dynamic quality that dissolves, diffuses and dissipates in order to recreate. And again, in his interpretation of Milton's comment on poetry as being "more simple, sensuous and passionate," Coleridge explains the second term thus: "that it should be sensuous, and by its imagery elicit truth at a flash." Organic form, the transmuting power of metaphor which is always remaking experience for us, and truth elicited at a flash by means of imagery—these are among the critical assumptions about the nature of poetry on which much of our criticism is based today.

Such a criticism is most valuable when it is applied to a certain kind of poetry—in this case intense, complicated and expressed through metaphorical language; poetry that is usually dramatic or lyrical in mode. Shakespeare, Donne, Coleridge, Keats and the moderns are the authors who make up our accepted tradition, but it is more difficult to fit into it Chaucer, Spenser, Milton and the Augustans. Natural, instinctive taste enabled Coleridge to appreciate Dryden's power and vigor, and he was in no doubt about the greatness of Milton, but his theory, with all its subtlety and insight into the nature of the imagination, drew him inevitably to Shakespeare and the mature Shakespearian style as a sort of norm against which all others could be measured. He admits only to reject as a poetic property "the great exquisiteness of language and sweetness of metre alone" in Pope's satires and epistles, observing "that is not poetry if it make no appeal to our passions or our imagination."

Our own critical rhetoric owes as much to Coleridge as the neo-classical owed to Aristotle; we too begin not from the craft or the languages, but from certain premises about the nature of imagination and of the creative activity, and if these premises are pursued too exclusively they may lead to errors of judgment or false emphases. The notorious attack on Milton in the nineteen twenties and thirties was not whimsically haphazard; it was a predictable outcome of too rigorous and academic an application of Coleridgean principles. Similarly some of the best work produced in the same period on Pope and Johnson as poets tended to consist of an examination of their witty devices of pun, zeugma, oxymoron and concealed imagery, rather than of their subject matter, metre, or the overall structure of their work and the critical principles on which it is based.

Those principles, when inflexibly applied, were as limiting as our own can be. We learn at an early stage about the sterility of neo-classical rules, so that we are sometimes tempted to feel that what is good in Dryden and Pope was achieved in spite of their beliefs. But just as it would be foolish to try to approach romantic poetry on the basis of the old rhetoric, so it is dangerous to wrench what we admire in Augustan poetry entirely to the pattern of the new. For in some ways the two are diametrically opposed. The classical theory of the function of poetry —that it instructs by pleasing—was accepted by Augustan and romantic poets alike, but what Wordsworth calls "the grand elementary principle of pleasure" is so much stressed by the romantics with their insistence on self-awareness and perception, and the exemplary or instructive aspect is so continually emphasized by the Augustans, that poetry itself, the subject of their discussions, seems hardly to mean the same thing to them.

When Pope said to Spence that it was easy to trace the main course of our poetry, the names he chose were Chaucer, Spenser, Milton and Dryden, while Shakespeare, whose stature he never questioned, was absent from the list. Here is a very different tradition from our own, and we can infer from it that Pope believed the epic kind of verse to be the backbone of our literature, and, in spite of the supreme genius of Shakespeare, that drama was so essentially different in kind that it could never take the same place in the main stream of the tradition. The poets of whom Pope is speaking were by no means all writers of epic, but their poetry, springing originally from the epic kind, is narrative or expository in style, objective and expansive rather than intense or concentrated, lucid and wide-ranging rather than complex and tightly-knit. It does not, in fact, lend itself easily to the Coleridgean approach, though there may be passages in the works of any of these writers which possess qualities of the imagination more usually found in dramatic or lyric verse.

To distinguish like this between kinds of verse is to follow the Renaissance and Augustan practice of categorizing various modes of writing—a useful exercise when this is the way in which the poets themselves looked at their art. But the Augustans had moved beyond the Renaissance position on this point. They paid respect to the doctrine of the kinds, but practised far fewer of them. Dryden and Pope never wrote the epics they projected. Dryden himself did not touch the pastoral, and by the time Johnson launched his attack on that form, the academic debate between the two kinds of pastoral, imitative and classical on the one hand and modern and realistic on the other, had been won not by dispute but by the emergence of a simpler descriptive poetry which gradually superseded the older form of Arcadianism. The movement of the period was, in fact, toward realism, and for several reasons. That whole world of myth and fable through which the Elizabethans had observed and interpreted nature, and which was the basis of their critical doctrines of invention and imitation, had crumbled under the influence of Cartesianism and the empirical attitude which would not countenance "false fabling," dark conceits, allegories and fictions, and which had even attacked metaphorical language. Though Dryden and Pope were conservative in their literary attitudes, they shared the opinions of their age with regard to truth or reality. Their poems do not "body forth the forms of things unknown"; they deal consistently with the forms of things known, with the world as it is, and in place of the myths of an earlier age they elevate the past, history, the ancients and the record of actual human experience.

In this, then, the Augustans differ from their Renaissance predecessors, and from their romantic successors who set out to recreate a new world from the individual perceiving power of the imaginative faculty. They are content with things as they are—or alternatively discontented enough to scourge the inadequacies of the age in satire. The whole idiom and structure of their poetry depends on this delicate balance between a desire to conserve the lasting and valuable elements in the tradition, and a determination to "publish the present age." Where the Renaissance poet thinks of himself as creating almost a new nature, and the Romantic as revealing the essential truth of experience in a flash of insight, the Augustan chooses to write, in Johnson's words, "to common degrees of knowledge," and adapts his style, his manner and his whole idiom accordingly.

His is a kind of poetry which continually throws us back on the importance of the subject matter and the pervasiveness of the ideas and attitudes to which it gives rise. When Pope in the *Essay on Criticism* wrote:

> But true expression, like th' unchanging Sun,
> Clears and improves whate'er it shines upon,
> It gilds all objects, but it alters none. . .

he anticipated the essential difference between his attitude and the Romantics'. No transformation has taken place in his idea of the act of composition, no metamorphosis; the objects, the material of his verse, remain unaltered. And because they must not be changed, because these phenomena are the reality with which poets must deal if they are to justify their claim to tell the truth, the words expressing them must be continually checked by the poet's judgment and prevented from proliferating into too wild a life of their own. Augustan precepts on the art of poetry make much of the separateness of the elements of composition. First comes the invention, or the finding of the thought, then the elocution or the clothing of it in fit words, and the stress is on the act of choice and discrimination which selects a language intelligible, lucid and embellishing. "Words too familiar or too remote defeat the purpose of the poet," Johnson remarks in his *Life of Dryden;* "they draw that attention to themselves which they should transmit to things."

What kind of style is it, then, which can take such a limited view of the potentialities of language, and submit so rigidly to its purely referential qualities? It will certainly not be a metaphorical style, though it may well be allusive, trying to substitute for the dimension metaphor normally brings, echoes and reverberations from other kinds of poetry by imitation or open reference to other works. Augustan poets are masters of implication, as they are also of periphrasis—or writing round an object and finding new terms in which to describe it without changing its essential nature. To call a pair of scissors "the glittering forfex" is accurate and exact, but it is also expansive. It amplifies the range of impressions without modifying the object itself in any fundamental way as a metaphorical image would. It does not please us by transmuting and fusing various elements; it defines and delights at the same time.

But it is not in allusion and periphrasis, or in the witty artifice of compressed figures of which Pope was peculiarly the master, that Augustan poetry achieves its appropriate form. More important than any individual device is the pattern of the work—not only its metrical structure, but its movement of thought and mood, its articulation as a whole. It is here that the influence of the epic tradition is most obvious. The epic is an expansive form, leisurely and ample in pace and scope, narrative in mode, but containing passages of exposition, of reflection, even of declamation. Its most characteristic figure of speech is the simile which enlarges the field of reference and is, as Johnson puts it, "a little descriptive episode" rather than an intense gathering together of many meanings, like a metaphor.

The whole nature of simile is an important clue to our understanding of the structure of this kind of poetry—not simply the prolonged simile, but any overt rather than implicit comparison. When Othello says of Desdemona

> O thou weed!
> Who art so lovely fair and smell'st so sweet
> That the sense aches at thee, would thou hadst ne'er been born,

it does not help to lay apart the elements of the comparison, to distinguish the weed, the flower and the woman, since all three are so closely woven together in the intricate texture of Othello's agony. As we apprehend them we are aware of a sensation of instantaneous interchange, rather like the effect of intoxication where everything seems distinct and yet to be perceived simultaneously. This kind of metaphor is a proper verbal form for passion; its effect is Coleridge's truth elicited at a flash by imagery. But Othello's elaborate simile when he vows relentless vengeance makes a completely different impression:

> Never Iago. Like to the Pontic sea,
> Whose icy current and compulsive course
> Ne'er feels retiring ebb, but keeps due on
> To the Propontic and the Hellespont,
> Even so my bloody thoughts, with violent pace
> Shall ne'er look back, ne'er ebb to humble love. . . .

This instantly checks the pace of the scene and holds it up by demanding a different kind of attention. The extent of the comparison gives it an intrinsic importance over which we must pause and reflect. It supports the theme—Othello's vengeance—but it is his own conscious rhetorical explication of his emotion, and the expansive style forces us to admire the aptness of the comparison, while at the same time we accept and recognize the nature of the feelings it illustrates. In his attempts to understand his situation, Othello frequently returns to this kind of rhetoric—to reflection on his past and explication of his present position—so that although the prevailing structure of the verse is always metaphorical and intense, we see how skilfully Shakespeare can introduce and exploit this other rhetorical mode both to define the character of his hero and to illustrate a variety of ways of looking at experience.

Augustan verse is generally reflective, expository and dominated by the simile, though, again, passages of metaphorical intensity can be contained within this prevailing structure, like those which many modern critics of Pope have frequently pointed out. But they are comprehended within a pattern of thought and movement which is leisurely in comparison to the dramatic mode, and which demands from us the "due distance" that a simile, for example, requires; that detachment in which we ponder over the idea of emotion proposed and the aptness and grace with which it is presented. No dissolution, no fundamental change seems to have taken place here; the effect is static and the style assumes a certain consent on the part of the reader that the subject and the attitudes are constant, valuable and absolute. To the Augustans this seemed as persuasive a form of rhetoric as that process of working on the imagination and the feelings which is evident in the more concentrated Coleridgean style. But Augustan poetry aims at conviction of a different sort; it intends to persuade the reader of the importance of the material by means of the accomplishment of the style.

At its simplest this Augustan technique can seem too static, and sometimes too ostentatious and superficial. Addison's famous simile of the angel in *The Campaign,* for instance, reads like a poetic version of some grand-style historical painting, in which the epic sublimity stands in isolation for its own sake:

> 'Twas then great Marlbro's mighty soul was prov'd,
> That, in the shock of changing hosts unmov'd,
> Amidst confusion, horror, and despair,
> Examin'd all the dreadful scenes of war;
> In peaceful thought the field of death survey'd,
> To fainting squadrons sent the timely aid,
> Inspir'd repuls'd battalions to engage,
> And taught the doubtful battle where to rage.
> So, when an Angel by divine command
> With rising tempests shakes a guilty land,
> Such as of late o'er pale *Britannia* past,
> Calm and serene he drives the furious blast;
> And, pleas'd th' Almighty's orders to perform,
> Rides in the whirl-wind, and directs the storm (11.279–292).

Johnson took pains to examine this comparison and judge whether the praise it had received was deserved. His conclusion is an interesting example of what he believed to be the nature of simile. He contends that this is not a simile at all, but an exemplification, because Marlborough and the angel are too alike, and the passage describes "a like consequence from a like cause, or a like performance by a like agency." This exemplification is compared to "two parallel lines which run on together without approximation, never far separated, and never joined." Johnson's criticism hints too at another fault in the passage. It has no real movement; it places things side by side but we are not aware of their relationship in connection with any prevailing tenor in the work. The poem has a simple narrative progression, interrupted from time to time by splendid or grandiose comparisons which draw attention to themselves far in excess of their importance to the whole structure.

Let us take in contrast a passage from Dryden where explicatory simile is brilliantly employed as the framework of the whole thing: the opening lines of the *Religio Laici:*

> Dim as the borrow'd beams of moon and stars
> To lonely, weary, wand'ring travellers
> Is Reason to the soul; and, as on high
> Those rolling fires discover but the sky,
> Not light us here, so Reason's glimmering ray
> Was lent, not to assure our doubtful way
> But guide us upward to a better day.
> And as those nightly tapers disappear
> When day's bright lord ascends our hemisphere;
> So pale grows Reason at Religion's sight;
> So dies, and so dissolves in supernatural light.

There can be no finer example of a structure which depends upon the expository, leisurely, defining character of simile but which, within that pattern, makes free use of metaphor. Dryden's love of figurative language often led him into those "beautiful faults," "the multitude of my similitudes," as he calls them in the dedication to *Eleonora.* He was enough of a poet of the seventeenth century to admire the line of wit, and his early metaphysical bias is always evident in his work until the very latest years. But what Johnson says of metaphysical conceits in his *Life of Cowley,* that "when they are expanded to perspicuity and polished to elegance, [they] may give lustre to works which have more propriety though less copiousness of sentiment," describes very well how Dryden employed his genius for coining images and comparisons.

In these lines from the *Religio Laici* the light imagery shimmers through the passage in endless variations—borrowed beams, rolling fires, Reason's glimmering ray, nightly tapers, day's bright lord, supernatural light—the first and the last of these being simple definitive terms, the rest essentially metaphors. But all of them are part of the argument; they are firmly controlled by the movement of the discourse. Dryden's pointing, his use of the iambic line, throws into relief the logic of his comparisons without diminishing the prevailing beauty of the imagery. The greatness of the lines, however, lies in the whole organization of their meaning. If we italicize the logical connective constructions we shall see how perfectly they fit Dryden's feeling for the medium and rhythm of the verse:

> *Dim as* the borrow'd beams of moon and stars
> *To* lonely, weary, wand'ring travellers
> *Is Reason to* the soul; and *as* on high
> Those rolling fires discover *but* the sky
> *Not* light us here, *so* Reason's glimmering ray
> Was lent, *not* to assure our doubtful way,
> *But* guide us upward to a better day.
> *And as* those nightly tapers disappear
> When day's bright lord ascends our hemisphere,
> *So* pale grows Reason at Religion's sight,
> *So* dies, and *so* dissolves in supernatural light.

The repetition of the same constructions interspersed by modifying clauses is as syntactically lucid as in any piece of prose. It also stresses the natural periodic rhythm which Dryden emphasizes by the other rhythm of the heroic couplet and its variations of triplet and alexandrine. The movement is as much a part of the beauty of the passage as the imagery, and the movement depends on a syntactical sense of discourse or argument as much as the imagery depends upon a general framework of simile, or overt explicatory comparison.

All this may seem very self-evident, but it is often overlooked in considering Augustan poetry that almost all that is best in it, not only in argumentative verse but in satire or narrative or descriptive works, depends upon this kind of movement. If in Augustan ideas of the nature of poetic composition subject matter is all-important, and the kind of style does not allow transformations or metaphorical transpositions, then the poet's imagination will find itself forced into other channels. It expresses itself in the play of mind and mood over the subject, in transitions from one idea to the next rather than through the flash of insight which reveals the truth in a moment. In narrative or moral verse it will tend to range allusively or reflectively over the consecutive span of time—past, present and future, which reflects the actual pattern of our experience, rather than look for those moments "when the light of sense goes out, but with a flash that has revealed the invisible world." Its concern is not with those illuminations which seem to interrupt, with an eternal significance, the temporal rhythm, but with the flow of time and the record of human experience.

Two very fine examples of this movement occur in Pope's *Essay on Man* and Johnson's *Vanity of Human Wishes,* both of them illustrations of the folly of human ambition. Pope and Johnson turn to history to support their moral theme, and the structure of the two passages, though in each case part of a moral-satirical discourse, is narrative. In each case again the survey of various or individual human experience rises to a final moral assertion to which the whole flow of the verse is directed. Here first is Pope, in the 4th Epistle of the *Essay on Man:*

> If all united thy ambition call,
> From ancient story learn to scorn them all:
> There in the rich, the honour'd, famed and great,
> See the false scale of happiness complete!
> In hearts of Kings and arms of Queens who lay,
> How happy, those to ruin, these betray.
> Mark by what wretched steps their glory grows,
> From dirt and seaweed, as proud Venice rose;
> In each how guilt and greatness equal ran,
> And all that rais'd the Hero sunk the Man:
> Now Europe's laurels on their brows behold,
> But stain'd with blood, or ill-exchanged for gold;
> Then see them broke with toils, or sunk in ease,
> Or infamous for plundered provinces.
> O wealth ill-fated! which no act of fame
> E'er taught to shine, or sanctified from shame!
> What greater bliss attends their close of life?
> Some greedy minion, or imperious wife.
> The trophied arches, story'd halls invade
> And haunt their slumbers in the pompous shade.
> Alas! not dazzled with their noontide ray
> Compute the morn and ev'ning to their day;
> The whole amount of that enormous fame
> A tale that blends their glory with their shame (II. 285–308).

The whole of this passage has an effect of complication which might give a modern reader the illusion of imagery, when in fact its contortions are achieved by grammatical compression, and its emotional impact by simple generalized comparisons of a stock nature. The depth and agility of the lines are conveyed through the change of tenses—"Mark by what wretched steps their glory *grows*"; "In each how guilt and greatness equal *ran*"; the imperatives *mark, see, compute* form the framework of the passage and these govern the past participles and the changing tenses until the apostrophe "O wealth ill-fated" changes the whole tone and prepares us for the rhetorical question and the exclamation which resolve into the final sentiment—"The whole amount of that enormous fame, A tale that blends their glory with their shame." The movement of these lines is so compelling that they rightly drive us on without too perceptible a pause to the opening of the next section, from the false scale of happiness to the true one:

> Know then this truth, enough for man to know,
> Virtue alone is happiness below . . .

and in their context a simple aphorism becomes a convincing statement of wisdom.

Johnson's exemplum of the vanity of human ambition and glory has a characteristically heavier pace and a greater simplicity of structure within the individual lines:

> On what foundation stands the warrior's pride,
> How just his hopes let Swedish Charles decide;
> A frame of adamant, a soul of fire,
> No dangers fright him, and no labours tire;
> O'er love, o'er fear extends his wide domain,
> Unconquer'd lord of pleasure and of pain;
> No joys to him pacific sceptres yield;
> War sounds the trump, he rushes to the field;
> Behold surrounding kings their pow'r combine,
> And one capitulate and one resign;
> Peace courts his hand, but spreads her charms in vain;
> "Think nothing gain'd," he cries, "till nought remain,
> On Moscow's walls till Gothic standards fly
> And all be mine beneath the polar sky."
> The march begins in military state,
> And nations on his eye suspended wait;
> Stern Famine guards the solitary coast,
> And Winter barricades the realms of Frost;
> He comes, nor want and cold his course delay,
> Hide, blushing glory, hide Pultowa's day:
> The vanquish'd hero leaves his broken bands,
> And shews his miseries in distant lands;
> Condemn'd a needy supplicant to wait,
> While ladies interpose, and slaves debate.
> But did not Chance at length her error mend?
> Did no subverted empire mark his end?
> Did rival monarchs give the fatal wound?
> Or hostile millions press him to the ground?
> His fall was destined to a barren strand,
> A petty fortress and a dubious hand;
> He left the name, at which the world grew pale
> To point a moral or adorn a tale.

A greater rigidity within the individual line is apparent in Johnson's verses, and this is as much a matter of metrical feeling as of syntax. He could not match the complication of Pope's "In hearts of Kings and arms of Queens who lay, How happy! those to ruin, these betray," where the Latinate constructions force certain words and phrases into positions of emphasis, so that all the emotional overtones of the words *happy, ruin, betray* are knit together by the involved syntactical and metrical rhythm of the lines. But the pattern of this long exemplum is again governed by discoursive organization. The tone is declamatory, but in spite of Johnson's repetition of certain constructions it is not by any means unvaried. He works by accumulation and suspense. The periodic sentences hold up the resolution of each statement; in the first line, for instance, what appears to be an expression which is directly interrogative—"On what foundation stands the warrior's pride," after a delay, when we reach the main clause, "let Swedish Charles decide," diminishes into an indirect question. This in turn is counterpointed by the series of direct rhetorical questions that lead us to the final summary of Charles's fate. The most remarkable lines in the passage are, in some sense, metaphorical:

> Stern Famine guards the solitary coast,
> And Winter barricades the realms of frost. . .

but the figure is one of those Johnson made peculiarly his own, where an inanimate noun is turned into an active agent through the force of the imaginative conception. Here the nouns are wrenched into a new significance through the activity of the verbs, but though Famine and Winter are behaving like generals, they still remain themselves; they are not transformed in the process. This kind of personification is one solution to the Augustan problem of retaining the defined meaning of a word but at the same time forcing it into some new and imaginative context. Johnson seldom if ever uses Pope's favorite device of periphrasis; he preferred the more direct and logical precision of this figure.

The concluding lines of the passage from *The Vanity of Human Wishes,* like those which end the passage from the *Essay on Man,* are full of allusive echoes: "A tale, told by an idiot, full of sound and fury, Signifying nothing." Here is the characteristic emotional mood of Augustan poetry, the sense, not of sudden transformation, but of gradual change—"quantum mutatus ab illo," elegiac and reflective. To survey experience and take a perspective of time and action easily arouses this mood, and inclines the reader to resignation or acquiescence. The suspended resolution of the periodic sentence itself is the logical counterpart to this habit of expatiating over a wide field of experience, and finally coming to rest in some affirmation of a simple and unquestioned common truth.

The movement of this kind of verse is also peculiarly suited to narrative, for the control and flexibility of the manner drives the relation on to its climax and never interrupts our sense of sequence. Its advantages reveal themselves if we compare Shakespeare's *Venus and Adonis* as a narrative poem with Marlowe's *Hero and Leander*, for the latter is curiously Augustan in some ways. Shakespeare moves at a clogged pace, hesitating over conceits, turning back on himself, drawing our attention to detail so that, as Johnson said of Richardson's novels, if you were to read for the story you would hang yourself. But though Marlowe's poem is full of elaborate descriptions, it is written in the smoothest and most highly organized of Renaissance metres, the elegiac couplet (a form of heroic couplet) which moves on with something of the easy transition and flow of early eighteenth century style. It crystallizes at times into aphorisms or digresses into fable, but it never completely loses the onward thrust that keeps us concerned with what happens next. And we are aware of a detachment in the author, which, as in Chaucer's narratives, produces overtones of ironic reflection. The distance Marlowe keeps from his subject allows him to introduce commentary on what is happening; we are invited to smile at Leander's simplicity and his sophistry, and at Hero's innocent coquetry. Venus's lust in Shakespeare's poem, on the other hand, is a cosmic experience in which the whole of nature seems involved, but Marlowe preserves due distance from his lovers and can thus produce an almost Augustan effect of sympathetic observation. Our response to this kind of style is a mixed one; we are concerned with the story, aware of the skill with which it is written, and always conscious behind the style of the attitude of the narrator. Dryden's great admiration for Chaucer derived from his recognition of this quality in his style, and his own ability to command it to some extent.

The characteristics of Augustan idiom and structure are well described by Johnson in *Idler* 63 where he is writing about the arts of rhetoric and poetry:

> the regulation of figures, the selection of words, the modulation of periods, the graces of transition, the complication of clauses, and all the delicacies of style and subtleties of composition, useful while they advance perspicuity and laudable while they increase pleasure. . .

It sometimes seems that this connectiveness, this insistence on the modulation of periods and the complication of clauses applies as much to prose as to poetry, and there is some truth in the idea. It was once fashionable to think of the eighteenth century as an age of prose, and to agree with Matthew Arnold and Leslie Stephen that Dryden and Pope were masters of our prose, not of our poetry. There is only one sense in which this is significant, however, the sense in which syntax, particularly in periodic constructions, can be said to have its own rhythm which imposes a certain structure on prose or verse. If we take this well-known passage from Raleigh's *History of the World,* the similarity becomes evident:

> O eloquent, just and mighty Death! whom none could advise, thou hast persuaded; what none hath dared, thou hast done; and whom all the world hath flattered, thou only hast cast out of the world and despised; thou hast drawn together all the far-stretched greatness, all the pride, cruelty and ambition of man, and covered it all over with these two narrow words, *Hic jacet!*

The complication of the clauses here has an almost liturgical quality; it gives rise to the counterpointing of significant and definitive words, contrasting with each other: *advise, persuaded; dared, done; flattered, cast out.* The rhythm of the last long half of the first part of the sentence stresses the repetition of "world"; the last part reverses the periodic structure of the first and moves directly and simply to the exclamatory conclusion. But though we might even say that Augustan poetry in its structure is curiously nearer to seventeenth century periodic prose than is the poetry of the seventeenth century, this great difference remains—that the strict metrical pattern of the couplet demands a far greater rhythmic complication of the poet than the open rhetorical declamation of the prose writer.

But Augustan verse is not the only kind that bears some relation to prose. There is always a close if secret connection between the structure of verse and prose within certain limits, which we can recognize, for instance, in the late eighteenth and nineteenth centuries. As the strongly marked caesura and the periodic constructions of the Augustan style begin to collapse with the passing of time, a new, flowing, associative manner of writing starts to develop. Goldsmith in *The Deserted Village* retains the couplet form, but practically eliminates the caesura for an effect of private and personal meditative recollection. This is even clearer in a later work like Coleridge's conversation poem *The Nightingale,* where, in the loosely associative manner, transitions from one recollection to the next, from one image to another, are made not through grammatical inflection or the complication of clauses, but by the simple use of the conjunction, linking one passage to the following. The emphasis is immediately thrown onto the vision-like quality of the recollections, and the unity of the poem depends on how certain images and impressions are knit together. For instance, the "bright, bright eyes" of the nightingales, "both bright and full" which gleam in the moonlight, are taken up again into the memory at the end of the poem where Coleridge describes his child's eyes, full of tears, glistening in the yellow moonbeam.

Nineteenth century descriptive prose at its best uses a similar technique to this. It is descriptive, moving from picture to picture, from scene to scene, so that the logical transitions are muted and the individual images thrown into high relief. Ruskin, making his contrast between English Gothic architecture and Venetian Byzantine—a contrast which is philosophical and historical as well as aesthetic, pursues his argument simply by means of two extended descriptions of Salisbury cathedral and St. Mark's. The skill with which he manages this has perhaps been as little noticed as that other skill with which, for instance, Gibbon can involve vivid descriptive detail within an overall rational argument. Ruskin can be thought of as a writer of ornate prose merely, and Gibbon as a monumental and stately periodic stylist, but in fact each represents a different way of looking at experience. The historian of the decline and fall of the Roman Empire, like the Augustan poet, must never lose sight of his pervading theme and argument which modifies the structure of his style and its details. The nineteenth century aesthetician, like the romantic poet, writes of experience, immediate visual experience, which is the physical correlative of insight, and his style, therefore, is a tissue of visual elaborations, of scenes and reactions to them, from which argument may be elicited, like Coleridge's poetic truth, at a flash, by imagery.

If I were to look for a word by which to describe the prevailing idiom of Augustan poetry, I would choose *discoursive,* retaining the obsolete spelling because it distinguishes the exact meaning more clearly. Johnson in his Dictionary defines it thus:

> having the character of discourses, whether meaning reason, or conversation, passing by intermediate steps from premises to consequences, containing dialogue; interlocutory, conversable, communicative.

He gives as his example this relevant passage from Dryden's *Essay on Dramatic Poetry:* "the epic is everywhere interlaced with dialogues; discoursive scenes." The essential point of the definition is that discourse as a mode "passes by intermediate steps from premises to consequences." The general pattern and the individual devices we have examined in the passages from Dryden, Pope and Johnson all share this characteristic. Many others could be found, too, to illustrate how discoursive poetry may be like conversation as much as like declamation, how its variations from narrative to talk, its transitions of mood and manner of address match its transitions of structure and metre, and, particularly in Pope's *Epistles,* give vivacity to works of which the subject matter is essentially steadfast and fixed. Johnson insists on the need for this connected discoursive element in literature as against the sudden flashes of brilliance, the dazzling images which draw attention to themselves at the expense of the whole. In *Rambler* 158 where he is complaining of false rules of lyric poetry drawn from the irregular example of Pindar, he writes:

> From this accidental peculiarity of the ancient writers, the critics deduce the rules of lyric poetry, which they have set free from all the laws by which other compositions are confined, and allow to neglect the niceties of transition, to start into remote digressions and to wander without restraint from one scene of imagery to another. To proceed from one truth to another, and connect distant propositions by regular consequences, is the great prerogative of man. Independent and unconfined sentiments, flashing upon the mind in quick succession may, for a time, delight by their novelty, but they differ from systematic reasoning, as single notes from harmony, as glances of lightning from the radiance of the sun.

Here we have the bare difference between the Augustan and romantic attitudes; between Johnson and Coleridge; between an older rhetoric and our new critical approach. The appropriate form to which Augustan poetry aspires in works of true genius is discoursive; it represents harmony rather than vision, above all it relates to a completely different conception of truth. The poet who proceeds from one truth to another needs to be sure of what those truths consist in. He is not feeling his way by experience; he is acquiescing in generally accepted ideas and presenting them persuasively to readers in whom he assumes a certain consent. Pope, writing that virtue alone is happiness below, did not conceive of a time when men might ask "what do you mean by virtue?" or "what is happiness?" He is content to prove his point through the whole structure and argument of his verse, but he does not ask us to experience the truth with him. So that the effect of his kind of poetry is not to make us aware of originality, novelty or new-found illumination. It is to remind us of what is already known and has been accepted by men for centuries, of what human experience has taught us, and to delight us by virtue of recognition rather than of surprise.

We have already seen that this idiom is related to the epic, the long exemplary narrative, and that its characteristic devices are simile rather than metaphor, and a structure which is discoursive rather than intuitive. It does not depend upon what Coleridge called organic form, the shape which grows from within and creates itself. But it would be unfair to call its form "mechanic," as if this represented a purely artificial imposition on the subject. It depends fundamentally on the Augustan attitude to the fixed, realistic, unchangeable nature of the subject matter—of truth, reality, objective things. Nor should we imagine that such poetry lacks emotion. Passion is not its strength, but it is instinct with pathos, irony, the reflective elegiac emotion that comes from looking backwards and forwards over the span of time, and the indignation provoked by comparing disorder, inadequacy, folly and vice with the harmony, sufficiency, wisdom and virtue which constituted the Augustan ideal of truth.

This should warn us of the dangers of approaching Augustan poetry with a Coleridgean and modern rhetorical bias. If we begin by studying the poet's images, we are likely to be disappointed. An analysis of Pope's cleverest devices (and he is the most figurative of all the Augustans), his most subtle metaphors, while satisfying in itself, will almost always end by making us uneasy with his work as a whole. It never seems to equal the sum of these parts. The parts fall into place only when we have recognized the intention, the mood and the assumptions of the whole. We have to submit ourselves to these before we can happily recognize the skill with which the devices play on our response. This is a point of view very foreign to us. We are not used to a common consent; we do not expect a poet to require it. In the dramatic, lyrical tradition the poetry itself does the work for us. The whole magnificent process of dissolving, diffusing and dissipating in order to recreate makes its own world and its own values, so that as we read we can, as Coleridge saw, suspend our disbelief. But Augustan discoursive poetry asks us to be aware of our belief and the poet's at the very beginning. It is as well to be honest about this, because dissent from the poet's point of view, though it may be a genuine disadvantage in Augustan poetry, does not mean that we cannot understand or admire such poetry, any more than the theological basis of *The Divine Comedy* prevents an unbeliever from delighting in it as a poem. But we must first know what is required of us before we can fully adjust ourselves to work as different in its whole outlook from our own. To love Augustan poetry is to be prepared to accept in their simplicity great commonplaces like those of which Gray's *Elegy* is composed, to recreate the frame of mind in which these seemed the proper substance of poetry, and then to approach the style itself in the same spirit that its author wrote. There is more than one way of living, of feeling, thinking and writing. These two traditions of verse are a striking example of the fact, for styles and structures always bear a deep relationship to ways of thinking and feeling in an age. To understand the discoursive idiom of Augustan poetry, as well as the organic form of the romantic style, is to recognize something of the richness and variety, the multifarious truth of poetry as a means of human expression.

josephine miles

THE SUBLIME POEM

We can, I think, construct a clear image of a sublime poem if we are willing to consider the basic simplicities of the modes in which most eighteenth-century poets wrote. If we were to look at all the leading poets of the century, thirty or forty of them perhaps, we should find a few, especially at the beginning, writing in that balanced, coupleted, cultivated mode which has been called classical; we should find a few, especially at the end, writing in that narrative lyrical ballad mode which has been called romantic; and we should find the rest, in the years from 1700 to 1770 and beyond, writing enthusiastically in a clearly definable harmonic and panoramic mode which has so far been called by no name of its own. One might call it picturesque or Pindaric, to suggest its artistic allegiances; Georgian, to suggest the reigns during which it prospered; Gothic, to suggest its sweep above and beyond classicism. All these terms, however, have limiting connotations awkward for the poetry. Closest to stylistic terms are Warton's "sublime" and "pathetic," representing a realm of emotional and dimensional discriminations adopted with interest by the critics in the century.

I propose to use sublime as a descriptive term for the whole realm of interest including the pathetic, for the whole ethos-pathos range of discernment; it too has its disadvantages of connotation, as in some of the specifications of Burke; but at least it is the era's own term, and suggestive even now of the sweeping, lofty, harmonious, emotional concerns which characterized poetic choices in the eighteenth-century mode. I shall try progressively to substantiate and clarify my use of it for that poetry which had its specific complex of traits: an epithetical, phrasal, participial, and compounding sentence structure, an unrhymed or irregular ode line, a vocabulary of passion and magnitude.

We may remember the classical distinction between ethos as human action and pathos as human suffering—suffering at the hands of fate, of

Reprinted from *Eras and Modes in English Poetry* (Berkeley, The University of California Press), pages 48–77, by permission of the author and publisher. Copyright 1957 by the Regents of the University of California.

the gods. Pathos was the wider, the more mysterious, the encompassing and tragic term; ethos was the term of social choice and custom, even of comedy. In ethics, man initiated; in pathetics, the gods proposed and disposed, and man endured. The great figure of ethos carried beyond its sphere, to become the extreme of pathos, is Prometheus. It was in such great pathetic figures and scenes that the eighteenth century was interested. Ethos for them had lessened, in "manners" as a matter of fashion, and as a term almost completely subordinated; pathos remained as high and moving, and to it was added the high and moving sublime of Longinus, newly sponsored by Boileau. Klaus Dockhorn, in his two monographs on Wordsworth and the sublime (Göttingen, 1944 and 1949), has shown us how exactly the formula seemed to get reversed, the classical high pathos becoming the neoclassical low and particular pathetic; and he has been troubled, as many historians have been, about the moment and the manner of this reversal. At least it may be suggested that English sublime-pathetic poetry itself carries a clue, perhaps a clearer one than its critics articulated, in its "simple, sensuous, and passionate" subject matter.

For Sylvester, Fletcher, More, Milton, the sensuous and passionate in poetry were high and lofty and coincident with sublimity. Heroic narrative was narrative of sublime pathos, of great figures in a great scene. But with and after them,[1] as narrative declined and description gained in literary force, as nature in its way took over the heights from man, and the gods became more and more a part of natural force, more mountainous, stormy, cosmic, yet retaining Longinus' Biblical sublimity, the human seemed to be diminished, its suffering set against the great storms of natural forces, made more local and perceivable, and so "pathetic" in its newly diminished sense. The mass of eighteenth-century poetry, the Dodsley collection for example, shows this new quality vividly: the new subject matter of natural force towering over and sublimating human passion, as in image it is a counterpart and analogy. We must turn to look at the poetry more closely to watch the development of the mode.

Intimations of sublimity grew slowly through the seventeenth century. The rich note of Spenser and his followers came to seem antiquated. The newer and more cosmic tone was Sylvester's in the *Divine Weekes,* and this is the sound that grew, for Milton especially, and for the later Cowley, Denham, Waller, and the Pindarists: the high style as it resounded in the spheres. We remember how at mid-century Hobbes

[1] Josephine Waters Bennett points out (English Institute *Essays,* 1951) that Spenser and Milton are the first great poets of Protestant revolt. See also Norman Maclean's "From Action to Image," in *Critics and Criticism,* ed. R. Crane (Chicago, 1925), and the Ramist models for Fraunce in Sister Miriam Joseph's *Shakespeare's Use of the Arts of Language* (Columbia Univ. Press, 1947).

and Davenant reargued the levels of style, and set again the highest as courtly and heroic. But courtly and heroic materials were not to be the active ones; rather, Protestanism was to turn them even further toward satire. For Protestanism it was the heavenly court, the heavenly city, the heavenly hero that mattered. So the style gradually rose up from the secular to the cosmic, with the combined aids of heroic theory, Sylvestrian practice, and Longinian *Peri Upsous*.

Davenant wrote to Hobbes in his Preface to *Gondibert* (London, 1651), "And surely Poets (whose business should represent the World's true image often to our view) are not less prudent than Painters, who when they draw Landschaps, entertain not the Eye wholly with even Prospect; and a continued Flat; but (for variety) terminate the sight with lofty Hills, whose obscure heads are sometimes in the clouds." He wrote also that "wise Poets think it more worthy to seek out truth in the Passions, than to record the truth of Actions; . . . it being nobler to contemplate the general History of Nature, than a selected Diary of Fortune." Davenant wrote with conscience, he said, and he chose to deal with Christian characters, with distant scenes, with wit, "the dexteritie of thought, rounding the world, like the Sun, with unimaginable motion; and bringing swiftly home to the memorie, universal surveys."

Hobbes replied with assent, equating heroic with celestial: "For there is in Princes, and men of conspicuous power (anciently call'd *Heroes*) a lustre and influence upon the rest of men, resembling that of the Heavens, and an insincereness, inconstancie, and troublesom humour of those that dwell in populous Cities, like the mobilitie, blustering, and impuritie of the Air; and a plainness, and (though dul) yet a nutritive facultie in rural people, that endures a comparison with the Earth they labour."

The universal analogies were so clear that the poet could easily proceed, in theory, but Davenant himself had not the sense of the new heroic meter and vocabulary. Too conceptual, too homely, too popular, his quatrains rattled:

> Of all the Lombards, by their Trophies known,
> Who sought Fame soon, and had her favour long,
> King Aribert best seem'd to fill the Throne;
> And bred most bus'ness for Heroick Song.

What Cowley and Waller praised him for in their introductory verses was his generality, his breaking away from the antique fictive spell of pagan gods and magic toward a more social and religious truth, in lines

> Which no bold tales of Gods or Monsters swell,
> But humane Passions, such as with us dwell.

What Davenant needed to fulfill his motives was a fuller power of elaboration, and it was this that Cowley began to capture in the *Davideis*, as Denham and Waller did in their surveys, so that the great power which Milton achieved had been anticipated by a growing purpose and familiarity. For all the relative failure of Cowley's heroics, his fellow Denham could praise them,

> When Heroes, Gods, or God-like Kings
> They praise, on their exalted wings
> To the Celestial orbs they climb,
> And with th' Harmonious Spheres keep time; . . .
> ("On Mr. Abraham Cowley," *Poems*, London, 1668)

And for all Denham's own immersion in the metaphysical style, he could begin to try the sort of line and phrasing which Dryden in turn would praise: the descriptive and lofty analogy, as in the middle of "Coopers Hill":

> But his proud head the aery Mountain hides
> Among the Clouds; his shoulders and his sides
> A shady mantle cloaths; his curled brows
> Frown on the gentle stream, which calmly flows,
> While winds and storms his lofty forehead beat:
> The common fate of all that's high or great.

Part of this increasing sense of nature's divinity and humanity came from Protestantism, from Platonic and Biblical sources, as in the work of Spenser, Sylvester, the Cambridge Platonists and Thomas Burnet, as, indeed, from the King James version of the Bible itself and the sublimity of preaching based upon it. Cowley's support of Davenant in his poem of praise was explicitly anti-Catholic, pro-Hebraic; and we can watch in paraphrases like those of Sandys the growth of a sensuous Biblical vocabulary into English.

Part of the sublime style, too, was to be found in classical poets, even the most mundane like Horace. In pastoral scenery, Christian and pagan could join to find significance. While Ovid had been the classical poet for the sixteenth century, and Virgil would be for much of the eighteenth, in between Horace provided a good guide, and everybody from Jonson to Roscommon tried him in translation. The English which translated him grew more and more suitably furnished and proportioned, though his true rich classical balance was difficult for native English to achieve. The famous beginning to his Ode IX, of Book I, much liked in the seventeenth century, even in its simple translation by Thomas Creech, suggests the new vocabulary of scene and sense:

See how the Hills are white with Snow,
  The Seas are rough, the Woods are tost,
The Trees beneath their Burden bow,
  And purling Streams are bound in Frost.

Or, even more lofty, the end of Ode III:

With Wings, which Nature's Laws deny,
First Daedalus did boldly dare
    To beat the Empty Air,
And wander thro' the liquid Sky.

Thro' Hell the fierce Alcides ran,
He scorn'd the stubborn chains of Fate,
And rudely broke the Brazen Gate;
    Nought is too hard for Man.

Grown Giants in Impiety,
Our Impious Folly dares the Sky,
We dare assault Jove's glorious Throne;
Nor still averse to his Command,
Will we permit his lifted Hand
    To lay his Thunder down.
        (*Odes, Satyrs. Epistles, of Horace,*
        6th ed., London, 1737)

This is soaring as "unclassical" as Blake's, and in Blake's vocabulary.

Horace's very consciousness of the varieties of style brought new possibilities to seventeenth-century attention, as he discussed suitability of method and subject in his "Art of Poetry":

Some scatter here and there few gawdy Lines,
Which glister finely, when a Grove's their Theme,
A pleasant Wood, or else a purling Stream:
How with the Flood, their Fancies smoothly flow!
How variously they paint the Heav'nly Bow!
But now perhaps none of these Themes agree.
Perhaps thou hast some Skill to paint a Tree,
But what of that? What will this Art perform?
Wert thou to draw a Shipwrack, or a Storm?

These had not been the subjects or the problems of English poets. They were the problems of painters, as Horace said; and of this likening the English now took strong note. How to paint a tree? How to paint a storm? It would remain for James Thomson to try the problem most wholeheartedly.

In Creech it was already the new "classical" Horace that was speaking and advising toward the new poetry. Hear how different the old colloquial Horace sounded, in the more English English of Oldham's translation: the same passage has for Oldham the miscellaneous jumble of earlier satire.

> Some, who would have us think they meant to treat
> At first on arguments of greatest weight,
> Are proud, when here and there a glitt'ring line
> Does through the mass of their coarse rubbish shine.
> In gay digressions they delight to rove,
> Describing here a temple, there a grove,
> A vale enamell'd o'er with pleasant streams,
> A painted rainbow, or the gliding Thames.
> But how does this relate to their design?
> Though good elsewhere, 'tis here but foisted in.
> A common dauber may perhaps have skill
> To paint a tavern sign, or landscape well;
> But what is this to drawing of a fight,
> A wreck, a storm, or the last judgment right?
> (*Poetical Works* of John Oldham, London, 1854)

This is the Oldham of the "Satires against the Jesuits" of 1683, the great admirer of Ben Jonson, one of the poets of the dregs, whips, and scourges of the satirical tradition; and both his technique and his vocabulary are strongly traditional, making little allowance for the mood of the classics which was dawning on the landscaped world of Dryden. In the satirists we see the conventionalists, the holders to English tradition, against the sweep of Miltonism; even in Marvell we see the force of the old terms in his State Poems, crowding out the green shade of his earlier rich pastoralism. Therefore the change was slow; the rational and bitter persisted; but translation by translation Horace was sweetening and his countryside winning out.

Swift in most of his poetry[2] and Gay in his *Fables* prolonged the vernacular satiric line a short way into the eighteenth century, but after them there was little of colloquialism in poetry until Burns and Coleridge and Byron brought it back again under different auspices, the active narrative simplicity of lyrical balladry.

Meanwhile, the Roman classical mode of the late seventeenth century had also somewhat subsided in the eighteenth. The balanced terms and structures of Joseph Hall, Marvell, Dryden, Addison, and Parnell continued temperately in some of Pope's work, and in Johnson's and Goldsmith's. But otherwise its force was minor, not to be renewed until late in the century, in the new classicism of Crabbe and Wordsworth.

The prevailing eighteenth-century poem was the sublime poem, risen from sources in English efforts at heroic poetry, strengthened by

2 Swift's *Battle of the Books,* like *The Rehearsal* earlier and Pope's *Peri Bathous* later, mocked the new sublimity.

new versions of classical practice, and fully established by the combined forces of the Bible, Milton, Fénelon, and Longinus. The sublime poem was written throughout the century, from Pomfret, Prior, Blackmore, Brooke, and Thomson, through Gray, Akenside, and Collins, through Blair and Dyer and Armstrong, through Mason, Lyttelton, and Somerville, to the Wartons and Blake and Bowles, even to Keats. Thereafter, with exceptions in Whitman,[3] Wilde, Henley, and some of the Imagists, we have had less of its nature. But for one whole century it dominated the world of English poetry.[4]

How may the sublime poem be distinguished? First of all, by its cumulative phrasal sentence structure, its piling up of nouns and epithets, participles and compounds, with a very minimum of clausal subordinations and active verbs. Second, by its vocabulary of cosmic passion and sense impression. Third, by its internal rather than external patterning of sound, the interior tonal shadings and onomatopoeias of its unrhymed verse. In combination, these three major traits make for an exceptionally panoramic and panegyric verse, emotional, pictorial, noble, universal, and tonal, rising to the height of heaven and of feeling in the style traditionally known as grand or sublime.

We may look at John Philips' "Blenheim" or "Cyder" as examples, to see how the consciously Miltonic style functions in blank-verse pomp, at the century's beginning. "Blenheim" begins:

> From low and abject Themes the Grov'ling Muse
> Now mounts Aerial, to sing of Arms
> Triumphant, and emblaze the Martial Acts
> Of Britain's Heroe; may the Verse not sink
> Beneath his Merits, but detain a while
> Thy Ear, O Harley, . . .

The lines proceed to show Albion in action:

> Now from each Van
> The brazen Instruments of Death discharge
> Horrible Flames, and turbid streaming Clouds
> Of Smoak sulphureous; intermix't with these
> Large globous Irons fly, of dreadful Hiss,
> Singeing the Air, and from long Distance bring
> Surprizing Slaughter; on each side they fly
> By Chains connex't, and with destructive Sweep
> Behead whole Troops at once; the hairy Scalps

[3] Gay Wilson Allen in his *Whitman Handbook* (Packard, 1946) clearly describes for Whitman the mode I have called "sublime": the panoramic images, linear units, cumulative structures, and phonic iterations.

[4] John Arthos' *Language of Natural Description in Eighteenth-Century Poetry* (Univ. of Michigan Press, 1949), pp. 2, 14, 42, makes this point particularly clear in his own terms, relating to the styles of Lucretius and Du Bartas.

Are whirl'd aloof, while numerous Trunks bestrow
Th' ensanguin'd Field; . . .
(Lines 143–153; *Poems,* ed. M. G. Lloyd Thomas, Blackwell, 1927)

This is the sort of sublime excess we have found even more in Blake's Prophetic Books than in Milton; it has the drive and richness of much compacted detail in massive range. The more famous "Cyder" is more pastorally peaceful, but still in its destruction scene reaches magniloquent heights.

Horrible Chasm, profound! with swift Descent
Old Ariconium sinks, and all her Tribes,
Heroes, and Senators, down to the Realms
Of endless Night.
(Bk. I, lines 227–231)

Fall and *rise* were, indeed, the characteristically most used verbs in eighteenth-century poetry; along with the nouns *air, sky,* and *scene,* they indicated the sort of cosmic atmosphere and activity that prevailed, while *dear, soft, tender, virtue, song, joy* for the first time in English poetry made feeling explicit, and the nouns *breast, head, maid, muse, youth* bodied forth the feeling figures. They were, as we may see from Philips and others, partly classical figures, the presences of gods and muses, more than life-size; they were partly and increasingly northern titanic figures, with a Jehovan presence; the first were often related to the "beautiful," the second to the "sublime," but even beauty in the eighteenth century grew more and more sublime as it grew from the classical terms of *happy* to late-century *sad,* from *new* to *wild,* from *nature* to *cloud,* from *art, fate,* and *friend* to *woe* and *weeping,* even from *mighty* to *little,* as the sublimity of passion came down to smallest essences, and the whole realm became one with the pathetic. This was the road which sublimity traveled: it grew out of classical beauty and it grew into classical pathos, moving always by way of the heights and the depths.

So Pomfret begins in 1699 with the classical picture in "The Choice":

Horace and Virgil, in whose mighty Lines
Immortal Wit, and solid Learning, shines;
Sharp Juvenal, and am'rous Ovid too,
Who all the Turns of Love's soft Passion knew:
He that with Judgment reads his charming Lines,
In which strong Art with stronger Nature joins,
Must grant his Fancy does the best excel:
His Thoughts so tender, and express'd so well;

With all those Moderns, Men of steady Sense,
Esteem'd for Learning, and for Eloquence.
(*Poems,* London, 11th ed., lines 19–25)

Then he proceeds to intensify, as in the last sections of "Love Triumphant over Reason":

The glorious Fabrick charm'd my wondring Sight;
Of vast Extent, and of prodigious Height:
The Case was Marble, but the polish'd Stone,
With such an admirable Lustre shone,
As if some Architect Divine had strove
T' outdo the Palace of imperial Jove, . . .

And then, in the "Divine Attributes," more wildness (sec. VI):

Did not th' Almighty, with immediate Care,
Direct and govern this capacious All,
How soon would Things into Confusion fall!
Earthquakes the trembling Ground would tear,
And blazing Comets rule the troubled air;
Wide Inundations, with resistless Force,
The lower Provinces o'erflow,
In Spite of all that human Strength could do
To Stop the raging Sea's impetuous Course.
Murder and Rapine ev'ry Place would fill,
And sinking Virtue stoop to prosp'rous Ill; . . .

Such variety and degree of power in 1699 presaged the range and variety of the whole century to come, all in a style "higher" than even Homer or Virgil had managed to achieve. Their lines and structures were classically balanced; these reached out to an evangelist heaven and hell.

The early practicers did not at first manage to break away from rhyme, as Pomfret here did not, and Blackmore even earlier (see *A Collection of Poems* by Sir Richard Blackmore, London, 1718 ed.). The mode was not yet clearly established, and Blackmore received the scorn of the wits for his high appeals to imagination and passion. But even in couplets the sublimity was evident. For example see "Advice to the Poets," fifth section:

The Solar Orb did from the South retreat,
And thro' the Air diffuse reviving Heat,
Solace the Soil, exhilerate the Swain,
And Nature loose from Winter's Chrystal Chain,
When the Great Chief, at Anna's high Command,
Return'd to chear Batavia's joyful Land:
Dreadful in Arms he march'd to Brabant's Coast,

> And Terror struck thro' Gallia's shuddring Host,
> Whose Cohorts o'er the Ground, like Locusts, spread,
> Each Herb devour'd, and crop'd each verdant Head.

The rhymes and antitheses are of the 1690's; the emotions and images, of the next generation; Blackmore, like Pope, was pulled two ways, and Pope, as in *Peri Bathous,* recognized the conflict, but would have been the last to give Blackmore any credit for the pioneering. Consciously and earnestly Blackmore followed Davenant's and Cowley's recommendations for Christian subjects; faithfully he advised the use of noble Spenserian diction; too humorlessly for the school of Dryden, he set about stretching the "radiant Wings" of poetry's messenger to "Heavn's eternal Gate." And he treated his detractors, the wits, like invading insects which "crop each budding Vertue's tender Head," in the same locust simile he had used before, now made central to the "Satyre upon Wit."

Even the prose of the preface to his most famous "Nature of Man" works in the terms of the new poetry. "The Design of this Poem, is to express how far the Disparity of the intellectual Faculties, Dispositions and Passions of Men is owing to the different Situation of their Native Countries in Respect of the Sun; . . ." And the poetry:

> Bright Humane Nature does no less demand
> An Air adapted, and peculiar Land.
> In vain you hope Illustrious Youth will shine
> Beneath th' Æquator, or th' Ecliptick Line;
> Where Sun-burnt Nations, of a Swarthy Skin,
> Are sully'd o'er with blacker Clouds within.
> Their Spirits suffer by too hot a Ray,
> And their dry Brain grows dark with too much Day.

But for the purposes of clarification of the mode, rather than praise the maligned Blackmore for being ahead of his day we had better scrutinize a poet more thoroughly characteristic, James Thomson for example. He was one whom his contemporaries and successors praised for just those qualities which he thoroughly contributed to the sublime: the fidelity of descriptive image, the vocabulary of nature and emotion, the smooth cumulative sound and structure of the verse. His "Winter" begins:

> See, Winter comes, to rule the varied year,
> Sullen and sad, with all his rising train—
> Vapours, and clouds, and storms. Be these my theme;
> These, that exalt the soul to solemn thought,
> And heavenly musing. Welcome, kindred glooms!
> Cogenial horrors, hail! . . .

In his preface, it was Job and Virgil that Thomson praised, and "the choosing of great and serious subjects, such as at once amuse the fancy, enlighten the head, and warm the heart," as an influence "towards the revival of poetry." His ostensible subject, the seasons, served to parallel both the history of civilization in survey, and the anatomy of man's passion in detail. See, for example, such description of a parallel emotion some hundred of lines into "Spring":

> Senseless and deformed,
> Convulsive Anger storms at large; or, pale
> And silent, settles into full revenge.
> Base Envy withers at another's joy,
> And hates that excellence it cannot reach.
> Desponding Fear, of feeble fancies full,
> Weak and unmanly, loosens every power.
> Even Love itself is bitterness of soul,
> A pensive anguish pining at the heart; . . .

Then see again how closely parallel runs the phrasing of his politics, as in "Liberty," IV:

> "Awhile my spirit slept; the land awhile,
> Affrighted, drooped beneath despotic rage.
> Instead of Edward's equal, gentle laws,
> The furious victor's partial will prevailed.
> All prostrate lay; and, in the secret shade,
> Deep-stung but fearful, Indigation gnashed
> His teeth. . . ."

The whole long poem is a compendium of the language of eighteenth-century Whiggish verse which would reach its height of power in Blake. Or again, as in the "Castle of Indolence," we may see that somewhat softer version of the sublime, which was to find its final elegance in Keats. Canto I, stanza XXXIX:

> Each sound too here to languishment inclined,
> Lulled the weak bosom, and inducèd ease.
> Aerial music in the warbling wind,
> At distance rising oft, by small degrees
> Nearer and nearer came, till o'er the trees
> It hung, and breathed such soul-dissolving airs
> As did, alas! with soft perdition please:
> Entangled deep in its enchanting snares,
> The listening heart forgot all dutie and all cares.

In all these ways, in the poetry of sensuous sensibility, the poetry of politics and universal survey, the poetry of massive personification, the poetry of patient detailed description, Thomson built up the book of eighteenth-century verse. He drew from the psychology of sense impression, from the painterly tradition, from the new philosophical feeling of cosmos and of anatomy more than life-size, and from the literary developments we have been observing, making even Spenser serve the new landscape. His work was the center of a century's mode.

Even so early as Parnell's writing of his "Essay on the Different Styles of Poetry," in 1714, the relation of new mode to old was so clear that it could be assumed and generalized upon. Parnell treated four difficulties for poetry: metaphysical verbalism, dry sententiousness, artificial pastoralism, and bombast. Then he treated the parallel virtues: the beautiful images of description, the forms that rise from reflection, the narrative liveliness of court or countryside, the true height of poetry of the passions.[5] The virtues are virtues of what he feels to be reality: observable images of natural scenes, thoughts, actions, and passions. The vices are the tricks of unreality in correspondent realms: image distorted into far-fetched metaphor, thought abstracted rather than personified, the countryside made unnatural, the natural sublime made fantastic or monstrous. He recommends as devices, modest metaphors, beauteous similes, repetitions, questions, emotions, personifications, exclamations, rising sentences, and smooth transitions, the very characteristics of eighteenth-century poetry as distinguished in itself:

> Whence images, in charming numbers set,
> A sort of likeness in the soul beget,
> And what fair visions oft we fancy nigh
> By fond delusions of the swimming eye,
> Or further pierce through Nature's maze to find
> How passions drawn give passions to the mind.

For this early conservative critic, as for Trapp and many other conservative theorists in the century, as indeed for Bysshe[6] in his standard compendium, the criteria of the naturalists from Hobbes and Locke and the deistic admirers of the observable universe had been acceptable and assumable; poetry lay in the sky, the mountain, the field, the human breast. It grew from sensation into thought and passion. It was essentially literal, essentially reportorial, reflecting a literally and reportorially sublime universe.

Not only Samuel Monk's *The Sublime,* but also such recent studies as Cecil Moore's *Backgrounds of English Literature, 1700–1760,* Ernest

[5] Note how these have been elaborated toward nature and passion from more technical medieval distinctions (J. W. H. Atkins, *English Literary Criticism: The Medieval Phase,* Cambridge Univ. Press, 1943; and Ernest R. Curtius, *Europäische Literatur und lateinisches Mittelalter,* Bern, 1948).

[6] For contemporary recognition of Bysshe's "sublimity" see Preface to *The British Muse,* ed. Thomas Hayward, London, 1738.

Tuveson's *Millennium and Utopia*, J. E. Congleton's *Theories of Pastoral Poetry in England, 1684–1798*, Donald Davie's *Purity of Diction in English Verse*, John Arthos' *Language of Natural Description in Eighteenth-Century Poetry*, Samuel Kliger's *The Goths in England*, John Butt's *The Augustan Age*, R. L. Brett's *The Third Earl of Shaftesbury*, and Jean Hagstrum's *Samuel Johnson's Literary Criticism* have made us increasingly aware of the brief tenure of neoclassicism in the eighteenth century, and the looming power of a cosmic art beyond the classic. In pulling away from the metaphysical fictive extreme, the century moved to another, natural, extreme, that of the sublime, where trope gave way to simile, and concept to body, and microcosm to the natural world. Thus the "Whiggish" poetry of the Shaftesburians, in the wake of Milton and Addison and Locke, the central century's poetry of Shenstone, Akenside, Thomson, Collins, the Wartons, even at times by Pope. Thus the poetic debate in Joseph Spence's *Essay on Pope's Odyssey*, 1626, between the classicist who loved plain nature, as Wordsworth later would, and the *modernist* (not a metaphysical reactionary) who loved "pictures! passions! charming imagery!" (Austin Wright's *Joseph Spence*, p. 17), all the "glittering and elevation" against which Wordsworth would eventually rebel.

The orderly harmonies of classicism had seemed and would seem again a relief after the extremes of metaphysical speculation, of sublime embodiment and extension. But meantime the reaches of sublimity were invigorating to eighteenth-century poets, and all tried to see how much particularity, how much error and flaw, the rising harmony might be able to sustain, beyond the confines of mere beauty and ethos. As early as the 1690's, while forty were reading Rochester to every one reading Milton (John H. Wilson, *The Court Wits of the Restoration*, p. 106), Robert Wolseley was nevertheless writing in his "Preface to Valentinian" (*Critical Essays of the Seventeenth Century*, ed. Spingarn, III, 12), "every ass that's romantick believes he's inspir'd." By 1761 Shenstone was writing to a friend: "The taste of the age, as far as it regards plan and style, seems to have been carried to the utmost height, as may appear in the works of Akenside, Gray's Odes and Church-yard verses, and Mason's Monody and Elfrida. The public has seen all that art can do, and they want the more striking efforts of wild, original, enthusiastic genius. It seems to exclaim aloud with the chorus in Julius Caesar,

> " 'O rather than be slaves to these deep learned men,
> Give us our wildness and our woods, our huts and caves again!' "
> (Quoted by John Butt, *The Augustan Age*, p. 138)

Akenside himself, along with Goldsmith, in his "Pleasures of Imagination (Enlarged)," stressed the inclusive powers of the sublime:

> . . . what human breast
> E'er doubts, before the transient and minute,
> To prize the vast, the stable, the sublime?

And though conservative critics like Johnson liked the vast to be magniloquent rather than mysterious, explicit rather than implicit, others like the Wartons were working constantly for more particularity, implication, speaking simplicity. As Edward Young phrased what Longinus and Boileau had said (*Night Thoughts,* IX, 1634 ff.):

> There dwells a noble pathos in the skies,
> Which warms our passions, proselytes our hearts, . . .
> Demonstrating great truth in style sublime,
> Though silent, loud! . . .

As these few lines represent the richer treasures of Collins and his contemporaries, we may let one quotation from Richard Hurd (*Works,* Vol. II, pp. 8–9) represent the vast store of mid- and late-century critical praise of sublime subject and style as distinguished from classical:

> "For there is something in the mind of man, sublime and elevated, which prompts it to overlook all obvious and familiar appearances, and to feign to itself other and more extraordinary; such as correspond to the extent of its own powers, and fill out all the faculties and capacities of our souls. . . .
>
> "Hence it comes to pass, that it deals in apostrophes and invocations; that it impersonates the virtues and vices; peoples all creation with new and living forms; calls up infernal spectres to terrify, or brings down celestial natures to astonish, the imagination; assembles, combines, or connects its ideas, at pleasure; in short, prefers not only the agreeable, and the graceful, but, as occasion calls upon her, the vast, the incredible, I had almost said, the impossible, to the obvious truth and nature of things."

The rationale for the phrasal and cumulative mode, with its language of sensory embodiment, is implicit in these terms; and they are not merely "Gothic" but also Biblical and classical terms, in the Grecian classicism of Plato, Longinus, Lucretius, and Pindar, as well as in what T. S. Eliot was to call, in "The Function of Criticism" (*Criterion,* II, 31 ff.), the Whiggery of the Inner Voice.

The "specific sort of feeling in the face of the awful and great" which Shaftesbury's *Characteristics* called sublime here blends with feeling itself, with greatness, with personification and implication, so that we may be sure of its all-encompassing power. By the late century, when there was a reaction toward classical balance, many poets, like Rogers, Blake, Bowles, and Keats, found still such satisfying wealth of both soaring statement and implicative height in the sublime style that they enthusiastically prolonged the use of it.

To Rogers' *Pleasures of Memory* the Introduction (1793) reads:

Oh could my Mind, unfolded in my page,
Enlighten climes and mould a future age;
There as it glow'd, with noblest frenzy fraught,
Dispense the treasures of exalted thought;
To Virtue wake the pulses of the heart,
And bid the tear of emulation start!
Oh could it still, thro' each succeeding year,
My life, my manners, and my name endear;
And, when the poet sleeps in silent dust,
Still hold communion with the wise and just!—
Yet should this Verse, my leisure's best resource,
When thro' the world it steals its secret course,
Revive but once a generous wish supprest,
Chase but a sigh, or charm a care to rest;
In one good deed a fleeting hour employ,
Or flush one faded cheek with honest joy;
Blest were my lines, tho' limited their sphere,
Tho' short their date, as his who trac'd them here.

These lines provide a standard context for the decade's key terms. Eighteenth-century *mind, clime, age, thought,* glow in increasing light. *Heart* and *tear* wake to *virtue, cheek* flushes with *joy. Life* and *name* endure through *world* and *time,* a *fleeting hour.* The wish or prayer in its cumulative couplets here gives us accustomed generality atremble with sensibility. The concluding lines of the "Ode to Superstition" are even more elaborate, in their physical sense of truth as light.

Lord of each pang the nerves can feel,
Hence, with the rack and reeking wheel.
Faith lifts the soul above this little ball!
While gleams of glory open round,
And circling choirs of angels call,
Canst thou, with all thy terrors crown'd,
Hope to obscure that latent spark,
Destin'd to shine when suns are dark?
Thy triumphs cease! thro' every land,
Hark! Truth proclaims, thy triumphs cease:
Her heav'nly form, with glowing hand,
Benignly points to piety and peace.
Flush'd with youth, her looks impart
Each fine feeling as it flows;
Her voice the echo of her heart,
Pure as the mountain-snows:
Celestial transports round her play,
And softly, sweetly die away.

She smiles! and where is now the cloud
That blacken'd o'er thy baleful reign?
Grim Darkness furls his leaden shroud,
Shrinking from her glance in vain.
Her touch unlocks the day-spring from above,
And lo! it visits man with beams of light and love.

Truth with glowing hand points to peace, feeling flows, voice echoes heart, the cloud shrinks, the dayspring visits man with beams of light and love—here again we have the central scene anatomized as in the earlier eighteenth century, but, in *nerve, feeling, echo, smile, voice,* and *touch,* that anatomy made now more inwardly expressive.

Southey is another to present this norm, in his "Bion" poems of 1795. His proportioning is average, his verse forms vary from old couplet to new sonnet, and of his subjects, as he says with Lovell in the Preface, "Much novelty cannot be expected." So he too writes of Memory in "The Retrospect," its closing lines of invocation,

Why wilt thou, Memory, still recall to view
Each long-past joy, each long-lost friend anew?
Paint not the scenes that pleas'd my soul of yore,
Those friends are gone, those long-past joys no more;
Cease to torment me, busy torturer, cease,
Let cold oblivion's touch benumb my soul to peace!

Older friends and scenes are blended with new joy and peace. And in "Romance":

Fain would the grateful Muse, to thee, Rousseau,
Pour forth the energic thanks of gratitude;
Fain would the raptur'd lyre ecstatic glow,
To whom Romance and Nature form'd all good:
Guide of my life, too weak these lays,
To pour the unutterable praise;
Thine aid divine for ever lend,
Still as my guardian sprite attend;
Unmov'd by Fashion's flaunting throng,
Let my calm stream of life smooth its meek course along;
Let no weak vanity dispense
Her vapors o'er my better sense;
But let my bosom glow with fire,
Let me strike the soothing lyre,
Altho' by all unheard the melodies expire.

In standard phrases and linear variations, Southey calling on Rousseau brings new and old together, *glowing, pouring, soothing* the era's sort of verb, and *calm stream of life* its metaphor, and *all unheard* the melodies. In the Sonnets are ruins, knells, nightingales, and other such appurtenances, yet such remarked simplicities as "My friendly fire, thou blazest clear and bright."

In satire, however crudely used, the same interplay is stressed, as by Gifford in the *Baviad*, which achieves the norm by making fun of it:

> If comedy be yours, the searching strain
> Gives a sweet pleasure, so chastis'd by pain,
> That e'en the guilty at their sufferings smile,
> And bless the lancet, tho' they bleed the while.
> If tragedy, th' impassioned numbers flow
> In all the sad variety of woe,
> With such a liquid lapse, that they betray
> The breast unwares, and steal the soul away.

His vocabulary is more of past than of future, more sweet fate, power, and bodily terms than the language of nature, soul, and truth in its more evanescent forms; but such it must be to keep poetry's feet on the ground, as he feels, and he feels in a very suitable and orthodox way. Amused by the vogue he makes fun of, his readers may also directly enjoy it, so strong are eighteenth-century forces still.

Some of the poets of the 1790's were even more than the average devoted to middle eighteenth-century measures: Blake, who pushed many measures to their limits, and Campbell, who preserved them faithfully over a long span, and William Bowles, who meant inspiration to the young Wordsworth. These were poets of full flowing lines, who shared especially the terms of power and sublimity, *eternal, dark, divine, beautiful, sacred, stormy, fate* and *rapture, cliff* and *vale* and *view*. Yet they are deeply personal, as Bowles says in introducing his sonnets. The very first provides an example:

> As slow I climb the cliff's ascending side,
> Much musing on the track of terror past,
> When o'er the dark wave rode the howling blast,
> Pleas'd I look back, and view the tranquil tide
> That laves the pebbl'd shore: and now the beam
> Of evening smiles on the grey battlement,
> And yon forsaken tow'r that time has rent:—
> The lifted oar far off with silver gleam
> Is touch'd, and hush'd is all the billowy deep!
> Sooth'd by the scene, thus on tir'd Nature's breast
> A stillness slowly steals, and kindred rest;
> While sea-sounds lull her, as she sinks to sleep;
> Like melodies which mourn upon the lyre,
> Wak'd by the breeze, and, as they mourn, expire.

Bowles's are not what we think of as lyrical sonnets; they are heavily descriptive in the same way that blank verse and heroic couplet might be: so devoted were these late-century poets to the emotional and substantial *mass* of verse, that even Blake's long lines (in *America*) do not seem alien:

> . . . the vale was dark
> With clouds of smoke from the Atlantic, that in volumes roll'd
> Between the mountains; dismal visions mope around the house . . .

and Campbell could give the sense of vast and mournful scope whether he used the newest experimental stanza forms or the conventional couplets with which he opened and closed his career. His youthful and famous "Pleasures of Hope" in 1798, despite its forward-sounding specific vocabulary of romantic usage in *dim, dream, father, child, home, star, wind,* the infiltration of new content into old form, was on the whole a model of a sublime poem, outdoing itself in the old glooms and splendors of expression and unable to suffer any real sea-change.

> Auspicious Hope! in thy sweet garden grow
> Wreaths for each toil, a charm for every woe;
> Won by their sweets, in Nature's languid hour,
> The way-worn pilgrim seeks thy summer bower;
> There, as the wild bee murmurs on the wing,
> What peaceful dreams thy handmaid spirits bring!
> What viewless forms th' Aeolian organ play,
> And sweep the furrowed lines of anxious thought away!
>
> Angel of life! thy glittering wings explore
> Earth's loneliest bounds, and Ocean's wildest shore.
> Lo! to the wintry winds the pilot yields
> His bark careering o'er unfathom'd fields;
> Now on th' Atlantic waves he rides afar,
> Where Andes, giant of the western star,
> With meteor-standard to the winds unfurl'd,
> Looks from his throne of clouds o'er half the world!
>
> Now far he sweeps, where scarce a summer smiles,
> On Behring's rocks, or Greenland's naked isles:
> Cold on his midnight watch the breezes blow,
> From wastes that slumber in eternal snow;
> And waft, across the waves' tumultuous roar,
> The wolf's long howl from Oonalaska's shore.
> Poor child of danger, nursling of the storm,
> Sad are the woes that wreck thy manly form!
> Rocks, waves, and winds, the shatter'd bark delay!
> Thy heart is sad, thy home is far away.

It is difficult to stop quoting from Campbell; he blends with such enthusiastic unoriginality the homely pathos of Goldsmith and Cowper with the sublime natural forces of Bowles and Blake into the finest sort of "preromantic" mélange.

Now how did this century-old pattern of cosmic, emotional, exclamatory pentameter change gradually into the romantic poetry of stanzaic implication? I think it did not. The preromantic sublime does not become romantic poetry, but goes on in its own way for Wordsworth, Keats, Campbell, Kirke White, and others high and low, to Tennyson, Whitman, Wilde, and to Dylan Thomas. Romantic starts new and individual, a fresh spring beside the old tumultuous river. The sources of this spring were in the Ballads wherever they might be found and read; but for a long time, as in Chatterton and some of Percy's *Reliques* themselves, these sources were swamped and overgrown with Spenserianism in the eighteenth-century antiquarian form which served to conceal the pure new motion of ballad lyric and ballad narrative.

In the 1790's there were manifold unconcealable new signs: Blake's *Songs*, Scott's narratives, Burns's hesitant new beginnings. The short implicative line of song demanded a different vocabulary and a different sentence structure, with less of exposition and more of echo.

> "Does the spring hide its joy
> When buds and blossoms grow?
> Does the sower
> Sow by night,
> Or the plowman in darkness plow?"
> (Blake, "Earth's Answer")

or,

> Such is the fate of artless Maid,
> Sweet flow'ret of the rural shade!
> By Love's simplicity betray'd,
> And guileless trust,
> Till she, like thee, all soil'd, is laid
> Low i' the dust.
> (Burns, "To a Mountain-daisy," 1786)

For Scott and Coleridge, as for Burns, the deepest source of invention appeared in a minor form, not in prime vocabulary or mode but in lines of lyrical understatement—"Does the spring hide its joy . . ." and "Low i' the dust."

> But not alone the bitter tear
> Had filial grief supplied;
> For hopeless love and anxious fear
> Had lent their mingled tide:
> Nor in her mother's alter'd eye
> Dar'd she to look for sympathy.
> (Scott, *Last Minstrel,* I, x)

So acceptance of the ballad tradition subtilizes old materials for the *Last Minstrel,* and adds the new particularity of detail.

> From the sound of Teviot's tide,
> Chafing with the mountain's side,
> From the groan of the wind-swung oak,
> From the sullen echo of the rock,
> From the voice of the coming storm,
>   The Ladye knew it well!
> It was the Spirit of the Flood that spoke,
>   And he call'd on the Spirit of the Fell.
> "Sleep'st thou, brother?" . . .
> (I, xiv, xv)

From such writing it is a step, though a magical one, to the lines of *The Ancient Mariner:*

> And the coming wind did roar more loud,
> And the sails did sigh like sedge;
> And the rain poured down from the black cloud;
> The Moon was at its edge.
>
> The thick black cloud was cleft, and still
> The Moon was at its side:
> Like waters shot from some high crag,
> The lightning fell with never a jag,
> A river steep and wide.
>
> The loud wind never reached the ship,
> Yet now the ship moved on!
> Beneath the lightning and the Moon
> The dead men gave a groan.
>
> They groaned, they stirred, they all uprose,
> Nor spake, nor moved their eyes;
> It had been strange, even in a dream,
> To have seen those dead men rise.

This poetry of implication, of half-heard sound and meaning, of active predicative structure, is as far as we can get from the sublime poem, and was its immediate successor as the metaphysical had been its immediate predecessor, with a brief era of classical balance to temper each change. Wordsworthian classicism worked between his most soaring predecessors, sublime masters such as Blake, and the new extremes of suggested depth in Landor, Byron, Coleridge. The one great follower of the sublime tradition in the romantic era was Keats. No real ballad man, he chose rather the old eighteenth-century inheritance of Spenser and the richest classical poets, the vocabulary of sense and passion, the phrasal and harmonic abundance unchecked by balanced structure. What he did draw from his own contemporaries was the sense of suggested depth as well as height, the nameless as well as the namable in the anatomy of sensation, so that he was able to blend the effectiveness of two whole traditions in his intensification of them. His is one more, and an intenser one, of the sublime odes to Melancholy.

No, no, go not to Lethe, neither twist
  Wolf's-bane, tight-rooted, for its poisonous wine;
Nor suffer thy pale forehead to be kiss'd
  By nightshade, ruby grape of Proserpine;
Make not your rosary of yew-berries,
  Nor let the beetle, nor the death-moth be
    Your mournful Psyche, nor the downy owl
A partner to your sorrow's mysteries;
  For shade to shade will come too drowsily,
    And drown the wakeful anguish of the soul.

2.

But when the melancholy fit shall fall
  Sudden from heaven like a weeping cloud,
That fosters the droop-headed flowers all,
  And hides the green hill in an April shroud;
Then glut thy sorrow on a morning rose,
  Or on the rainbow of the salt sand-wave,
    Or on the wealth of globed peonies;
Or if thy mistress some rich anger shows,
  Emprison her soft hand, and let her rave,
    And feed deep, deep upon her peerless eyes.

3.

She dwells with Beauty—Beauty that must die;
  And Joy, whose hand is ever at his lips
Bidding adieu; and aching Pleasure nigh,
  Turning to poison while the bee-mouth sips:
Ay, in the very temple of Delight
  Veil'd Melancholy has her sovran shrine,
    Though seen of none save him whose strenuous tongue
Can burst Joy's grape against his palate fine;
  His soul shall taste the sadness of her might,
    And be among her cloudy trophies hung.

Here in the combination of extremely sensuous particularity with emotional forms and personifications, the varied and interior odal structure, the full vowel harmony, the language of anatomy and ceremony, we read an essence of the poetry which Hobbes early blessed, which Milton and Thomson and Collins forwarded, which was the eighteenth century's own; in the sublime poetic scene of the universe, the enduring passionate figures, larger than life.

w. k. wimsatt, jr.

ONE RELATION OF RHYME TO REASON

Vous ferez rimer ensemble, autant qu'il se pourra, des mots très-semblables entre eux comme SON, et très-differents entre eux comme SENS.—Théodore de Banville, Petit Traité de Poésie Française

The view of rhyme which I wish to discuss in this essay has been formerly advanced[1] but has never, I believe, been widely entertained. It seems never to have been expounded in English and has never become a part of English literary theory in the sense of being illustrated from English poetry. English prosodists have discussed rhyme as a degree of likeness in word sounds and have catalogued its approximations: alliteration, assonance, slant rhyme, eye rhyme, analyzed rhyme, dissonance, and so forth. But about the meaning of rhyme words they have had little to say. In this essay I wish to develop the idea that verse in general, and more particularly rhyme, make their special contribution to poetic structure in virtue of a studiously and accurately semantic character. They impose upon the logical pattern of expressed argument a kind of fixative counterpattern of alogical implication.

II

It would be only an exaggeration, not a distortion, of principle to say that the difference between prose and verse is the difference between homoeoteleuton and rhyme. "Non modo ad salutem ejus exstinguendam sed etiam gloriam per tales viros infringendam," says Cicero, and Quin-

Reprinted from *The Verbal Icon* (Louisville, University of Kentucky Press) pages 153–166, by permission of the author and publisher. Copyright 1954 by The University of Kentucky Press.

[1] The most formal statement seems to be that of Goethe's friend J. S. Schütze, *Versuch einer Theorie des Reimes nach Inhalt und Form* (Magdeburg, 1802). I have been unable to consult this work and owe my knowledge of it to a summary in Dr. Henry Lanz's *Physical Basis of Rime* (Stanford University, 1931), 162–66.

tilian quotes[2] it as an example of homoeoteleuton or like endings. Here the *-endam* and the *-endam* are alike, logically and legitimately alike; each has the same meaning, or is the same morpheme, and each supports the logic of the sentence by appearing in a certain place in the structure. Stylistic parallels or forms of meaning of this sort seem to come fairly to the aid of logic; they are part of the normal framework of prose. The difference between these and rhyme in prose may be illustrated by the following examples from St. Augustine: "Lingua clamat, cor amat"; "Praecedat spes, ut sequatur res." Here not only the endings but also the roots rhyme, and the result is an effect of alogicality, if not of excess and artificiality. It is not really to be expected that the roots should rhyme. The same may be said for all parallels of sound which do not inhere in some parallel meaning of the words themselves, but acquire their parallel merely through being placed in parallel structures. Such, for example, is the transverse alliteration of Lyly,[3] where the series of parallel consonants has logically nothing to do with the antithetic parallel of the words. Of somewhat the same character is the cursus or metrical ending. And if a prose writer were to reinforce a pair of parallel or antithetic clauses by making each one an iambic pentameter, we should say that this was decidedly too much, that the metrical equality was hardly interesting unless it combined with a vein of logic that ran differently.

It is possible to point out examples, in balladry and in other primitive types of poetry, where the equalities of verse coincide with the parallels of meaning. Even in sophisticated poetry such as Tennyson's *In Memoriam* one may find some stanzas where a high degree of parallel is successful.[4] But on the whole the tendency of verse, or certainly that of English verse, has been the opposite. The smallest equalities, the feet, so many syllables, or so many time units, are superimposed upon the linear succession of ideas most often without any regard for the equalities of logic. Two successive iambs may be two words, or one word, or parts of two words, and so on. The larger units, the lines, also are measured without reference to logically parallel sections of sense. Even in heavily end-stopped verse, such as that in Shakespeare's early plays, the complete phrase of which each line is formed stands in oblique

[2] *Pro Milone,* II, 5; *Institutio Oratoria,* IX, iii, 73 ff. Cp. Aristotle, *Rhetoric,* III, 9.

[3] "Althoughe hetherto Euphues I have shrined thee in my heart for a trustie friende, I will shunne thee heerafter as a trothless foe." *Euphues* (*Works,* R. Warwick Bond, ed., Oxford, 1902, I, 233); cp. I, 123.

[4] The parallels of Hebrew poetry are, of course, the outstanding exceptions to the generality which I propose, but in this connection I believe it ought to be observed that the lines and half lines of Hebrew poetry are not equal with the metrical exactitude of classical and modern European verse. The number of accents is the same, the number of syllables indeterminate, and the parallel of sense plays an important role in strengthening the equality and pattern of the verse.

relation to the lines before and after. The lines do not parallel one another but spring ahead, one from another, diversely.

The more primitive and forthrightly emotional the poetry, as in balladry, the less it may demand the sensory resistance of verse non-parallel to logic. The more sophisticated and intellectualized the poetry, the more it will demand such resistance. The point is worth illustrating from the blank verse of *Paradise Lost*—one of the most artful verse forms in the range of English literature. An important phrase in Milton's own prescription for blank verse is "sense variously drawn out from one verse into another." This various drawing out he accomplishes for the most part by his ever various, subtly continuous, confused, and tenuous syntax, by which the sense drips down from line to line and does not usually run parallel in any successive lines. But if it does run parallel, there will be certain careful and curious dislocations that prevent the lines from seeming to be the unit of logical measure.

> Abhorred *Styx*, the flood of deadly hate;
> Sad *Acheron* of sorrow, black and deep;
> *Cocytus*, named of lamentation loud
> Heard on the rueful stream; fierce *Phlegethon*,
> Whose waves of torrent fire inflame with rage.

It is I who have italicized the names of the four infernal rivers. These are the four heads of the parallel—moving back toward the front of the line, from Styx to Cocytus, then leaping to the end with Phlegethon. The modifiers of the first two are of about the same length and place in the line; that of the third is longer and runs through two lines; that of the fourth fills just one line. Thus comes the sense of weaving back and forth, of intellect threading complexity, rather than a cool, simplifying triumph of classification.[5] The same handling of parallel can sometimes be seen in single lines.

> *Un*res'pit*ed'*, *un*pit'*ied*, *un*'re*prieved'*
> *Un*shak'en, *un*'seduced', *un*ter'rified'

> *Thou'* art' my fa'ther, *thou'* my au'thor, *thou'*
> My being gavest me.

The italicized syllables escape a prosaic parallel by falling in different metrical positions, now in thesis, now in arsis. The third "thou" is thrust out alone at the end of the line. The verse runs sinuously, intertwining with the sense and making a tension and resilience.

[5] Cp. the morning *laudate* of Adam and Eve—recited in "holy rapture" and "various style." *Paradise Lost,* V, 146–47, 192–99. This passage affords an instructive comparison with the King James version of Psalm cxlvii, 2–4, 8–10, where the Hebrew parallel of sense and rhythm is largely preserved.

III

We come then to rhyme, the subject of our argument. And first it must be admitted that in certain contexts a high degree of parallel in sense may be found even in rhyme. Even identical words may rhyme. In the sestina, for example, the same set of rhyme words is repeated in six different stanzas. But here the order changes, and so does the relation of each rhyme word to the context. That is the point of the sestina. Somewhat the same may be said for a refrain when it does not rhyme with any other line of the context. In the broadest sense, difference of meaning in rhyme words includes difference of syntax. In fact, words have no character as rhymes until they become points in a syntactic succession. Hence rhyme words (even identical ones) can scarcely appear in a context without showing some difference of meaning. The point of this essay is therefore not to prove that rhyme words must exhibit difference of meaning, but to discuss the value of the difference and to show how a greater degree of difference harmonizes with a certain type of verse structure.

Under certain conditions (much more common than the sestina or refrain mentioned above) the opportunity and the demand for difference of meaning in rhyme may be slight.

> Scogan, that knelest at the stremes hed
> Of grace, of alle honour and worthynesse,
> In th'ende of which strem I am dul as ded,
> Forgete in solitarie wildernesse,—
> Yet, Scogan, thenke on Tullius kyndenesse.

The three identical "nesse" rhymes could be mere prosy homoeoteleuton if the three words occurred in positions of nearly parallel logic or syntax. But Chaucer's sense, meandering like the stream through the stanza, makes no great demand upon these rhymes, and weak though they are, they are strong enough. Even in Chaucer's couplets the same continuity of sense through the verse may be discovered, and the same tendency in rhyming, as we shall illustrate in the comparison which follows.

Pope is the English poet whose rhyming shows perhaps the clearest contrast to Chaucer's. Chaucer found, even in Middle English, a "skarsete" of rhyme.[6] There would come a day when an even greater scarcity of easy rhymes would create a challenge to the English poet and at the same time indicate one of his most subtle opportunities. In the course of three hundred years English lost many of its easy rhymes, stressed Germanic and Romance endings, *y, ing, ere, esse,* and *able, age, al, aunce, aile, ain, esse, oun, ous, ure,* so that Pope perforce rhymed

[6] *Complaint of Venus.*

words differing more widely in meaning. The characteristics of Pope's couplet, as opposed to Chaucer's are, of course, its closure or completeness, its stronger tendency to parallel, and its epigrammatic, witty, intellectual point. One can hardly imagine such a couplet rhyming "wildernesse" and "kyndenesse," or "worthynesse" and "hethenesse," as Chaucer does in one couplet of the knight's portrait.

Most likely it is neither feasible nor even desirable to construct a scale of meaning differences to measure the cleverness of rhyme. The analysis which I intend is not in the main statistical. But an obvious, if rude, basis for classification is provided by the parts of speech. It may be said, broadly, that difference in meaning of rhyme words can be recognized in difference of parts of speech and in difference of functions of the same part of speech, and that both of these differences will be qualified by the degree of parallel or of obliquity appearing between the two whole lines of a rhyming pair. The tenor of the comparison which follows will be to suggest that Pope's rhymes are characterized by difference in parts of speech or in function of the same parts of speech, the difference in each case being accentuated by the tendency of his couplets to parallel structure.

A large number of rhymes in both Pope and Chaucer, or indeed in any English poet, are rather neutral to our inquiry.

> Whan that Aprille with his shoures soote
> The droghte of March hath perced to the roote.

Here the rhyme makes its contribution to difference of sense against equality of verse, but because the oblique phrases themselves make a fundamental contrast to the metrically equal lines, and the rhyming parts of speech are a function of the phrases, the rhyme is not likely to be felt as a special element of variation. There is a higher proportion of such rhymes in Chaucer than in Pope.[7] In general Chaucer relies for variation more on continuous sense and syntax than on rhyme, and when his rhyme words are the same part of speech, he is apt to give us a dullish rhyme:

> Me thynketh it acordaunt to resoun
> To telle you al the condicioun.

In similar constructions Pope is apt to find some quaint minor contrast in length and quality of words:

[7] I base my statements in this part of the essay on a general impression which has been borne out in a line-by-line analysis of four passages from each author: Chaucer (*Works*, F. N. Robinson, ed., Boston, 1933), *Legend of Good Women*, Prologue F, lines 1–148; *Canterbury Prologue*, lines 1–148; *Knight's Tale*, first 148 lines, 1355–1502; *Nun's Priest's Tale*, first 148 lines, 2821–2968; Pope (*Complete Poetical Works*, H. W. Boynton, ed., Boston, 1903), *Essay on Criticism*, I, lines 1–148; *Rape of the Lock*, I, lines 1–148; *Epistle to Dr. Arbuthnot*, lines 1–148; *Dunciad*, Book IV, lines 1–148.

> What guards the purity of melting maids,
> In courtly balls, and midnight masquerades?

It is in couplets of parallel structure, however, that the rhyming of Pope is seen to best advantage. More of these couplets in Pope have rhymes of different parts of speech than in Chaucer, and their effect is more pronounced in Pope because the parallel within the closed couplet of Pope is likely to be smarter. Chaucer will write:

> And everemoore he hadde a sovereyn prys;
> And though that he were worthy, he was wys.

Pope will write:

> Oft, when the world imagine women stray,
> The Sylphs thro' mystic mazes guide their way.

> When Florio speaks, what virgin could withstand,
> If gentle Damon did not squeeze her hand.

In these two examples, though the syntax is oblique, the sense is parallel and antithetic. Pope's couplets, no matter what their syntax, tend to hover on the verge of antithesis and hence to throw a stress upon whatever difference of meaning appears in the rhyme words.

One might expect to find that a parallel both of general sense and of rhyming parts of speech would produce a quality of flatness, a sort of minimum rhyme such as we found in St. Augustine—"Lingua clamat, cor amat"—only the first step beyond homoeoteleuton. One thing that may prevent this and may lend the rhyme a value of variation is that through some irregularity or incompleteness of parallel the rhyming words have oblique functions. Thus Chaucer:

> No deyntee morsel passed thurgh hir throte;
> Hir diete was accordant to hir cote.

And Pope:

> From each she nicely culls with curious toil,
> And decks the Goddess with the glitt'ring spoil.

There are more of these couplets in Pope than in Chaucer, and with Pope the rhyme difference is more likely to seem the result of some deft twist or trick.

> Some are bewilder'd in the maze of schools,
> And some made coxcombs Nature meant but fools.

There is a kind of inversion (from pupils to schools and back to the pupils in a new light) which in some couplets appears more completely as chiasmus, an effect concerning which I shall have more to say.

The two types of rhyme difference which characterize Pope's poetry (that of different parts of speech and that of the same part of speech in different functions) are a complement, as I have suggested, of his tendency to a parallel of lines. To recognize this may affect our opinion about how deliberately or consciously Pope strove for difference of rhyme, but it should not diminish the impression which the actual difference of rhyme makes upon us. Such rhyme difference may be felt more clearly as a characteristic of Pope if we examine the rhymes in a passage where the parallel is somewhat like that which Chaucer at times employs. It is difficult to find passages of sustained parallel in Chaucer. The usual narrative movement of his couplets is the oblique forward movement of actions in a sequence. But in the character sketches of the *Canterbury Prologue* a kind of loose parallel often prevails for ten or twenty lines, as one feature of a pilgrim after another is enumerated. The sense is continuous, in that the couplets tend to be incomplete, but the lines are all members of a parallel bundle. A clear example may be seen in the yeoman's portrait.

> And he was clad in cote and hood of grene.
> A sheef of pecock arwes, bright and kene,
> Under his belt he bar ful thriftily,
> (Wel coude he dresse his takel yemanly:
> . . . .
> Upon his arm he baar a gay bracer,
> And by his syde a swerd and a bokeler,
> And on that oother syde a gay daggere
> Harneised wel and sharp as point of spere;
> A Christopher on his brest of silver sheene,
> A horn he bar, the bawdryk was of grene.

"Thriftily" and "yemanly," "bracer" and "bokeler," "sheene" and "grene," rhymes like these (aside even from the use of final syllables, "ly" and "er") I should call tame rhymes because the same parts of speech are used in closely parallel functions. To see the difference in this respect between Chaucer and Pope we may turn to the classic lines of another portrait:

> Bless'd with each talent and each art to please,
> And born to write, converse, and live with ease;
> Should such a man, too fond to rule alone,
> Bear, like the Turk, no brother near the throne;
> View him with scornful, yet with jealous eyes,
> And hate for arts that caus'd himself to rise;
> Damn with faint praise, assent with civil leer,
> And without sneering teach the rest to sneer;
> Willing to wound, and yet afraid to strike,

Just hint a fault, and hesitate dislike;
Alike reserv'd to blame or to commend,
A tim'rous foe, and a suspicious friend.

The parallel of lines is continuous, but the rhymes are always different parts of speech. The portrait continues:

Dreading ev'n fools; by flatterers besieged,
And so obliging that he ne'er obliged;
Like *Cato,* give his little Senate laws,
And sit attentive to his own applause.

Here the same parts of speech are rhymed, but one verb is passive, one active; one noun is plural, one singular. The functions are different, in each case what he does being set against what he receives.

It is to be noted that in the yeoman's portrait such rhymes as "grene" and "kene," "thriftily" and "yemanly" are of the sort which we described above as minimum rhyme, only one step away from homoeoteleuton. Rhymes of this type often escape the extreme, as we saw, by some irregularity of parallel. But it is significant to add now that even when Pope does not escape the extreme he has resources of piquancy. Here and there he will be guilty of a certain flatness:

Each motion guides, and every nerve sustains,
Itself unseen, but in th' effects remains.

Often, however, he conveys some nice contrast in the parallel.

True wit is Nature to advantage dress'd,
What oft was thought, but ne'er so well express'd.

Here the two rhyme verbs are not merely parallel examples. One is literal, one is figurative, and in being matched with each other they express in brief the metaphor on which this classic critical doctrine is based, that to express is to dress.

Th' adventurous Baron the bright locks admired;
He saw, he wish'd, and to the prize aspired.

Here the difference between "admired" and "aspired," the swift ascent of the Baron's aspiration, is precisely the point.

One speaks the glory of the British Queen,
And one describes a charming Indian screen.

Do thou, Crispissa, tend her fav'rite Lock;
Ariel himself shall be the guard of Shock.

From "British Queen" to "Indian screen," from "Lock" to "Shock," here is the same bathos he more often puts into one line—"When husbands, or when lapdogs breathe their last."

IV

What I conceive to be the acme of variation occurs in a construction to which I have already alluded, chiasmus. The basis of chiasmus will be a high degree of parallel, often antithetic. The rhyme may be of the same part of speech or of different parts. If it is of the same part, the chiastic variation will be a special case of the "schools"–"fools" rhyme already quoted, where a twist in the meaning gives different functions to the rhyme words. If the rhyme is of different parts, the variation will be a special case of that already discussed, where different parts of speech rhyme in parallel lines.

> Whether the nymphs shall break[1] Diana's law,[2]
> Or some frail China jar[2′] receive a flaw.[1′]

In the first line the breakage, then the fragile thing (the law); in the second line another fragile thing (the jar) and then its breaking (the flaw). The parallel is given a kind of roundness and completeness; the intellectual lines are softened into the concrete harmony of "law" and "flaw." The meaning is locked in a pattern of inevitability.

> What dire offence from amr'ous causes[1] springs,[2]
> What mighty contests rise[2′] from trivial things.[1′]

> Love, Hope, and Joy, fair Pleasure's[1] smiling train,[2]
> Hate, Fear, and Grief, the family[2′] of pain.[1′]

> Fear[1] to the statesman,[2] rashness[1] to the chief,[2]
> To kings[2′] presumption,[1′] and to crowds[2′] belief.[1′]

> Thus critics of less judgment[1] than caprice,[2]
> Curious,[2′] not knowing,[1′] not exact,[1] but nice.[2]

In the last example the antithesis is tripled, and the order being successively chiastic, returns upon itself, which is sufficient complication to make "caprice" and "nice" a surprise. Then one is an adjective and one a noun, and "caprice" has two syllables.[8]

The contemplation of chiastic rhyme, the most brilliant and complex of all the forms of rhyme variation, leads me to make a brief general remark upon the degree of Pope's reputation for rhyme. I have relied heavily upon examples of rhyme from Pope because he takes such clear and frequent advantage of the rhyming quality with which I am concerned. To that extent, and it seems to me an important extent, he is one of the finest English rhymers. Yet a critic of Pope's rhyme has

[8] For three exquisite examples of chiasmus from three other poets, see the rhymes of "dust" and "lust" in Andrew Marvell's "Coy Mistress," "thrush" and "brush" in Christina Rossetti's "Spring Quiet," and the double chiastic rhyme of "leaping" and "sleeping," "laid" and "fade" in A. E. Housman's "With rue my heart is laden."

spoken of "true" rhymes and "false" rhymes and "rimes to the eye" and has been concerned to discover that of 7874 rhymes in Pope 1027 are "false." Another has approved of Pope's "correctness" in excluding polysyllables from his rhymes, but has found Pope's repeated use of the same rhyme words "monotonous in a high degree and a very serious artistic defect." The same critic has actually spoken of Pope's "poverty of rhyme." One of the purposes of my argument is to cut the ground from under such judgments. They can spring only from a limited view of rhyme as a form of phonetic harmony—to be described and appraised in terms of phonetic accuracy, complexity, and variety—in other words, from a failure to connect rhyme with reason.[9]

V

We have so far considered rhyme as it makes variation against the parallels of verse. If we think now of the meaning of the words as the basis of comparison, thus beginning with variation or difference, we can discuss the sameness of the rhyme sound as a binding force. Rhyme is commonly recognized as a binder in verse structure. But where there is need for binding there must be some difference or separation between the things to be bound. If they are already close together, it is supererogatory to emphasize this by the maneuver of rhyme. So we may say that the greater the difference in meaning between rhyme words the more marked and the more appropriate will be the binding effect. Rhyme theorists have spoken of the "surprise" which is the pleasure of rhyme, and surely this surprise is not merely a matter of coming upon a similarity which one has not *previously* anticipated. It cannot be a matter of time. Even after the discovery, when the rhyme is known by heart, the pleasurable surprise remains. It must depend on some incongruity or unlikelihood inherent in the coupling. It is a curious thing that "queen" should rhyme with "screen"; they are very unlike objects. But Pope has found a connection between them, has classified them as topics of chat, and then the parallel of sound comes to his aid as a humorous binder.

> The hero William, and the martyr Charles,
> One knighted Blackmore, and one pension'd Quarles.

"Charles" did not actually pension "Quarles," but we are well on the way to believing that he did; the rhyme at least is a *fait accompli.*

The most extreme examples of this kind of humor are the extrava-

[9] Professor Tillotson, looking in the right direction, has recorded his impression that Pope prefers "a verb for at least one of the rime-words in a couplet" and that "a verb at the end of the first line is often followed by its object in the next line." *On the Poetry of Pope* (Oxford, 1938), 124.

gant double or triple rhymes of a Butler, a Swift, a Byron, or a Browning. One stanza from Byron will do.

> He was a Turk, the colour of mahogany;
> And Laura saw him, and at first was glad,
> Because the Turks so much admire philogyny,
> Although their usage of their wives is sad;
> 'Tis said they use no better than a dog any
> Poor woman, whom they purchase like a pad:
> They have a number, though they ne'er exhibit 'em,
> Four wives by law, and concubines "ad libitum."

If Byron had rhymed "philogyny" and "misogyny," it would not be very funny, for one expects these two words to sound alike; they are formed alike from the Greek and make the end words of a natural antithesis. They are mere homoeoteleuton. "Mahogany" makes a comic rhyme with "philogyny" because of the wide disparity in meaning between the words. Mahogany, the Spanish name of a reddish hardwood, is not a likely companion for the learned Greek abstraction, but once an ingenious affinity in meaning is established, the rhyme sounds a triple surprise of ratification. Then comes "dog any," and difference of meaning in rhyme has proceeded to the point of disintegration and mad abandon. What convinces us that "dog any" belongs in this stanza is not so much its inevitable or appropriate meaning as the fact that it does rhyme.

VI

"Rime," says Henry Lanz, "is one of those irrational satellites that revolve around reason. It is concerned not with the meaning of verse but only with its form, which is emotional. It lies within the plane of the a-logical cross-section of verse."[10] It is within the scope of my argument to grant the alogical character of rhyme, or rather to insist on it, but at the same time to insist that the alogical character by itself has little, if any, aesthetic value. The music of spoken words in itself is meager, so meager in comparison to the music of song or instrument as to be hardly worth discussion. It has become a platitude of criticism to point out that verses composed of meaningless words afford no pleasure of any kind and can scarcely be called rhythmical—let them even be rhymed. The mere return to the vowel tonic (the chord or tone cluster characteristic of a vowel) is likely to produce the emotion of boredom. The art of words is an intellectual art, and the emotions of poetry are simultaneous with conceptions and largely induced through the medium of conceptions. In literary art only the wedding of the alogical with

[10] *Physical Basis of Rime*, 293.

the logical gives the former an aesthetic value. The words of a rhyme, with their curious harmony of sound and distinction of sense, are an amalgam of the sensory and the logical, or an arrest and precipitation of the logical in sensory form; they are the icon in which the idea is caught. Rhyme and other verse elements save the physical quality of words—intellectualized and made transparent by daily prose usage.[11] But without the intellectual element there is nothing to save and no reason why the physical element of words need be asserted. "Many a man," says Dr. Lanz at the close of his book, "was cruelly put to death for a 'daring rhyme.'" And he regards it as a "triumph of modern science that, instead of marveling at the mystery of this force, we can 'dissect it as a corpse.'" These notions seem set up to provoke the retort that men are cruelly put to death not for melodies but for ideas, and that it is only when reduced to a purely "physical basis" that rhyme becomes a "corpse."

> When Adam dalf and Eve span,
> Who was then a gentilman?[12]

If there is something daring in this rhyme of John Ball's, it is certainly not in the return to the overtone of 1840 vibrations per second characteristic of ă [æ], but in the ironic jostle by which plebian "span" gives a lesson in human values to aristocratic "gentilman."

[11] Cp. G. W. F. Hegel, *The Philosophy of Fine Art,* F. P. B. Osmaston, tr. (London, 1920), IV, 7–10, 84, 90–91, part III, subsection III, chap. III.

[12] Lanz, *Physical Basis of Rime,* 121, 342.

edward hubler

FORM AND MATTER

The notion of Shakespeare as the natural poet, the artist of direct self-expression, is now an old one. It has survived many literary fashions and many revolutions in thinking about nature. To the young Milton, Shakespeare was "fancy's child" and his poetic effects were both "wild" and "native." At about the time that Milton was referring to Shakespeare in this way, John Benson found the sonnets, in his 1640 edition of them, "serene, cleere, and eligantly plaine"; and ever since then there have been critics to praise them for their naturalness and simplicity, although they are, in all truth, difficult enough. If the matter is considered relatively—the sonnets in relation to other contemporary sonnets, and the verses in general in relation to, say, Milton's—there is some justification for the opinion. Some of the sonnets are simple, and sometimes Shakespeare's dramatic writing is simpler than that of any other poet who has achieved comparable effects. No other English dramatist in a similar context has dared to be as simple as he is in the "Good-night, sweet prince" speech toward the close of *Hamlet.* He had learned to write, and, in Miss Stein's phrase, it had become a "natural thing to do. But there are others who learn how, they learn to read and write, but they read and write as if they knew how."[1] It is well said. Although he had a talent for the natural and simple, the power of simple expression was not his from the beginning; it grew with his art and is only one aspect of it, but the one which, how often and how wrongly! is taken for the whole. In the commonly held view simplicity equals sincerity, and, conversely, complexity is artificial. The praiseworthy thing is the simple thing. "An artist," writes Hesketh Pearson in a discussion of the sonnets, "does not fool about with words when expressing his true emotion."[2] Pearson's study of Shakespeare is a deservedly popular book, popular enough to

Reprinted from *The Sense of Shakespeare's Sonnets: Form and Matter* by Edward Hubler by permission of Princeton University Press. Copyright 1952 by Princeton University Press.

1 Gertrude Stein, *Four in America,* Yale University Press, New Haven, 1947, p. 120.

2 Hesketh Pearson, *A Life of Shakespeare,* Penguin Books, 1942, p. 27.

have been distributed to the armed forces during the Second World War.

The view of the sonnets which has dominated learned criticism for the past fifty years is at first glance a different matter. It was given currency by the late Sir Sidney Lee, who, toward the end of the last century, was engaged in demonstrating Shakespeare's indebtedness to his predecessors and contemporaries. Lee, having pointed out with notable clarity and learning the existence of certain sonnet conventions, concluded that the sonnets were conventional and little more, for he tended, like Pearson, to value only the spontaneous. In one of his sonnets Shakespeare had written,

> When I have seen the hungry ocean gain
> Advantage on the kingdom of the shore,

and Lee, noticing that Shakespeare had come across the idea in Golding, supposed that Shakespeare's statement was without meaning.[3] We need not look into the logic of this; still less should we wonder if Shakespeare really had seen the phenomenon. The point is that for Sir Sidney repetition constituted convention, convention was empty, and the sonnets therefore appeared to be insincere. In this view of poetry a poem's value is finally determined by reference to documents other than the poem itself, and this is very much like Pearson's second measure of value. He tells us that we can recognize the sincerity of certain passages in Shakespeare by, first, their simplicity, and, second, "because they tell us what we already knew about him."[4] In both the learned and the popular view there is, then, a limitation on the function of poetry which Shakespeare was not willing to admit. A reading of the sonnets makes it quite clear that Shakespeare believed, or wanted the reader to believe, that they were a true expression of his individuality. "Every word doth almost tell my name," he wrote in one of them, "Showing their birth and where they did proceed." Shakespeare has a good many remarks on his particular purpose in writing the sonnets, and on poetic theory in general, and I think that the student should not reject them without due consideration. I hope that it will not be idle to consider them in relation to Shakespeare's poetic practice.

The most cursory reading of Shakespeare will make it clear that he liked to play with words, sometimes with wretched effect; and it ought to be equally plain that no man without an interest in words and word patterns ever became a poet. Shakespeare's native interest in words was encouraged by the tradition of his time which considered the art of writing to be based on a body of precepts and saw no reason to think

[3] Sir Sidney Lee, *A Life of William Shakespeare*, The Macmillan Company, New York, 1931 (14th ed.), p. 32.

[4] *op. cit.*, p. 30.

of craftsmanship as an affectation. Craftsmanship was then known to be what it is—the means by which the thing is said. Now it happens that it is in the nature of conscious artists to be seduced at times into an overemphasis of their craft, and this matters very little to an age which takes an interest in technique. In such times there is an allowance, and quite without condescension, for the performer's pride in skill. The composers of concertos used to allow the performer to provide his own cadenza, to do, in effect, what he could, and simply in order to show what he could do. There was a tendency in Shakespeare's time, and earlier, to admire the formal dexterity of ingenious word play, and this is nowhere better illustrated than in the sonnet tradition. Petrarch, whose exquisite taste saved him from the greatest excesses, was a master at it. One of his sonnets is an elaboration of an image comparing his lady to the sun. She is the sun; her person, her face, her eyes, her hair are suns. If the sun rises before her, he shines brightly; but when she arises, he is dimmed. Petrarch loved to play upon the similarity of his lady's name (Laura) to *l'aura* (the breeze) and *laurea* (the laurel) and to resolve words similar to her name (*laureta,* for example) into its syllables and expand them in terms of praise. All this can be boring enough in Petrarch; in his imitators it often becomes a dreary elaboration of empty virtuosity.

Shakespeare, too, sometimes let his virtuosity get the better of him, as certain spectacular failures in the sonnets to the young man testify:

> To me, fair friend, you never can be old,
> For as you were when first your eye I ey'd. . . .[5]

The modern reader wonders how Shakespeare brought himself to do it. Such passages occur too often to be oversights, and what we know of Shakespeare's poetic practice does not allow us to think that he disliked them. The banished Romeo grieves that he must go to Mantua while every other person and every thing may stay in Verona with Juliet: "This flies may do, but I from this must fly." Considered simply as form, the line is superb—ten monosyllables arranged almost in their prose order, yet managing to involve two antitheses: the pun and the double use of "this." Shakespeare places "but I" in the middle of the line, leaving on either side phrases of exactly the same duration. The words, as it is customary to remark of the lights in Times Square, would be beautiful if only we did not know what they meant. It should be remembered that such passages are most frequent and most flagrant in the poetry written when Shakespeare was learning his craft and taking pride in what he learned. It should be observed, too, that it is his

[5] Sonnet 104.

admiration of the phrase, and not his concern for the metrical form, the scene, or the genre, which sometimes dominates his judgment.

Shakespeare's weakness, since it was of his age, passed almost unnoticed. There was, of course, some adverse criticism. The players, speaking of the ease with which Shakespeare composed, had said that he scarce blotted a line. "Would he had blotted a thousand," was Ben Jonson's response. This seems to be fair enough, but when Jonson proceeds to specific comment we notice that his criticism is not directed at Shakespeare's weakness. He objects to Shakespeare's making Caesar say that he "never did wrong, but with just cause." Although this is a better and wiser line than the one Shakespeare later substituted for it, Jonson nevertheless finds it ridiculous—not formally, mind you, but as an idea. Jonson's objection seems to assume that there is always a right way and that a just action never involves injustice. It is an extraordinary assumption for a man of Jonson's intellect, but, in a way, it is characteristic of him. It indicates his comparative singleness of vision, which, in turn, does much to account for the greater virulence of his comedy and his inability to conceive a living tragedy. Jonson's thought is often clearer than Shakespeare's, his poetry less textured—and precisely because of the greater simplicity of what he had to express. With him there was not the same danger of loss in pruning a phrase. He was not much interested in tangential and associated meanings. To Shakespeare, intensely aware of the many-sidedness of meaning, the play on words was a ready instrument.

In our time we seem to have agreed that the pun is worthless. It is now good form to greet a pun with groans, and not even the punster is offended. There seems to be an assumption that the pun, resulting from the accidental resemblances of words, can have nothing essential about it and is incapable of expressing value. Yet the pun persists in spite of our conviction of its frivolity. Punsters apologize, but they go on punning; and a man is allowed to pun if he deprecates the enjoyment. In Shakespeare's time the pun was a rhetorical figure, and the rhetoricians considered it solemnly, dividing it into four categories and dignifying each with a long name. In those days word play was not necessarily frivolous, and our loss of the point of view which lent puns dignity is not clear gain. A poet is made as well as born, and in the sixteenth century the making was a conscious process. The fledgling poet learned what could be done with words by studying the figures of speech. The man of our time tends to notice only the figures which do not succeed, which are not figures of thought as well as figures of speech. He cries out against the excesses and fails to notice the others, the near relations. Would he call the use of *bier* and *beard* in the following passage a pun?

When lofty trees I see barren of leaves
Which erst from heat did canopy the herd,
And summer's green all girded up in sheaves,
Born on the bier with white and bristly beard. . . .[6]

If it is a pun, do we wish it otherwise? And why not? And what are we to think of the schematic placing of *unfair* and *fairly* in the fourth line following?

Those hours that with gentle work did frame
The lovely gaze where every eye doth dwell,
Will play the tyrants to the very same,
And that unfair which fairly doth excell. . . .[7]

The line can be paraphrased, "and make unbeautiful that which now excels in beauty," but the paraphrase for all its clarity is prose. Is there any gain in the repetition of the syllable and the emphasis on the related and unrelated parts of the words? The truth is that Shakespeare's interest in words produced some of his best as well as some of his worst effects.

There are two sonnets, numbers one hundred thirty-five and one hundred thirty-six, which are elaborate four-way puns on his name, Will, which, then as now, also meant *volition* and *obstinacy.* In his day it had the additional meaning of lust. The first begins,

Whoever hath her wish, thou hast thy *Will,*
And *Will* to boot, and *Will* in overplus. . . .

Although it would be possible to write a paraphrase giving the multiple meanings of each repetition, no one should be asked to read it. Readers attracted by the ingenuity will find, on piecing out the poems, that they are successful works of a kind no longer admired. They make sense, and their sense is appropriate to the context in which they are found; but they no longer impress. They are bravura pieces in an outmoded manner, and they do not pretend to be anything more. They are, moreover, the only such pieces Shakespeare ever wrote.

Since he was a poet, he inevitably admired formal graces; and since he was very human, he sometimes indulged his admiration; but his admiration never altered his conviction that matter should take precedence over form. He seems to have been primarily attracted to a given form by its potential utility, by its appropriateness to his purpose and talent. It was his way to take a known form and wrest it to his uses, transforming it, sometimes, into an instrument of an effectiveness its inventor could not have foreseen. Then when he had humbled it to his uses,

[6] Sonnet 12.

[7] Sonnet 5.

it was his way to move on to something else. His technical practice throughout his career bears witness to this basic attitude, and his use of the sonnet form he adopted is a case in point. Although in two-thirds of his sonnets he placed the main pause after the twelfth line, it comes after the eighth line in twenty-seven of them, and is irregular in the remaining few. Sonnet number ninety-nine has fifteen lines, sonnet one hundred twenty-six has twelve, and is written in couplets. Number one hundred forty-five is in tetrameter verse, and all the rimes in sonnet twenty are double.

Shakespeare's sonnet form had been invented early in the century by Henry Howard, Earl of Surrey. Its fourteen lines were divided into three quatrains and a concluding couplet. In Shakespeare's characteristic use of it, the quatrains state a subject and the couplet sums it up, most often through the application of the subject to a specific situation. In the first quatrain of the familiar seventy-third sonnet, the poet compares himself to autumn leaves; in the second, to twilight; and in the third, to dying embers. From the gathering together of these images, and the poet's application of them to himself, there emerges the idea of approaching death. Then comes the couplet directed to the friend to whom the poem is addressed and stating the idea to be derived from the situation set forth in the quatrains.

> That time of year thou mayst in me behold
> When yellow leaves, or none, or few do hang
> Upon those boughs which shake against the cold,
> Bare, ruin'd choirs where late the sweet birds sang;
> In me thou see'st the twilight of such day
> As after sunset fadeth in the west,
> Which by and by black night doth take away,
> Death's second self, that seals up all in rest;
> In me thou see'st the glowing of such fire
> That on the ashes of his youth doth lie,
> As the death-bed whereon it must expire,
> Consum'd with that which it was nourish'd by;
>   This thou perceiv'st which makes thy love more strong
>   To love that well which thou must leave ere long.

There is a pause after each quatrain, the greatest coming after the third. It was his customary usage. There are seven rimes: *abab cdcd efef gg*. Shakespeare might have chosen the Italian sonnet with its five rimes, arranged *abba abba* in the octave, and its variety of rime schemes (*cde cde,* for instance) in the sestet. But the fewer rimes of the Italian sonnet make it a more difficult form, and the absence of the couplet makes it less suited to the explicitness Shakespeare favored. The Italian sonnet was magnificently used by Milton (a more fastidious craftsman than

Shakespeare), who returned to it throughout his long career as a poet, leaving on his death only eighteen sonnets in English. Apart from the sonnets in his plays, Shakespeare wrote one hundred and fifty-four, ranging in excellence from the best lyrics in the language to quite poor stuff. Given his talent, it was impossible for him to write a worthless poem, but sometimes in the sonnets it is a near thing. One gathers that he worked at a sonnet for a while, and, if it proved recalcitrant, wrote another, not always throwing the first one away. It is notable that the English poets distinguished for their craftsmanship have almost always preferred the Italian sonnet form.

The sonnet, of whatever form, has an affinity for intensity, and the best sonnets, of whatever time and place, are those devoted to the development of a single mood, the elaboration of a single image, or the expression of a single thought. The long line (five feet in English, six in French) is admirably suited to dignified and serious expression, and the number of lines is appropriate to the sonnet's singleness of purpose. A poem intending to be both unified and intense must be long enough to permit development and short enough to allow the reader a retention of everything his eye takes in, from the first to the last words. For this purpose fourteen lines were found to be right. A few more or less would have done, but half as many would have been too few, and half again the number would have been too many. When the sonnet form was in the process of creation, sonnets were written in varying lengths; but the form crystallized at fourteen lines for the reasons given. Within this form it is necessary to make everything contribute to the proposed effect, for the tightness throws into relief everything which does not contribute, or does so only obliquely. The sonneteer intent on unity must either increase the matter to fit the form or fuse both with all the skill in his power. If he permits himself to stretch the matter, there can be no intensity; and, in any case, verbal expansion was not Shakespeare's way. He had no need to pad his lines; the talent for the right word was in his flesh like blood. Although the need for a rime sometimes forces him into brief verbosity, he has nothing at all like "Ten times in the revolving year plus three," a line of our century which stretches the idea of thirteen times a year to pentameter length. But at times he would not trouble to develop his thematic structure to a coincidence with the sonnet form, or to articulate the parts.

In the sonnets of characteristically Shakespearean structure, the first aspect of the idea carries through the quatrains, leaving as the technical problem of greatest difficulty the articulation of the couplet. The proportion of failures in meeting this problem is smaller in those sonnets in which the main pause comes after the eighth line, or thereabouts, leaving in the remainder of the poem (equivalent to the sestet in the Italian sonnet) enough scope to avoid the oversententious and sometimes casual tone into which the brevity of the couplet sometimes trapped him. One of these sonnets, number thirty-five, is a case in point. It is one of Shakespeare's lesser poems, yet in his treatment of the couplet he achieves a greater coherence than is usual with sonnets of like calibre written in his accustomed form. His success with modestly ambitious poems in which the main pause comes after the eighth line is not without exception, but it is normal enough to be worth notice. His technical practice in the sonnets is of a piece with that of his plays. It is sometimes perfect, often brilliant, too often impatient and content to let well enough alone.

In the sonnets he states his admiration for the craftsmanship of the rival poet, but the importance he accords to it does not permit him to admire the poems, for he always grants priority to substance. There is nothing in his works indicating anything but dislike for the "fools . . . that for a tricksy word defy the matter."[8] He praises plain speaking and sends satiric shafts at the spinners of "taffeta phrases, silken terms precise" that blow one "full of maggot ostentation."[9] The attitude is everywhere expressed—in the young courtier who so outraged Hotspur, and in Osric, whom Hamlet found not worth his scorn. Shakespeare was a professional writer, but he was not a man of letters; his love of literature did not lead him to tolerate the "literary." He never accepted the idea of style as an end in itself. We are sometimes told that his plays disclose a low view of the writing profession, but I think it is rather that his comic genius kept him aware of the eccentricities of his craft. Hotspur's contempt for "mincing poetry" discloses the common attitude of the man of affairs; it also discloses Shakespeare's awareness of the too frequent justification of it. Some poetry *is* mincing, and some writers are fools, as Shakespeare well knew. From time to time he falls into the "literary," but these descents are failures of taste and, usually, of youth. His conviction was always against the subordination of the thought to the word.

In the sonnets addressed to the young man he contrasts his own expressions of devotion with the "strained touches rhetoric can lend"[10] to the works of other poets, assuring the reader that the old strain needs no variation and declining to employ the latest literary mannerisms.[11] He tells the reader that he wants the sonnets to represent him as he is, and that he believes they do.[12] On another occasion he remarks that the sonnet is sent "to witness duty, not to show my wit."[13] The assur-

[8] *The Merchant of Venice,* 3.5.74.
[9] *Love's Labour's Lost,* 5.2.409.
[10] Sonnet 82.
[11] Sonnet 76.
[12] Sonnet 76.

ance must be taken with the realization that there is no necessary contradiction between showing both duty and wit in the same poem, for it is obvious that in poetry a condition of complete artlessness is impossible. The appearance of artlessness is another matter. And surely the normally complex reader can be moved by a poem and admire its art at the same time. There can be no question of content *or* art; there must be both; it is a matter of proportion and purpose. The truth is that quite often the sonnets do not show the craftsmanship they should, that the reader sometimes finds the lack of variation all too apparent and is too often confronted with statement that is only partially realized as poetry. The matter of some of the sonnets would be more available if they had more art.

The poet's problem was to formalize and verbalize his thought. It is, of course, only an egregious obstinacy which would refuse to suppose that sometimes it was not the other way about, that at times the phrase came first, demanding to be used. But it could not have been generally so. With him *invention,* as with the Elizabethans as a whole, had the primary meaning of finding, not the means of expression, but subject matter for composition; and the sonnets which discuss invention assure us that the subject matter (the friend and the poet's relation to him) is *given.* That is never questioned. What troubles Shakespeare is his inability to handle the subject matter. He insists on the inadequacy of "my pupil pen," a phrase which recalls the references to "my unpolished lines" and "my untutored lines" in the dedications to *Venus and Adonis* and *The Rape of Lucrece.* Although the attitude they express is opposed to Shakespeare's promises of immortality, one would have to have a very wooden notion of mankind to suppose them meaningless. With the greater number of persons confidence is not unwavering, especially professional confidence at the beginning of their careers, and the lives of poets for whom documentation is adequate show periodic resurgences of doubt to be a common experience. Such is the case in the sonnets, but we should notice that it is not a simple alternation of confidence and fear. The poet's sense of inadequacy is set forth in relation to particular matters: he is not equal to his theme, or he is not of the calibre of the other poet, or both. In sonnet number seventy-nine he says that the greatness of this theme deserves the "travail of a worthier pen," and in the succeeding poem he calls the rival poet a "better spirit" and refers to "my saucy bark, inferior far to his."

It is customary to say that the praise of the other poet is grudgingly given, and it is clearly far from wholehearted. Yet there are aspects of the other man's writing which won Shakespeare's admiration. What he

[13] Sonnet 26.

disliked about the rival poet was the character of the man. In the eighty-sixth sonnet there is the well-known and enigmatic passage about the "affable familiar ghost" which "nightly gulls" the other poet with intelligence. We cannot know to what rumored events the phrase refers, and we may dispute the meaning of some of the words, but it is clear that Shakespeare suggests something specious about the content of the rival's poems. We gather from many references that Shakespeare considered him an opportunist who praised the young man for reasons other than those of honest friendship. To this pretension, he says, even the graces of the subject can bring only a superficial virtue; they can "but mend the style."[14] The context of the verses about the rival poet is complicated, and their force is far from single, yet the element of deference, varied in expression and stated at times with bitterness, is present, called forth by the other poet's style—"the proud full sail of his great verse."[15] What Shakespeare praises in the other poet is technical proficiency. What he deplores in his own work is the lack of it.

Since the identity of the other poet is unknown, we cannot weigh the truth of Shakespeare's estimate of him, but it is obvious that his opinions of his own work are on the whole just. In the sonnets the lowest level of excellence is low indeed, but the subject matter of the worst verses is usually that for which in other poems he has been able to find adequate expression. Clearly the normal difficulty is not one of substance; it is the failure to mold the subject matter into a coherent poem. Sometimes he begins a sonnet in an excellent vein and ends it wretchedly. Number one hundred eleven is a case in point. Up to the couplet a poem of considerable stature, it is boundlessly interesting as a statement of a recurrent attitude toward his life in the theatre. With the couplet there is a change in tone and a shocking decrease in magnitude. The idea in the couplet is of course pertinent to what goes before, if only because an assurance of friendship is always proper to a series of poems addressed to a friend; but in this case the assurance comes with such a diminution of force that one wonders why it was allowed to stand.

O, for my sake do you with Fortune chide,
The guilty goddess of my harmful deeds,
That did not better for my life provide
Than public means which public manners breeds.
Thence comes it that my name receives a brand,
And almost thence my nature is subdu'd
To what it works in, like the dyer's hand.
Pity me, then, and wish I were renew'd;
Whilst, like a willing patient, I will drink

[14] Sonnet 78.
[15] Sonnet 86.

> Potions of eisel 'gainst my strong infection;
> No bitterness that I will bitter think,
> Nor double penance, to correct correction.
>   Pity me then, dear friend, and I assure ye
>   Even that your pity is enough to cure me.

The artistic failure of the couplet is so accentuated by the double rime that one wonders if at the time of composition the ingenuity of the rime seemed to justify the couplet.

Perhaps we can learn more of Shakespeare's poetic practice if we turn to a structural pattern with which he always succeeded. No sonnet beginning with "When" is an undistinguished poem. Naturally there is nothing magical in the word. It is simply that "when" introduces a subordinate clause which must, perhaps after more subordinate matter, lead to a main clause, thus creating an arrangement of logically ordered elements in an emphatic sequence. When the arrangement can be readily made to coincide with the sonnet length, the structure avoids Shakespeare's most characteristic faults as a sonneteer—the tacked-on couplet and the broken back. He is almost certain to succeed when the parts of the sonnet stand in a "When I, Then I, Then I, So" relationship, or in some variant of it. It was an excellent pattern for a poet impatient with technical problems. But if the pattern did not reach to the end of the sonnet, or if there was no "so" or "for" notion to follow the logical sequence, the couplet, as in the fifteenth sonnet, stood in danger of seeming to be tacked on. Too often the development of the idea ends with the quatrains, and the couplet fails to share the power in which the quatrains were conceived. In such instances the couplet is poetically, but not intellectually, false. It seems, to use Shakespeare's words, to have been begotten in "the ventricle of memory . . . and delivered upon the mellowing of occasion."

> Not marble nor the gilded monuments
> Of princes shall outlive this powerful rime,
> But you shall shine more bright in these contents
> Than unswept stone besmear'd with sluttish time.
> When wasteful war shall statues overturn,
> And broils root out the work of masonry,
> Nor Mars his sword nor war's quick fire shall burn
> The living record of your memory.
> 'Gainst death and all-oblivious enmity
> Shall you pace forth; your praise shall still find room,
> Even in the eyes of all posterity
> That wear this world out to the ending doom.
>   So, till the judgement that yourself arise,
>   You live in this, and dwell in lovers' eyes.[16]

[16] Sonnet 55.

A deservedly famous poem, it ends in a couplet of diminished force, but not because of what the couplet *says*. The promise of immortality so pallidly stated in the couplet is expressed with vigorous conviction in the preceding lines, with which, spiritually, the poem ends. The quatrains had used up the poet's emotion, leaving no power for a repetition of only formal necessity. The couplet serves chiefly to fill out the form and betray critics who, noticing the relaxed feeling, assume hastily that the theme is alien to Shakespeare's sensibility; but this cannot possibly have been the case, for the idea had been congenial enough only a few lines earlier. In general the couplet is used most expertly when its idea follows in logical sequence from the thematic structure of what has gone before, or when its function is a clear and positive summing up or application of the preceding matter, as in the seventy-third and the one hundred and sixteenth sonnets.

Tucker Brooke observed[17] that the couplet sometimes "introduces a surprise or negation which suddenly swings the reader into a point of view antithetical to that developed in the quatrains." It may be of some significance that of the thirteen sonnets[18] using the couplet in this way only one, number thirty, is among the best known, and it, perhaps, hardly deserves the distinction that has been accorded it. Presumably it has won its place in the public's esteem through the beauty of its opening lines:

> When to the sessions of sweet silent thought
> I summon up remembrance of things past . . . ,

for much of what follows is overweighted with decoration. The alliteration of "And with old woes new wail my dear times waste" is not as drearily flamboyant as Poe's "weary way-worn wanderer," but it is a close call. In this sonnet the casualness of the couplet is saved from emphasis by the relaxed lines which lead up to it. But generally Shakespeare's failures with the couplet are owing to the danger inherent in the sonnet form which he chose and to his impatience with formal problems.

There are other failures arising from sources quite beyond the poet's control, just as there are graces which providence seems to have conferred uniquely on him. Both of them can be readily noticed in the sonnets written on the subject of absence.[19] None of these sonnets is among Shakespeare's most distinguished poems. Too often they seem to have been written only to witness duty, and at their worst they are his nearest approach to frigidity. The least interesting are those most wholly

[17] Tucker Brooke, *Shakespeare's Sonnets*, Oxford University Press, London-New York, 1936, p. 4.

[18] Sonnets 19, 30, 34, 42, 60, 84, 86, 91, 92, 131, 133, 139, 141.

[19] The sonnets clearly written in absence are: 27, 28, 36, 37, 38, 39, 43, 44, 45, 46, 47, 48, 49, 50, 51, 56, 57, 58, 59, 97, 98, 113, 114.

devoted to absence, and the cause of their lack of distinction is apparent. It was the habit of his time to think of friendship's community of interest in terms of identity (one soul in two bodies), a metaphorical extravagance for which he has been censured, but which is absurd or meaningless only to those of a literal turn of mind, or to those who would reserve it for the poetry of romantic love. In Shakespeare's time it was an accepted manner of speaking about a psychological fact, as Euripides wrote about Aphrodite without, presumably, believing in her physical reality. For Shakespeare it was, as an ideological structure must always be for a poet, a formalized extension of his own perception.

In his selection of already formalized ideas, the poet always takes a chance. He cannot pick them with an eye to posterity, for he has no means of knowing which ideas will endure and which will not. He must write for himself and the readers of his own generation, and for the rest he can only hope. He must, as Day Lewis remarks,[20] "hope for the pure luck that Donne had with the compass legs—that men still use compasses, though they have discarded epicycles and planispheres." For us the identity metaphor in the context of friendship has gone the way of the planisphere. And that is not the worst of it, for it was Shakespeare's habit to think of friendship in terms of both identity and the outmoded theory of the four elements (fire, air, earth, and water) of which all things were thought to be made. The belief was that physical things were made of the heavier elements, earth and water, and things of the mind and spirit of the other two. In Shakespeare's time references to the belief were, of course, immediately understood and spontaneously credited. In a pair of sonnets, numbers forty-four and forty-five, the poet wishes that he were entirely made of the lighter elements so that he could leap the distance to his friend, as his thoughts and wishes, being incorporeal and therefore free of earth and water, were able to do. One imagines that the poems were never vital, but their pretty ingenuity must have been more telling, and their thought more forceful, when the identity metaphor was taken seriously and the content of the idea of the elements was readily available.

Only a small portion of that content is now conveyed to the average reader. The association of tears and water is plain enough to be a perpetual commonplace, and it was hardly fresh when Shakespeare used it—but it was not empty. Water being then associated with earth and opposed to fire and air, the water-tears conjunction in poetry could carry the suggestion of heaviness and earth in separation from warmth and light. This gave meaning to such passages as that in which Laertes declines to shed tears for his drowned sister: "Too much of water hast

[20] Cecil Day Lewis, *The Poetic Image*, Oxford University Press, New York, 1947, p. 92.

thou, poor Ophelia." At the time of its composition the line was not simply the word play it has now become; it then suggested that her body had returned, cold and lifeless, to the heavier elements. But time has taken the content of the line away, and for most of us it is an irritatingly commonplace assertion, suggesting little but crassness in the speaker and forcing the actor to hope that in the richness of the scene the line will pass unnoticed.

Sometimes conceits no longer admired in themselves are effectively employed, for the decay of an idea need not be fatal to its use in a poem, provided the force of the idea *as employed* is not single. The dramatic function of the weird sisters at the opening of *Macbeth* is immediately apparent, quite apart from the spectators' belief or disbelief in witches, because the reality of the thing for which they are the emblem is undeniable to all intelligent playgoers. In a like manner the old conceit of the conflict between the eye and the heart, or the mind and the eye, is used powerfully in the dark lady sonnets because it is there invested with the force of a moral struggle; but in the sonnets written in absence to the young man, the conceit is used ingeniously for its own sake, and time has left little but the ingenuity. Other uses of the conceit, as in sonnet one hundred fourteen, succeed because they are endowed with a collateral intellectuality:

> Or whether doth my mind, being crown'd with you,
> Drink up this monarch's plague, this flattery?
> Or whether, shall I say, mine eye saith true. . . .

Other sonnets written in absence are interesting for what they glance at, for what they give us of the poet's mind.[21] Still others[22] derive their power from the poet's fears for the dissolution of the friendship under the blows of circumstance. These can more appropriately be considered later. The thing to notice here is the relation between the power of the poems and their subject matter. Absence was not in itself a subject which the poet could work into enduring poetry. He writes best in absence when he celebrates the friendship itself, or fears for it, or writes of absence in images which for him were always figures of thought and feeling as well as figures of speech.

He saw nature precisely and was always able to find the right words for her loveliness—"proud-pied April," for example. It is to the exercise of this talent that the absence sonnets of widest fame owe their renown. Two of them ("How like a winter" and "From you I have been absent," numbers ninety-seven and ninety-eight) are remembered for passages of unobtrusive melody and lines of easy grace:

[21] See Sonnets 35, 37, 38, 58, 59.

[22] See Sonnets 36, 49, 57.

> Nor did I wonder at the lily's white,
> Nor praise the deep vermilion in the rose. . . .

It is clearly not the summit of Shakespeare's art, but it is one of his peculiar achievements, this seemingly effortless poetry of nature: "The teeming autumn big with rich increase" and such phrases as "What old December's bareness everywhere." No other English poet has phrases of that quality, and, as far as I know, none of Shakespeare's translators has been able to approximate it in other languages. Shakespeare always wrote well on nature's morning loveliness and her plenitude. Subjects for which he had an affinity, they gave these poems an excellence beyond anything that the contemplation of absence inspired in him. It is one of the most striking *données* of his poetic talent. To it even more impressive powers were shortly to be added.

With writers of stature, the development of style stands in a reciprocal relation to intellectual and spiritual growth. A writer's style can persist unchanged to the end of his career only if he remains minor. In the first years of the 1590's the young Shakespeare, mainly under the influence of Marlowe, formed a style admirably suited to his early powers. The rhythmic unit was the blank verse line, and generally the memorable phrases were those of a Marlovian rotundity, or descriptive passages of his own peculiar loveliness. One could not say of it, as Eliot said of the style of *In Memoriam,* that it was intimate with the poet's depths, for there is nothing in the first works that can properly be called depths. But he soon became conscious of the depths, and a new style had to be evolved to disclose them. By the time he was writing *Richard II,* the first style was already inadequate to the new perception, and was felt to be. He was able to characterize Richard by making him the connoisseur of surfaces and the artist in words, and by bringing him to a realization of the speciousness of appearance—in short, by endowing him with a share of his own sensibility.

Richard's most moving speeches have a greater flexibility than the best verse of the preceding plays, but their metrics are not markedly different. While Richard is less inclined to think in blank verse lengths than his predecessors, the line is still the rhythmic unit, and the run on rhythms tend to end at the caesura:

> For within the hollow crown
> That rounds the mortal temples of a king
> Keeps Death his court, and there the antic sits,
> Scoffing his state, and grinning at his pomp,
> Allowing him a breath, a little scene,
> To monarchize, be fear'd, and kill with looks,
> Infusing him with self and vain conceit,

As if this flesh which walls about our life,
Were brass impregnable; and humour'd thus
Comes at the last, and with a little pin
Bores through his castle wall, and—farewell king![23]

Or, through its propriety to the character of the hero, the poet makes effective dramatic use of his ornate style, as in the descent from the ramparts of Flint Castle, where the magnificent showmanship is both Shakespeare's and Richard's:

Down, down I come; like glist'ring Phaeton,
Wanting the manage of unruly jades.
In the base court? Base court, where kings grow base,
To come at traitors' calls and do them grace.[24]

But at other times the formalism obscures, almost obliterates, the meaning:

Ay, no; no, ay; for I must nothing be;
Therefore no no, for I resign to thee.[25]

Throughout the play there is little of what we are later to have in abundance, and toward the end of the play when the theatricality is over and the inwardness of Richard is the dramatist's first concern, the disparity between the ornate style and the deeply felt content, between the achieved style and the newly realized depths, is the concern of Shakespeare's deposed and imprisoned artist-hero. We discover him in Pomfret Castle brooding on the difficulty of putting his misery into words:

I have been studying how I may compare
This prison where I live unto the world,
And for because the world is populous,
And here is not a creature but myself,
I cannot do it; yet I'll hammer it out. . . .[26]

With Shakespeare himself it was never hammered out in these terms. His most deeply revealing passages are never in a style which is at once in contrast to and congruent with the depths disclosed. That is the glory of Racine, who in that respect is unchallenged. Shakespeare found a more direct solution.

There is little to suggest the solution in his first works, where in general he searched for depths with Marlovian means, or with his own adaptation of the styles of Marlowe and Spenser. But when the profundity came, when, as in the later tragedies, it was at its greatest, it was

[23] *Richard II,* 3.2.160–170.
[24] *Ibid.,* 3.3.178–181.
[25] *Ibid.,* 4.1.201–202.
[26] *Ibid.,* 5.5.1–5.

sometimes expressed in a style having at once homeliness and splendor, as in Macbeth's "I have supp'd full with horrors. . . ." In his early works he tended to reserve homeliness for prose, a practice he quickly outgrew; indeed, he departed so completely from it that by the time he wrote *King Lear* the rhythmic distinction between prose and verse had disappeared, and the movement from prose to verse is, in the greatest passages, not always to be distinguished by the ear; and when it can be, it is a difference without a distinction in kind. In *King Lear* the unpatterned rhythm of the prose is the pulsing of its spirit, and the verse, if one has got it by heart, cannot be written down again in Shakespeare's lines without consulting the text. The reader is invited to try.

The seeds of this were in Shakespeare from the beginning, and as he learned to write the shoots began to appear. Their growth, in the way of such developments, was not constant. Sometimes purposely, sometimes without apparent awareness, he doubled back upon himself; but there was no stopping the fitful progression. In *Romeo and Juliet* there is early formalism and ornateness, there is fustian, there is sheer aria, and there are promises of things to come; Romeo, dreaming of his love, is greeted by his servant with the news of her death:

> Her body sleeps in Capel's monument,
> And her immortal part with angels lives.

Romeo replies in a speech of startling contrast to the lyric regularity of the servant's lines:

> Well Juliet, I will lie with thee to-night.

The accents have varied values, the rhythm is irregular, the line is just a little in excess of pentameter length. Homely words in their prose order making poetry as revealing of character as any dozen lines in the play! Yet they are not altogether simple, and in as far as they are simple, it is the simplicity of the master of language. The increasing frequency with which such passages appear is the most striking index of Shakespeare's ability to make his art the servant of his insights. It is, in Granville-Barker's phrase, "the power to show us reality behind appearance, or as Shelley said, to lift the veil from the hidden beauty—and, he could have added, the unrecognized horror—of the world." The power is more often demonstrated in the sonnets than in the plays contemporary with them, because, one supposes, of the greater difficulty of expressing perceptions in dramatic form. In any case his most considerable power flowered first in the poems.

What the reader remembers most vividly from the early *Venus and Adonis* are vignettes of nature—bits of natural description, and, above all, Poor Wat, the hare. What stays ineradicably in his mind from the early sonnets is the joy in plenitude, the sadness of mutability, beauty of phrase and beauty of nature, and the virtuosity of such rhythms as,

> Sap check'd with frost, and lusty leaves quite gone,
> Beauty o'er-snow'd, and bareness everywhere.

And while the reader will continue to find these things to the end of the sonnets, it is not long until he also finds: "then hate me when thou wilt," "give not a windy night a rainy morrow," "my love is as a fever," and,

> For I have sworn thee fair and thought thee bright,
> Who art as black as hell, as dark as night.

Examples swarm to be quoted, and in an instant pass from the depiction of homeliness to the unveiling of horror. In this unveiling Shakespeare sometimes displayed the old extravagance of his earlier ornateness. In an almost Strindbergian poem[27] on the power of lust, he writes,

> . . . lust
> Is perjur'd, murderous, bloody, full of blame,
> Savage, extreme, rude, cruel, not to trust. . . .

It is hortatory rather than persuasive, and there is some sacrifice of power to the exigencies of art. The anticlimactic position of "not to trust" is owing entirely to the need for a rime. But he does not make the sacrifice as often as in the earlier sonnets. He had no sooner mastered the homeliness than he employed it concretely and compactly to give immediacy—the constable, for instance, as the emblem of death:

> . . . when that fell arrest
> Without all bail shall carry me away. . . .

To us this vivid immediacy of the commonplace is not always as noticeable as it should be, since the dissonance of one age mellows into the harmony of the next. Time bestows a patina; an image used successfully in a poem acquires poetic associations. But when Shakespeare's homely images were new they must have been as startling as Eliot's "patient etherized upon a table" seemed to be just a generation ago.

Shakespeare's use of this new and startling homeliness (could we call it the second major aspect of his style?) is of a piece with his juxtaposition of grandeur and horror. The juxtaposition of comedy and tragedy had long been a part of the English tradition, but it was reserved for Shakespeare to make each a part of the other; and we may see the growth of his poetic use of homeliness in the sonnets. There could be no purer instance of this development than the juxtaposition of styles in the seventy-third and seventy-fourth sonnets, two sonnets which comprise one poem. The first ("That time of year thou may'st

[27] Sonnet 129.

in me behold") employs what had long been known to be poetic image and the language of poetry. The second concentrates on the homely and the ugly and ends in a couplet of the barest language. There is not a word in the couplet (except perhaps *worth*) which carries an overtone. Language could not be more completely stripped of connotation. There is nothing to distract the reader from the bare singleness of the thought. Yet the emotion of the quatrains carries over, and, in its context, the couplet is poetry. It is what he was later to do, perhaps more magnificently, with Lear's five *nevers.*

> But, be contented: when that fell arrest
> Without all bail shall carry me away,
> My life hath in this line some interest,
> Which for memorial still with thee shall stay.
> When thou reviewest this, thou dost review
> The very part was consecrate to thee:
> The earth can have but earth, which is his due;
> My spirit is thine, the better part of me:
> So then thou hast but lost the dregs of life,
> The prey of worms, my body being dead,
> The coward conquest of a wretch's knife,
> Too base of thee to be remembered.
> The worth of that is that which it contains,
> And that is this, and this with thee remains.

The simplest statement of the sonnet's meaning would be, "the essential is best." It is an idea of which Shakespeare never wearied, and nothing more readily recalled its truth to him than the contemplation of poetry. He asks that the sonnets be remembered for their content.[28] He says that it is their subject that makes the poems pleasing, and not what the poet brings to them.[29] He repeats that his powers are not worthy of their theme. And once, after a long silence, he invoked his muse to return again to his friend and "sing to the ear that . . . gives thy pen both skill and argument."[30] The young friend, except for these poems, is now unknown, and Shakespeare has become the greatest of English writers. This admiration for a man we do not know, and this derogation of poetic powers we esteem, may strike us at first as curious. But the sonnets tell of a time when Shakespeare was unknown, or almost so, and the young man was not only well-known, he was, in the poet's eyes, fair, kind, and good. In those days the poet's attitude was not curious; and it is still less so when thought of in relation to his tendency to hold the subject more highly than the means by which it finds expression.

[28] Sonnet 32.
[29] Sonnet 38.
[30] Sonnet 100.

catherine ing

THE LYRICS OF SPENSER, SHAKESPEARE, AND DONNE

Part 1

SPENSER

The poetry of Spenser which may be called lyrical in any true sense is a very small part of his work. It is, curiously enough, not the part which composers have set to music. There are settings of parts of *The Faerie Queene:* Carlton set stanza one of Book V, Canto vii, stanzas one and two of V, viii, and stanza one of VI, viii as numbers fourteen, nine, ten and fifteen of his *Madrigals To Fiue voyces* (London, 1601); Gibbons set stanza forty-nine of III, i as numbers ten and eleven of his *First Set of Madrigals And Motets of 5. Parts* (London, 1612). This is all madrigal work. There is also a setting by Kirbye, as numbers twenty-two and twenty-three of his *First set Of English Madrigals, to 4. 5. and 6 voyces* (London, 1597), of two stanzas of the dirge in the November Eclogue in *The Shepheardes Calender;* it is interesting that those too are set to madrigal music and not as airs. With the exception of Kirbye's settings, there is no known music for any of Spenser's lyrical poetry, and this is significant.

The poems of any value which we may call lyrics are: Hobbinol's "laye Of fayre *Eliza*" in the April Eclogue of *The Shepheardes Calender* (London, 1590); the "roundle" sung by Perigot and Willye in the August Eclogue; the sestina in the same Eclogue; the dirge in the November Eclogue; possibly *Another of the Same* (An Epitaph vpon the right Honourable sir *Phillip Sidney* knight), from *Astrophell* (1595); *Epithalamion,* from the group *Amoretti and Epithalamion* (1595); and *Prothalamion* (1596).[1] I have called these lyrics because some of them occur in a context suggesting singing, and the rest are, or are related to, odes, which are in origin songs.

Reprinted from *The Elizabethan Lyric* (London, Chatto & Windus, 1951), pages 209–236, with the permission of the author. Copyright 1961 by Catherine Ing.

[1] I use the text given by Ernest de Selincourt in *Spenser's Minor Poems* (Oxford, Clarendon Press, 1910).

The lay to Eliza is perhaps the best-known passage of *The Shepheardes Calender.* It is introduced by Hobbinol's consenting to sing Colin's "laye," "Which once he made, as by a spring he laye, And tuned it vnto the Waters fall." It begins with a nine-line stanza, of which the rime-scheme is ababccddc; the number of syllables in the lines is 10, 4, 10, 4, 10, 10, 4, 4, 8; the number of stresses is 5, 2, 5, 2, 5, 5, 2, 2, 4, and the arrangement of stresses is usually a repetition of x /, though line seven appears to begin / x and line nine either / x or \ \. There are thirteen stanzas in the poem. Now a lay is defined by the *New English Dictionary* as "A short lyric or narrative poem intended to be sung. Often *poet.* for 'song.'" Illustrative quotations include references to bird song. A poem of a hundred and seventeen lines is not very short, especially when sung. This poem, opening as it does with a stanza made up of an unusual arrangement of lines of different lengths, cunningly linked by rimes, has not the air of a short and simple song. Nevertheless, a quick glance at the pages on which the "song" is printed in any edition will show that, while the poem is not a short and "artless" song, it might well be intended for singing as airs were sung; that is, it consists apparently of thirteen stanzas all of the same form of mixed long and short lines, and all following the same rime-scheme. Much too long for the complications and repetitions of madrigal setting, it might be an air poem. If it were, we should expect to find each stanza formally an exact repetition of the first.

The second stanza repeats this form, and so does stanza three, with the exception of line eight, which has five syllables instead of the expected four, though probably still only two stresses. "And Primroses greene" could no doubt be sung to the same musical phrase as "Her worthy praise," with some division of the first note. Such division is not necessary for stanza four, but in stanza five it would be required for each of the four short lines, which are "vpon her to gaze," "it did him amaze," "Let him if he dare" and "His brightnesse compare." Stanza six also has four five-syllabled lines in place of the four-syllabled lines of the first stanzas, and the first two short lines of stanza seven have also five syllables each. So far, however, it might still be possible to fit these appropriately into equivalent musical phrases. With lines seven and eight of stanza seven, however, this becomes impossible. The two lines run:

> Shee is my goddesse plaine,
> And I her shepherde swayne,

and it is clear that each has not only six syllables but three stresses. Now this presents a very different problem from that of the five-syllabled lines. Where the number and placing of the stresses remained roughly similar, the alteration in number of syllables could be treated as a simple variant of the model form, and fitted into a similar, though not identical, rhythmical phrase. The third stress, however, alters the nature of the phrase, and if these three-stress lines were sung to a musical phrase truly suitable for the two-stress lines of the opening stanza, either music or words must suffer. In the remaining stanzas of the poem, some of the short lines return to the original form, but others break this form. "To fyll the fourth place," "Oliues bene for peace," "Binde your fillets faste" and "worne of Paramoures" could not possibly repeat the rhythmical effect of "Helpe me to blaze" or "Her worthy praise." That is, this poem could not possibly be used for an air poem of the kind we have studied and is not, in fact, suitable for setting to the characteristic Elizabethan kinds of music.

This does not, of course, in the least affect the beauty of the poem, but it does, I think, tell us something about the kind of poet Spenser was. There is here either unwillingness or inability to repeat a metrical form so perfectly that every embodiment of it would be as happy with a given tune as the first. Unlike most of the poets of the age who wrote lyric, Spenser, in writing what at first sight is a poem for a repeating air, does not apparently hear or feel the unchanging shape of a tune in the back of his mind as he writes. The introduction to the lay, which quite deliberately and specifically suggests singing as its manner of utterance, is simply a part of a poetic suggestion of appropriate atmosphere, a suggestion which is to be carried out by purely poetical means. It is very much "*poet.* for 'song.'" The idea of a song is given in the introductory verse, and the "lay" itself, so long as it is not in fact sung, beautifully carries out the idea. In reading, the short lines are always sufficiently different from the neighbouring long lines to continue giving at least the impression, "Here the stanza moves from long phrases to short," and the short lines are sufficiently far removed from each other for the differences between them to remain unobtrusive, and probably actually unnoticed. It is only the test of literally setting to music that will reveal the fact that this is not a "song" in the strict sense. Unsung, it is very like a song.

All its music lies in the words themselves. Throughout the poem Spenser uses alliteration freely but not excessively, often initially, but equally often, less obviously, medially. Thus 'b' 'l' and 's' play in and out of the first two stanzas, the second beginning also a use of 'g,' which in its turn comes freely into stanza three, together with the related 'k.' This relation between the voiced and unvoiced form of a consonant has already been used, 'v' and 'f' in the first stanza, 'b' and 'p' in the second. 'f' and 'v' are again used in the fourth stanza, together with full alliteration on 'r' and 'm,' 'g,' 'h,' 'b,' and 'f' are all used in stanza five, 's' and 'b' and nasals in stanza six, 'p,' 'b,' 's' and 'f' in stanza seven, 'p,' 'b,' 's' and 'h' in stanza eight, 'd' and 'r' in stanza nine, 'r,' 'p' and 's' in stanza ten, 'f,' 'd,' 't' and 's' in stanza eleven, and in the last two stanzas nearly all these consonants equally. In all these stanzas, minor alliterations occur in addition to the most obvious examples.

Vowel echoes, too, are used frequently. The 'a' sound as in "face" is very important throughout the poem, occurring often in rimes, and the 'e' of "bless" is also very frequent. The second stanza has 'ĭ' and 'ŏ,' the third 'ē,' ('ī'), the fifth 'ō,' and all have some share of the persistent 'a' (as above) and 'ĕ' sounds. In fact, the organization of consonant and vowel sounds in the poem is both rich and delicate, so rich that it might interfere with the hearing of a tune, so delicate that the more subtle relationships, as in medial alliteration or in assonances shifting their place in the line, might be unheard in the company of a tune. The poem is most musical, but its music is its own, and leaves no place for the music of an air. On the evidence of this poem, it might be said that in one sense Spenser is one of the most musical, in another sense one of the least musical, of Elizabethan poets.

The August roundelay on the whole confirms this impression. The lines are given alternately by Perigot and Willye, Perigot "singing" the narrative lines and Willye the "undersong." These lines divide themselves into groups of four, in which the second (Willye's first) always begins with "hey ho," followed by a repetition of a phrase or word from the first line. The fourth line (the second of the "undersong") is always some comment on or amplification of the third line (the second of the narrative). It is therefore the second line of each four-line group which is a kind of refrain, a practice unusual but not unique among Elizabethan lyrists.[2] The "hey ho" and refrain quality of this second line give the poem much of the feeling of the "hey nonny no" type of song, in which, because singing is the most important part, many nonsense syllables are freely used. In fact, however, the fourth line is used for far fuller and more indirect comment and expansion than is quite compatible with its apparent nature. Thus, while Willye sometimes gives the simple "she can trippe it very well" as the comment on "Tripping ouer the dale alone," he adds "so loue into thy hart did streame" to the group.

> *Per.* All as the Sunny beame so bright,
> *Wil.* hey ho the Sunne beame,
> *Per.* Glaunceth from Phœbus face forthright;

and this clearly is an addition to the narrative beyond what is expected of the undersong. That is, Spenser uses a metrical form of alternately

[2] Cf. No. 19 of *A Booke of Ayres* (London, 1601), by Rosseter and Campion.

riming quatrains of four-stress lines with a refrain line and another line that begins by appearing to be another, though more varied, refrain line. He thus suggests a simple, part-nonsense folk song by his metrical form, but, though the actual form maintains this suggestion, he fills it with more material than might be expected. Once again he uses a form which gives the associations of singing, but would, if actually sung, probably lose its capacity to communicate all that its words contain.

The sestina of the same eclogue shows clearly how completely Spenser is, technically, a poet of words. This very difficult form is not easy to follow in speech: with music it would hardly reveal itself at all. The sestina consists of six six-line stanzas, in which no line of the first rimes with any other, but every word occurring at the ends of lines in the first stanza is used again to end lines in the other stanzas in a revolving order constantly turned on by the use of the last word of one stanza as the end-word of the first line of the next. The rime order is therefore: ABCDEF, FABCDE, EFABCD, DEFABC, CDEFAB, BCDEFA. Then follows an envoy of three lines, in which the six end-words, in their original order, occur at the end of each half-line. The long separation of words from their rimes, with the exception of the turn by means of a couplet from one stanza to the next, means great concentration of attention if the form is to be observed; and the need to use the whole word for the rime involves the poet in shifts and complications of syntax which could not be followed in sung poetry. It is noticeable that the poetry for airs and madrigals customarily uses very simple and direct syntax and a grammatical structure allowing frequent coincidence between logical and metrical divisions; this practice enables the sense to develop clearly through singing. This is obviously untrue of a passage like this:

> And as my cryes
> (Which of my woe cannot bewray least part)
> You heare all night, when nature craueth sleepe,
> Increase, so let your yrksome yells augment.
> Thus all the night in plaints, the daye in woe
> I vowed haue to wayst, till safe and sound
> She home returne, whose voyces siluer sound
> To cheerefull songs can chaunge my cherelesse cryes.

The choice and successful use of a metrical form like this show that the poet is one who must find the music for his lyrics in his words. Any other music for it is unthinkable.

Colin's dirge in the November eclogue preserves its stanzaic form more perfectly than the Eliza lay by using a repeated refrain for the short line, "O heauie herse" and "O carefull verse" for the first eleven stanzas, and "O happye herse" and "O ioyfull verse" for the last four.

Nevertheless, Spenser at times shifts stress so sharply that his form is at least momentarily endangered. Where stanza one has "Let streaming teares be poured out in store," stanza seven has "Thereof nought remaynes but the memoree"—a line which plays such havoc with the given form as to be, I feel, simply metrically bad. After observing this, the reader is not surprised to find lines which fail in other ways to correspond with the pattern. Lines six and seven of each stanza, which immediately precede the first short line, usually have four stresses each, but they occasionally have five, and once three. This poem, then, is like the Eliza lay in that it is not in fact suitable for singing, but it is like it also in having a rich use of its own speech music, and in appearing to preserve, though it often departs from it, a complex stanza form; the pattern of this form is a ten-line stanza riming ababbccdbd, the lines containing 6, 5, 5, 5, 5, 4, 4, 2, 5, 2 stresses, and superficial readings would give the impression that the form was preserved.

The epitaph on Sidney, *Silence augmenteth grief*, is not very valuable poetically, and therefore not very important metrically, but it has one point of interest. Written in quatrains of poulter's measure, riming aabb, it uses heavy pause so regularly that it reads readily as a poem written in the 3 3 4 3 form of hymn measure, riming abcb. This is startling proof of the tendency of the long-lined form to break into some version of the shorter-lined measure, for Spenser of all our poets seems to have had least difficulty in writing many unbroken long lines. The alexandrine of *The Faerie Queene* stanza is evidence of this, but so also is the fact, observable in the poems we have studied, that when Spenser breaks his own set form, his tendency is nearly always to lengthen and not to shorten some line in the form.

We come now to Spenser's finest lyric achievements, the two great marriage odes. It will be sufficient to examine the *Epithalamion*, which is probably on the whole the finer of the two, and certainly includes, in its slightly larger scale, all the metrical characteristics of *Prothalamion*. Individual choice may waver between the *Epithalamion* refrain, with its slight variations, and the unchangingly beautiful

Sweete *Themmes* runne softly, till I end my Song

of the *Prothalamion*, but both perform the same function of persistently reminding the reader of the idea of singing, and with equal success. The *Epithalamion* gives to the reader the peculiar pleasure of hearing a poet's own triumphant bridal song, and it is almost unique in our literature as a prolonged celebration of happy love.

Epithalamion has twenty-three complete stanzas, and a short envoy. Each stanza ends in some version of the lines:

So I vnto my selfe alone will sing,
The woods shall to me answer and my Eccho ring.

The variants on this are used to link the lines in sense to the stanza, and they always leave unaltered the words "sing," "woods," "answer," "Eccho" and "ring." Of the twenty-three stanzas, the first, second, fourth, fifth and sixth have eighteen lines with the rime-scheme ababccdcdeefggff RR; stanzas 3, 7, 8, 12, 13, 14, 17, 18, 19 and 20 have nineteen lines with the rime-scheme ababccdcdeefggfhh RR; stanzas 10, 16, 21 and 23 have eighteen lines with slight variants on the first rime-scheme of their last nine lines, the rimes of the first nine being identical in order with those in the other stanzas; stanzas 9, 11[3] and 22 have nineteen lines with slight variants in the rime-order in the last ten lines; and one stanza only, number 15, has only seventeen lines, the first nine riming like the rest, the last eight varying slightly.

In every stanza the sixth and the antepenultimate lines are noticeably shorter than the rest, having three stresses where most of the rest have five or six, and every stanza except the short fifteenth has a similar short line as the ninth or tenth. Each short line rimes with the immediately preceding line. The continuing (and only slightly varied) rhythmical movement throughout is dissyllabic rising. Variations in the rime-scheme of lines after the ninth in each stanza do not occur until after the first eight stanzas, and occur freely only in stanzas 9, 10, 11, 15, 16, 21, 22 and 23; that is, whole groups of stanzas at the beginning and the middle and near the end of the poem are consistent. The last stanza is the same length as the first.

It should be clear from this description that the poem is made up of complex stanzas of great length handled with a remarkable balance between freedom and conformity. In no stanza (if the emendation in stanza eleven be accepted) is any variation allowed until after the ninth line. This establishes confidence in the form and a trust in the poet's capacity to continue in it, a necessary reassurance where the form is so long as it is here. The length is confident, but has resting-places: the short line riming with its immediate predecessor gives a point of rest, and lightens the texture by the space for silence it provides. The first marked variations in rime-scheme occur in the stanzas preceding the

[3] In stanza eleven I venture to suggest emending "womanhood" in the eighth line to "womanhead." As it stands, this is the only line in the whole of a richly rimed poem apparently unrimed. In all the other stanzas the first nine lines are absolutely regular in rime-order. According to this order, line eight would be expected to rime with line six, "(Medusaes mazeful) hed." "Womanhe(a)d" is a form common with Spenser: cf. *F.Q.* II, xii, 55 and V, ix, 45, where it occurs in rimed positions. If in *Epithalamion* we read "womanhe(a)d," stanza eleven has the rime-scheme ababccdcdeefgfghh RR, which is likely according to the example of all the other stanzas: if we read "womanhood," the scheme is ababccdedffghghjj RR, which is highly unlikely. Renwick incorporated this emendation in his edition.

central climax, giving a sense of freedom in the movement. The poem comes to its final rest on a stanza of the same length as the first stanza, enhancing the ode's processional air of movement up to a central point of importance and back to something like the starting-point. The structure of the whole goes far to explain why the poem, immensely rich in sensuous appeal as it is, is totally unsensual, and complete belief in the truth of the poet's claim that "the inward beauty of her liuely spright" is the lady's heart of beauty and the centre of his love for her; the stanzas referring to this "inward beauty," though they contain few words describing such beauty in comparison with the rich profusion of sensuous description throughout the poem, occur in the very centre of a poem whose rhythmical construction insists on making the centre the climax. Therefore, the very structure of the poem gives, by placing, to the claim of spiritual love an importance which convinces without explanation. Here is economy in the disposition of riches of description.

The wealth of description is equalled by the wealth of verbal music. Every use of vowel and consonant sounds open to the poet is apparent in *Epithalamion.* The words sing fully and richly, with a music leaving no hearing for other kinds of music. The poem is indeed a "song" in lieu of ornaments, and its rhythm, melody and harmony convey and deepen meaning through their steadily mounting and then falling movement and the long full syllables carried and linked by consonantal impulses and connections.

There is in Spenser's practice of versification some clue to the meaning of his title of "poets' poet." It may mean "poeta poetarum," but it means also something more precise. It means that his technique is so complete a use of the poet's methods of dealing with his material, words, that he is a "poet" in a full and exact sense, and that few but other poets may fully appreciate his use of material.

His tendency in some earlier poems to lengthen short lines and to use a line apparently merely formal (as in the August roundelay) to add to his meaning shows his need for room to say all he has to say. He has much to say, and he is therefore using words with full regard to their meanings and associations. Yet he is able at the same time to use them with full exploitation of their aural qualities. He makes words sing, partly because he is apparently little interested in playing tricks with rhythm; apart from certain curious experiments in, for example, the February eclogue of *The Shepheardes Calender,* he uses almost always divisions of passages in repeating dissyllabic rising rhythm, very rarely inverting, reducing or doubling stress, but allowing his flow of sounds to proceed uninterrupted by startling rhythmical complications. The regularity of his rhythmical movement is revealed and filled out by great complexity of the pitch and quality relationships of speech sounds.

The full value of the vowels and consonants constituting syllables is given by the verse's freedom from unprepared-for rhythmical changes, and so achieves a singing quality inherent in the speech sounds themselves. Reason and song, therefore, are secured by Spenser without dependence on the other singing art, and an ear acute as a poet's for the beauty of speech sounds is required to hear the rich variety of his winding lengths of phrase.

In fact, Spenser appears to write lyric poetry having the untroubled impersonal quality of sung lyric while using only the singing of speech, speech which is more often used in poetry with emphasis principally upon the personal emotional connotations of its meaning content. His versification, therefore, prepares his audience for his peculiar power of wedding meaning to physical embodiment with the closeness of complete fusion.

Part 2

SHAKESPEARE

Shakespeare's lyrics, unlike Spenser's, were intended for music, for most of them occur in the plays in contexts showing, with one exception, that the songs were to be literally sung. The exception is the introduction of the dirge in *Cymbeline,* where Arviragus says:

> And let us, Polydore, though now our voices
> Have got the mannish crack, sing him to the ground,

and Guiderius answers:

> I cannot sing: I'll weep, and word it with thee;

and later Arviragus says again:

> We'll say our song the whilst.

The likeliest way of accounting for this is that the boy-actors' voices, or one of them, had broken, and so necessitated an alteration in the intention of singing *Fear no more.* The alteration shows both the usual practice of singing Shakespeare's songs in the plays and also willingness to accept reading as a reasonable substitute. That is, we are confirmed in believing that Elizabethan songs, while admirably suited to singing, are capable of utterance independent of the singing voice, and that we merely follow the Elizabethans themselves in recognizing this independence. The rest of the songs, from those in *Love's Labour's Lost,* certainly an early play (printed 1598) to those in *The Tempest,* probably though not certainly Shakespeare's last play, were all sung. For some of the songs we have contemporary settings, for some settings probably contemporary (recorded in Playford's *Select musical Ayres,* 1653, *Select Ayres,* 1659 and *Musical Companion,* 1673, which may well preserve contemporary settings), and for the rest later settings by Arne, Schubert and twentieth-century composers. It is not our purpose to study the music, but simply to remember that the songs were songs in the literal sense.

It is neither possible nor necessary to examine all the songs from Shakespeare's plays in order to detect their nature. It will suffice to select a few from different periods of his years of practice as a playwright, which may well serve as examples of his lyric work. We may take *When daisies pied* from *Love's Labour's Lost,* and *Who is Silvia?* from *The Two Gentlemen of Verona* as examples of early lyrics; *Tell me where* from *The Merchant of Venice, Sigh no more* from *Much Ado about Nothing, Come away* and *When that I was* from *Twelfth Night,* and *It was a lover* from *As You Like It* as examples of the lyrics in mature comedy; *Take, O, take* from *Measure for Measure* as an example from 'dark comedies'; the Willow Song from *Othello* as an example of song in tragedy; *Fear no more* from *Cymbeline* and *Full fathom five* from *The Tempest* as examples of lyric in the late romances.[4]

The song from *Love's Labour's Lost* is a perfect example of air poetry. The stanza form established at the beginning is as follows:

```
x / x / x / x /      a
x / x / x / x /      b
x / x / x / x /      a
x / x / x / x /      b
x / x / x / x /      c
\ / x / x / x /      c
    / /              d
/ / / / x / x /      e
x / x \ x / x /      e
```

This is perfectly preserved by the second stanza, which exactly repeats the last five lines of the first, and follows completely the stress and rime-scheme of the first four lines. The third and fourth stanzas, which turn to winter from spring, again repeat the stress pattern, though it is only the last four lines of the first "winter" stanza that are repeated in the next. The "winter" stanzas should, I think, be so printed as to show the perfection with which the "winter" refrain can repeat the form of the "spring" refrain, thus:

[4] The text is that of the First Folio, with spelling modernized. The songs are conveniently collected in A. H. Bullen's *Lyrics from Elizabethan Dramatists* (London, 1889).

When blood is nipped, and ways be foul,
Then nightly sings the starting owl,
To-whit;
To-who, to-who, a merry note,
While greasy Joan doth keel the pot;

which perfectly follows the pattern of–

The cuckoo then, on every tree,
Mocks married men, for thus sings he,
Cuckoo;
Cuckoo, cuckoo,–O word of fear,
Unpleasing to a married ear.

It will be noticed that the onomatopœic bird cries occur in exactly corresponding positions. The riming throughout is perfect.

Who is Silvia? has three stanzas, each following the pattern:

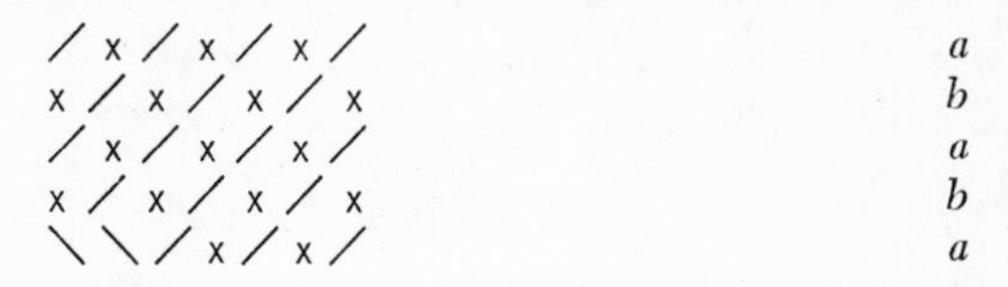

The rimes of lines two and four are double: "(com)mend her–lend her," "kindness–blindness," "(ex)celling–dwelling." These lines show the practice, very frequent in Elizabethan poetry for music, of ending on a a light syllable. The other lines are obviously whole phrases, neither falling-rhythm lines catalectic nor rising-rhythm lines lacking a light syllable at the beginning; this practice too is, as we have seen, common in Elizabethan lyric verse. There cannot, from beginning to end, be any difficulty in fitting the verbal phrases to music suitable for the first stanza.

Tell me where is clearly fitted for madrigal rather than for air music. It consists of two sections, question and answer, the second section different in form from the first.

```
      \ x \ x \ x \        a
  \ \ x / \ \ x /          a
      / x / x / x /        a
            x /b x /       b
  \ \ x / x / x /          c
  x / x /a x / x /         c
      x x / x / x /        c
    \ \ \ / / x /          d
    / x / x / / /          D
            / / /          D
```

It has often been pointed out that the "*a*" rime of this poem is a rime for "lead," the metal of the casket which is to be chosen as the song is sung. It has less often been noted that question and answer are beautifully linked in sound, both by the repetitions of the "*a*" rime of the first section in the "fed" of line two of the second section, and by the echoing response to "reply, reply" at the end of the first section in the rimes "eyes–dies–lies" of the second section. This poem has the whole phrasing of madrigal verse, carried by recurring x / movement, linked by rime and assonance, and using onomatopœic syllables "Ding, dong, bell" for singing purposes.

Sigh no more is an air poem, with double rimes and light endings for the even lines of the two eight-line stanzas, each of which consists of four lines and a four-line refrain. The pattern is as follows:

/ \ / / x / x /	*a*	*c*
\ / x / x / x	*b*	*e*
x / x / x / x /	*a*	*c*
x / x / x / x	*b*	*e*
x / x / x / x /	*c*	*c*
x / x / x / x	*d*	*d*
x / x / x / x /	*c*	*c*
\ x / / x / x	*d*	*d*

In reading, the first lines of the two stanzas phrase themselves with a subtle difference which, however, cannot interfere with the singing, "ditties" fitting neatly into the space for "ladies," though the grammatical connections are different:

Sigh no more, ladies, sigh no more
Sing no more ditties, sing no moe.

The "hey nonny, nonny" phrases are typical nonsense syllables for singing, and other syllables are used to give pleasurable sound-echoes; "deceivers ever" chimes within itself as well as with its rime "never," and the rimes "heavy–leavey" in the corresponding positions in the second stanza; the first rime of the second stanza "moe–so" picks up the "go–woe" rime of the refrain.

Come away is an interesting example of possible confusion in reading arising from reliance on a tune for first utterance of a poem. It seems to me that the first line might be stressed equally well / x \ / x \ / or \ x / \ x / /; the first line of the second stanza makes it clear that the stressing must be \ x / \ x / /. Line seven of the second stanza needs note-division to make it fit its position, for "Sad true lover never find my grave" must correspond to "My part of death, no one so true," though it may be that we ought to read "love" for "lover." Otherwise, both stanzas beautifully fit the pattern:

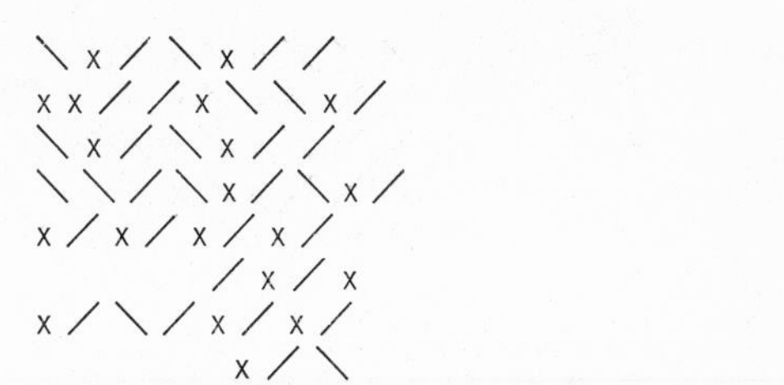

a
b
a
b
c
d
c
d

Particularly beautiful is the way in which "O, prepare it" of the first stanza demands a phrasing which makes the "O" sigh in the corresponding "Lay me, O, where" in the second stanza.

When that I was is principally interesting for its simple "popular" form, with the second and fourth lines of a quatrain as refrain, and the use of very loose syntax in the other lines to ensure perfect conformity to the tune pattern.

/ x x / x x / x / x /   *a*
x / / x / x x /   *b*
x / x / x / x /   *a*
x x / x / x / x /   *c*

The triplet hurry of unstressed syllables suggests an almost nursery-rime movement to make the syllables fit.

It was a lover is a sheer singing poem. Three of the five lines of each stanza are refrain lines, they use many nonsense syllables and a full chime on the "sing–ring–sing–ding" syllables. The remaining two lines are required only to fit into a very simple pattern.

x / x / x / x /   *a*
With a hey, and a ho, and a hey nonino,
x / x / \ \ x /   *a*
In the spring time, the only pretty ring time,
When birds do sing, hey ding a ding, ding,
Sweet lovers love the spring.

Take, O, take has only one stanza in *Measure for Measure,* but it appears in Fletcher's *Bloody Brother* with a second stanza. It may be that the song is Fletcher's and not Shakespeare's, but it may equally well be that Fletcher added a stanza to Shakespeare's poem when he came to use it. Certainly the one stanza stands as Shakespeare's in the first printing of *Measure for Measure* (First Folio). The stress and rime-schemes are:

/ / / x / x / *a*
\ \ / x / x / *b*
\ \ / x / x / *a*
/ \ \ x / x / *b*
/ x / x / x / *c*
/ x / *c*
/ x / x / x / *c*
/ x / *c*

It should be noted that the "*a*" rimes have assonance with the "*c*" and also with the opening "Take." The balanced drag of the line openings settles easily into the regular x / movement of the endings.

The Willow Song is not entirely Shakespeare's. It occurs in the *Gorgeous Gallery* (1578), in Howell's *Devices* (1581), in B. M. MS. Add. 15117 with lute accompaniment, and in various other contemporary and later collections. No one version is quite the same as any other. Shakespeare is adapting a well-known song, and what matters to us is his full retention of the refrain lines consisting entirely of the word "willow."

Fear no more, the spoken song, follows the stanza form nearly as strictly as a sung verse. Its three stanzas have the form:

/ x / x / x (x) / *a*
/ x / x / x / (x) *b*
/ x / x / x / *a*
(x) / x / x / x / (x) *b*
(x) / x / x / x / *c*
x / x / x / x / *c*

The envoy runs:

(x) / x / x / x *a*
/ x / \ / x *a*
/ x / x / x *b*
/ x / x / x *b*
/ x / x / x / *c*
/ x / x / x / *c*

The shift of movement in the first four lines of the envoy, and the closing up of the rimes into couplets, give heightened insistence to the spell of the envoy.

Of *Full fathom five* it should be noted that its "Ding, dong, bell" is a late use of singing syllables used earlier in *Tell me where.* The form is:

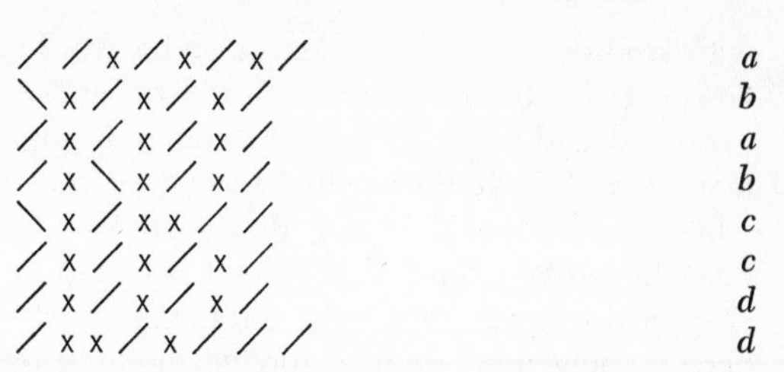

The "*b*" and "*c*" rimes have assonance with each other, and f and s alliterations are clearly audible.

Nothing strange has been found in the metrical structure of these songs except, possibly, the degree of their perfection. This is one of the most important points to be noticed about them. They are songs for singing, and Shakespeare has followed as closely as any of the large Elizabethan family of Anon. the needs of verse for music. There is here no sign of that phenomenon of "content bursting the bounds of the verse-form" which certain critics have professed to observe as characteristic of Shakespeare's mature work. The purpose of examining the selected poems has been to show that Shakespeare's metrical practice as a lyrist followed the conventions of his contemporaries who wrote verse for music; the selection was made to represent all the parts of his writing life, and it shows this conformity of practice from beginning to end. The poems are clearly "music" lyrics and, like other men's work of this kind, are carefully calculated in rhythmical phrases which may be repeated when an air is repeated, or made of complex phrases carried on a recurrent movement where there is no need for stanza repetition. Like other men's work, again, these lyrics are surely enough constructed in their use of stress to retain form when the music is removed. The place of the music is to some extent supplied, here as elsewhere, by arrangements of vowel and consonant sounds running through the poems. On the whole, the choice of syllables is such as to provide freely prolongable vowels for singing without the impediments of thick consonant groups. This choice is assisted and confirmed by the use in many of the lyrics of refrain lines of nonsense syllables valuable purely for rhythmical and melodic purposes. Rhythm and melody, in fact, are the most immediately noticeable characteristics of these poems; that is, their formal qualities are as important as their sense content. They have the typically impersonal, though not unemotional, nature of the true song.

It is, therefore, not surprising to find in their content much that is generalized in meaning with, for instance, a high proportion of abstract nouns in the vocabulary. Grace, beauty, kindness; fancy; death; life, love; learning, physic, slander, censure, joy and moan; these are the subjects and examples in the songs. They tell us that beauty lives with kindness; that the cuckoo sings his word of fear when the common flowers paint the meadows with delight and the owl hoots when blood is nipped and ways be foul; that fancy is engendered in the eyes; that men were deceivers ever; that the rain it raineth every day and a great while ago the world begun; that a life was but a flower and therefore take the present time; that golden lads and girls all must, as chimney-sweepers, come to dust; that coral is made of drowned bones. There is here nothing new, nothing foreign, nothing peculiar to the strange experience of rare natures. Yet these songs occur in plays concerning characters highly individualized and deeply understood, and many of them come at moments important to the action. They are not "turns" inserted to cover a lack of action, interludes between the parts of the play that matter. They are remembered with the plays, and remembered as parts of them. It is not a complete memory that retains Berowne's jesting wit and dismissal to painful lessons, and not the songs of spring and winter; the jealous rivalries of two gentlemen and not Silvia; Bassanio's ambition and the grief and cruelty and witty triumphs of a Venetian story, and not the song of fancy; the wit-plays and pains and victories of true love, and not the song that rebukes the sighing of ladies for inconstant men; the errors and jokes and tricks and self-deceits of Illyria, and not sad cypress and the wind and the rain; the weariness of courts and the humorously borne distress of love, and not the springtime lover and his lass; the struggle of loyalty and purity against perfidy and lust, and not the seals of love; the cruel jealousies of Cymbeline's Britain, and not the quiet consummation; the tempest and not the sea-nymphs' knell. That is, an essential part of plays showing a care and understanding of the idiosyncratic personality as strong as ever playwright has had is a kind of lyric which, by its reliance on aural qualities and its formal use of words, has tended always to an effect impersonal and generalized; the formal lyric belongs integrally to the treatment of developed human individuals. *Measure for Measure* startles and convinces equally by the leaping into momentary but three-dimensional life of the unimportant Barnadine and by the association of the mature human Mariana, with her vocation for wifehood, with the sweet far sadness of *Take, O take.* Desdemona, distinguished as she is by gaiety and courage from the stock figure of suffering heroine, sings an old song of the lovelorn poor soul sighing "Willow," and it is of the essence of this moving scene that, instead of speaking of her personal situation, she sings of the timeless poor soul.

The perfect formality and the perfect propriety of Shakespeare's songs in their given places give an indication of his greatness and special quality as a dramatist, and show why criticism of Shakespeare that has concentrated on his poetry and tended to forget the practical theatrical relevance of his scenes has nevertheless sometimes contributed much of value to the understanding of his work. His psychological knowledge and understanding and his experience of effective theatrical methods are, after all, valuable because they contribute to works of art. It is not the subtle complexity of the development of Hamlet's nature that is finally important in *Hamlet:* it is the fact that this is made into a work of art. This fact alone has preserved, as on a Grecian urn, the interest of his problem for our unending absorbed inquiry. All the human penetration of Shakespeare's plays in black ink still shines bright because it has found form, and all the interest of complex individuality has remained fresh for us because it has been held by its form in some relation with all other human experiences that have found form in art. Neither Shakespeare's plots nor his persons are mere types, but their relationship with types has given them focus and perspective in our view of them. The very fact of the strict formal perfection of his lyrics, and the other fact that they have a proper place in his plays, should warn us off using his writing as the raw material for disquisitions on psychology. They show clearly in miniature the importance of his art.

They show, too, something of the nature of that art. Their impersonal but often deeply moving generalizations occur in situations where the interest in his characters may merge with interest in the kind of experience or set of relationships in which they find themselves. The love-sick Duke of Illyria, the mad Ophelia, the varyingly cheated Beatrice and Hero, are revealed in themselves and in their likeness to others in the songs associated with them, for the songs embody situations and not people, and are yet relevant to these people in the situations in which they find themselves. The songs then show the dramatic imagination which deepens the emotion with which we respond to characters by relating them to the memory of past situations of feeling without destroying their individual experience of the situations. They show how the famous "universality" of Shakespeare's plays comes by the great and profound sense of proportion which, simultaneously, loves and admires and pities the lonely individual, and sees that though individual he is not in all his doings unique. The songs with their beautiful and shapely utterance of truisms hint the fact that the course of Shakespeare's stories is often towards the discovery that the truth in many human situations is a truism. Lear's Fool, with his echo of another fool in "When that I had and a little tiny wit," sings truths that Lear is toiling all his age to find, crying when he finds them "O, I have ta'en too little care of this."

Finally, the formal perfection of the songs is a type of the beauty which is the crown of artistic achievement. Their simple secure matter and manner have that delicacy of perfect shape which seems always fragile, and so makes the beholder feel almost with fear that their certainty is "securus" in its dangerous sense: a change of word, a careless touch, would spoil them. Yet we have no desire that they should seem more robust by being less perfect in form. Their triumph is worth having. This is closely akin to the singular beauty of Shakespeare's comedy, which is full of songs, and which moves in each play to a fullness of happy harmony so delicately balanced on resolved misunderstandings that again it moves us by the pathos in secure happiness. It is at once certain and vulnerable, and worth knowing, however short its life. The short and perilous life of human happiness is perpetuated by the formal beauty Shakespeare gives it. It is not for nothing that Feste sings of the wind and the rain that raineth every day, making a song of the dangers of the world he lives in.

This may seem a far cry from scanning verse. Yet I believe that to recognize the form in Shakespeare's lyrics is to have taken a step on the road to understanding his imagination.

Part 3

DONNE

Spenser was a poet whose lyrical work was antagonistic to the addition of music. Shakespeare's lyrics were intended for music. For some of Donne's lyric poems we have contemporary settings, for the majority none; we shall probably never know how many of them were intended for music. Of the *Songs and Sonets, Go and catch a falling star* has a tune found in B.M. MS. Egerton 2013; *'Tis true 'tis day* has a tune in Corkine's *Second Book of Ayres* (London, 1612), and it has also been suggested as an answer to Dowland's *Sweet, stay awhile,* which is set in *A Pilgrimes Solace* (London, 1612); *Send home my long-stray'd eyes* is printed, with variations, to a tune in Ritson's *English Songs* (London, 1783), but there is no knowing the date of this tune; *The Baite* is intended for the same tune as Marlowe's *Come live with me,* which appears in Corkine's *Second Book of Ayres* (London, 1612); *The Expiration,* with very slight differences, is set by Alfonso Ferrabosco in his *Ayres* (London, 1609). *To sue for all thy Love,* in Dowland's *Pilgrimes Solace,* has been ascribed to Donne. A tune for the *Hymne to God the Father* appears in MS. Egerton 2013. The only purpose in listing these settings is to remind ourselves that Donne's verses were sometimes intended for the strictness of musical setting, and that it may therefore be well to look in his lyric poems for strict metrical structure.

It cannot be pretended that Donne's lyrics have that directness of syntax and smooth development of word-order that we have found in typical Elizabethan music-poetry. It is therefore tempting to read his lyrics with complete submission to the emphasis accent, ignoring, or at least reducing, ictus where it is not obviously coincident with emphasis. Grierson, for instance, refers to Donne's poetry as "not perfect in form, rugged of line and careless in rhyme," and so reminds us of Jonson's censure of Donne for "not keeping of accent." Of late years rugged lines and not keeping of accent have been accounted to Donne for praise rather than blame, but the idea of his technique persists. I do not suggest that there are no imperfections, ruggednesses and careless rimes in Donne's poetry, but it may well be dangerous always to expect them. A search for irregularity may bring rewards.

To assume his carelessness in rime, for instance, leads to supposing that his rimes do not matter. Yet a study of his rimes in the *Songs and Sonets*[5] is interesting. Of the fifty-five poems printed by Grierson as *Songs and Sonets,* two only, *Confined Love* and the sonnet *The Token,* have no rimes on any of the personal pronouns; two, *The Canonization* and *A Valediction forbidding Mourning,* use only "it" of the pronouns in a rime position; *Communitie* has only "ours" in rime. That is, fifty-three poems use the personal pronouns in rimes, and many of them use them many times, persistently echoing "I," "they," "thee," "mee," "hee," "shee," "thou," "you," "wee," "us." One of the uses of "it," in *The Canonization,* is curiously insistent, and deliberately related to other pronouns:

The Phœnix ridle hath more wit
By us, we two being one, are it.
So to one neutrall thing both sexes fit,
Wee dye and rise the same, and prove
Mysterious by this love.

This has the further interest of being related to Shakespeare's *The Phœnix and the Turtle,* which is concerned with the "two being one":

Property was thus appalled,
That the self was not the same;
Single nature's double name
Neither two nor one was called.

Reason in itself confounded
Saw division grow together,
To themselves yet either neither,
Simple were so well compounded;

That it cried, How true a twain
Seemeth this concordant one.[6]

[5] I use the text of *The Poems of John Donne,* edited by Herbert J. C. Grierson, 2 vols. (Oxford, 1912).

[6] It is surprising that little attention is paid to Shakespeare in discussions of the Metaphysical Poets and the influences upon them.

and the Threnos says:

> Death is now the phœnix' nest,
> And the turtle's loyal breast
> To eternity doth rest,
>
> Leaving no posterity:
> 'Twas not their infirmity,
> It was married chastity,

which seems closely connected with *The Canonization's* theme of the mystery, legend and "patterne" of love between two perfect lovers. The "it" used for rime in this poem seems by this treatment to become as strongly "personal" a pronoun, by paradox, as any of the others. Now words in rime positions are important in the work of most poets, and no poet can prevent his rime-words from at least seeming important; therefore, unless we assume Donne to be incompetent in his use of form, an assumption hardly justifiable, we should follow the guidance given by his rime-words. I suspect that the persistent sounding of the personal pronouns, their note intensified by their use for rimes, through Donne's *Songs and Sonets,* is a main, though unsuspected, cause of one of our responses to his poetry. His love poems constantly convey a haunting and inescapable sense of personality, not of the details of appearance, behaviour and character, but of the inner sense of existence as an individual; Donne as lover is "I," his lady is no visible person, but "shee." He is filled with the baffling sense of the unbreakable "I-ness" of "I," of the "you-ness" of "you," of the "she-ness" of "she," and the love poetry is filled with the desire to turn this into the one-ness of "us," or even further into the "it-ness" of the phoenix. No poetry more strongly conveys the feeling of the defined individual existence we all sense in saying "I," as we never sense it in repeating our own names, which are rather the external signs to others of our characters; it is in using the pronoun that we imply "I am." No poetry more strongly expresses the desire to escape from, or to submerge, this invincible conviction of separate existence. The content states these feelings; but the form makes them live in the inexorability with which it dwells on the pronouns.

Once their note has been heard in the rimes, it becomes increasingly audible within the lines. It is surprising how often the pronouns occur in positions requiring ictus, and how easy it becomes, if the rimes have been followed, to give this ictus, where prose reading would deny it. So strong does this sound become that it may lead to questioning of a line's superficial meaning. It is possible to suspect the hint of a pun in *The Extasie:*

> Our eye-beames twisted, and did thred
> Our eyes, upon one double string.

"Eyes" occurs in the same position in the lines as "we," four lines earlier:

> Sat we two, one anothers best.

Donne certainly puns in the famous Hymn, where he plays throughout on "done" and "Donne," with painful intensity of meaning. His use of pronouns is almost like a continuous underlying pun on the meaning of most of his love poems.

Once we have found the power of his rimes to clarify his meaning, we may be prepared to look further for enlightenment from his metrical practice. In *A Valediction: of weeping* the first and second stanzas establish the underlying stress scheme of the third line as:

x / x / x / x / x /.

Now in the third stanza,

> O more then Moone,
> Draw not up seas to drowne me in thy spheare,
> Weepe me not dead, in thine armes, but forbeare
> To teach the sea, what it may doe too soone;
> Let not the winde
> Example finde,
> To doe me more harme, then it purposeth;
> Since thou and I sigh one anothers breath,
> Who e'r sighes most, is cruellest, and hastes the
> others death,

the natural prose reading of the third line gives / x x / x x / x x /, a very abrupt change of rhythm, and "not keeping of accent." It is clear that "Weepe" and "dead" and "armes" must have stress from their emphasis, but it is not impossible to include ictus in the speaking of the line. We then have / \ x / x \ / \ x /, which accords more nearly with the metrical pattern and also slightly adjusts the sense. If "me" and "thine" are given by ictus some slight degree of stress, then the line carries the extra implication of special poignancy in *her,* of all people, doing this to *him,* of all people. "W/eepe m\e not d/ead, in th\ine a/rmes, b\ut forbe/are" means more than the natural reading, and it means a "more" that is in keeping with the intent of this poem as of most of Donne's love poetry.

A clearer example occurs in *The Apparition.* If this is read with respect for the continuing rhythmical movement x /, which is clearly indicated, ictus will pick out for stress the pronouns of the first, second and third persons with a shocking insistence on the points of the ugly triangle. The poem ought to be read like this; until it is, it will never yield up the full painful force of its bitter threat. When it is so read, the sixth line has in it more than may be explained by the annotation that old superstition believed that a candle flickered in the presence of a ghost. It then gives also stress to "thy":

> Then *thy* sicke taper will begin to winke:

and thus concentrates the threat. As he has waned in his relations with and influence upon her, so must she wane in her influence upon the later lover. If the possibility of this meaning is doubted, it should be remembered that in *The Canonization,* Donne says, "We are Tapers too."

In these passages it is clear that care for the metrical form can clarify and deepen our understanding of Donne's meaning. It remains true that much of his lyric versification is irregular and difficult, but we ought at least to give it the chance of justifying itself as a container for his sense. Very often it will so justify itself, and when this occurs it gives the lie to the belief that Donne can write characteristically only when he tramples on form. When his form is followed, and allowed to make its contribution to meaning, it will be found, as in the examples given above, that its contribution is to give conviction and definition to our interpretation of his characteristic moods.

These three poets differ as widely from each other in the nature and effect of their work as any three poets well can who write in the same age. Their differences and their achievements are indicated by their metrical practices as surely as by their poetic statements. "The exact structure of his peculiar versification" is the embodiment of a poet's individual poetic nature.

walter jackson bate

KEATS'S ODES OF MAY, 1819

Until the time of the composition of the odes, Keats had employed conventional metrical and stanzaic forms which were immediately recognizable. He had in general confined himself to the couplet, blank verse, *ottava rima,* the Spenserian stanza, and, of course, the sonnet. In the remarkable journal-letter to his brother (February 14 to May 3, 1819), however, in which he enclosed the first of the odes, the *Ode to Psyche,* Keats revealed that he had been attempting a totally new stanzaic experiment.

During the month of April, Keats had composed two irregular sonnets, predominantly Shakespearean, but without either the three contiguous alternate rhyming quatrains or the concluding couplet: *To Sleep* (*ababcdcd bc efef*) and the second of the two sonnets *On Fame* (*ababcdcd efeggf*). He now expressed himself as dissatisfied with both the strict Petrarchan and the Shakespearean rhyme-schemes:

> I have been endeavouring to discover a better sonnet stanza than we have. The legitimate does not suit the language over-well from the pouncing rhymes—the other kind appears too elegiac—and the couplet at the end of it has seldom a pleasing effect—I do not pretend to have succeeded.[1]

He then copied out a newly-composed sonnet:

> If by dull rhymes our English must be chained,
> And, like Adromeda, the Sonnet sweet
> Fettered, in spite of painèd loveliness;
> Let us find out, if we must be constrained,
> Sandals more interwoven and complete
> To fit the naked foot of Poesy:
> Let us inspect the Lyre, and weigh the stress
> Of every chord, and see what may be gained
> By ear industrious, and attention meet;
> Misers of sound and syllable, no less

Reprinted from *The Stylistic Development of Keats* (New York, Humanities Press) pages 125–133, with the permission of the author and the publisher. Copyright 1958 Humanities Press Inc.

[1] *Letters,* p. 342.

> Than Midas of his coinage, let us be
> Jealous of dead leaves in the bay wreath crown;
> So, if we may not let the Muse be free,
> She will be bound with garlands of her own.

"I do not pretend to have succeeded,"[2] wrote Keats of this sonnet; and indeed, he wrote only three sonnets thereafter.[3] But it will be observed that this sonnet, of which the rhyme-scheme is *abcabdcabcdede,* like the other two sonnets of the same month, has neither the couplets of the Petrarchan octave, the concluding couplet of the Shakespearean form, nor the continued alternate-rhyming of the three successive Shakespearean quatrains.

Mr. H. W. Garrod,[4] in his analysis of the stanzaic structure of the *Ode to Psyche,* has advanced the suggestive conjecture that the ode-stanza of Keats was an outgrowth of the sonnet-form, and that in his construction of the stanza Keats succeeded in eliminating what he disliked in either form of the sonnet and yet at the same time retained from each what he considered of value. The soundness of Garrod's conjecture becomes more apparent with the analysis of all the ode-stanzas. Yet something may be added to what he says, and the connection of the ode-stanza with the sonnet may be even more firmly established.

Garrod assumes that the "legitimate" sonnet to which Keats refers is the Petrarchan, and that the "pouncing rhymes" to which he objects are the couplets of the Petrarchan octave. Such an assumption is certainly justified. Mr. M. R. Ridley, however, has questioned the equation of "legitimate" with Petrarchan:

> Now if that sentence [writes Ridley, referring to Keats's statement of his dissatisfaction with the sonnet form] ended at "effect," and was written by anyone but Keats, there could be no doubt of the way to take it; the dashes will mark a parenthesis and we shall have: "The legitimate does not suit the language over-well from the pouncing rhymes (the other kind appears too elegiac) and the couplet at the end of it has seldom a pleasing effect." . . . Keats uses the dash as a kind of perfunctory maid-of-all-work. . . . We can equally well assume that "the other kind appears too elegiac" is a parenthesis[5] in which Keats is dismissing the Petrarchan form from con-

[2] *Loc. cit.*

[3] The burlesque sonnet, "The House of Mourning" in the Petrarchan form, and the two Shakespearean sonnets, "The day is gone," and *To Fanny.*

[4] *Keats* (1926), pp. 85–90.

[5] As a matter of fact, Keats far more rarely employs dashes as parentheses than as periods, colons, or commas. Further, when Keats makes a sudden break within the body of the sentence, the dash he customarily uses is a short one elevated somewhat above the bottom level of the line; when he employs the dash as a period or semicolon, it is usually even shorter—scarcely more than an elongated dot at times—and placed at the lowest level of the line or else below it. The latter is the case with the dash appearing after "rhymes" (see the *ms.* in the Harvard Keats Memorial Collection); it is unquestionably intended to designate a full stop.

> sideration as he had almost entirely dismissed it from his practice. . . . Prima facie I should have supposed him a little more likely, in view of his adoption of the Shakespearean sonnet form to have described that form as the "legitimate" rather than the Petrarchan. "Elegiac" is a vague word on which to base much of a conclusion.

As for the "pouncing rhymes," they refer less to the couplets of the Petrarchan octave, says Mr. Ridley, than to the "rapid *tick-tack, tick-tack, tock-tuck, tock-tuck* of the alternating rhymes, often emphasized by the monosyllabic rhyme-words."[6]

The word "elegiac" would appear to have been a little more perplexing to critics of Keats than it should. It has usually been regarded as thematic in its reference, while Mr. Ridley believes that it denotes "the grave and sometimes almost melancholy sonority of the Petrarchan form."[7] From the middle of the eighteenth century until a century later, "elegiac" was commonly used in critical and prosodic writing to designate the pentameter *abab* quatrain.[8] Keats himself had employed the quatrain for his early elegiac stanzas *On Death.* In 1838, Guest, in his prosodic history, could still explicitly refer to the quatrain as the "elegiac stave" and add that the Shakespearean sonnet is simply a development of the "elegiac stave."[9] The use of the term is still occasionally found in present-day prosodic writing.

Mr. Ridley's belief that the term "legitimate" refers to the Shakespearean sonnet seems equally unwarranted. The sonnets of the eighteenth century were largely Petrarchan, or else variations from a Petrarchan basis; the Shakespearean form was usually considered a deviation from the norm. The epithets "legitimate" and "Petrarchan" were consequently used interchangeably in the prosodic writing of the eighteenth

6 Ridley, pp. 202–204. [M. R. Ridley, *Keats' Craftsmanship* (London: Oxford Press, 1933).]

7 P. 203.

8 Perhaps owing in part to its similarity to the classical "elegiac distich"—which, with its alternate hexameters and pentameters, produced a definite effect of alternate repetition—the pentameter quatrain, after Hammond's *Love Elegies* (1743), was almost invariably employed for the writing of elegiac verse. After the publication of the elegies of John Scott (1760) and Shenstone (1764), the quatrain ceased to be called "Hammond's meter" and was almost universally designated as the "elegiac quatrain." It was as such that it was employed in the elegies, for example, of Mickle, Graeme, Duncombe, Chatterton, and Cary; and when Blacklock, Langhorne, Jago, Smollett, and the pathetic Michael Bruce had elegies to compose, they followed custom and used the quatrain. Despite Johnson's questioning of the appropriateness of the stanza for elegy—"Why Hammond or other writers have thought the quatrain of ten syllables elegiac, it is difficult to tell" (*Life of Hammond, Lives,* ed. Hill [1905], II, 316)—the use of the stanza increased; sonneteers, like Charlotte Smith, who wrote upon elegiac themes, forsook the Petrarchan form and, in order to approximate the elegiac stave, employed the Shakespearean; Hayley, who had first used the quatrain for elegiac purposes in 1774, continued to do so; Bowles and Helen Maria Williams followed suit; and the 'nineties witnessed an output of elegies even more exclusively in the stanza—notably those of Southey.

9 *History of English Rhythms,* II, 377–378.

and early nineteenth centuries.[10] Leigh Hunt, for example, whose influence on Keats's sonnets from the beginning is very marked, employed the terms synonymously in his essay "On the Nature and Property of the Sonnet, Particularly the Sonnet Called the Legitimate."[11]

Keats, then, like Hunt before him,[12] wished to avoid, first, the hurry and snap of the couplets forming the Shakespearean conclusion and the "pouncing rhymes" of the Petrarchan octave, and, second, the continual alternate-rhyming of the three successive "elegiac staves" which form the body of the Shakespearean sonnet. Now it is plain that in his experiments in "How fever'd is the man," *To Sleep,* and particularly the sonnet enclosed in his letter, "If by dull rhymes," Keats is attempting, on the one hand, to do away with the "pouncing rhymes" of the couplets in the Petrarchan octave and of the concluding couplet in the Shakespearean sestet, and, on the other, to tighten and unify the sonnet by freeing it from the looseness which results from the successive alternate-rhyming quatrains of the Shakespearean form. The first of the odes, the *Ode to Psyche,* is constructed with a similar aim. Its first fourteen lines constitute an amended "Shakespearean" sonnet—*ababcdcdeffeef*—and is similar in rhyme-scheme to the first sonnet with which he experimented metrically, "How fevered is the man" (*ababcdcdefeggf*). The next lines are a broken series, consisting of a quatrain, two couplets, and a dangling line. The following twelve lines, which begin a new division of the ode, consist of a normal Shakespearean sonnet without the concluding couplet. The following fourteen lines are reminiscent in structure of the second of Keats's experiments with the sonnet, *To Sleep.* The rhyme-scheme of that sonnet had consisted of two quatrains, then two lines, apparently dangling but in reality repeating the rhymes of the first quatrain; and finally, a concluding quatrain. The rhyme-scheme of these fourteen lines in the third division of the *Ode to Psyche* consists of two quatrains, the second of which is *c d d c;* and following these, two lines, apparently dangling, but repeating rhymes in the preceding division of the ode, followed by a concluding quatrain, *e f e f.* The concluding division of the ode consists of an exact Shakespearean sonnet, with the

[10] Even so popular a sonneteer as Charlotte Smith, who writes for the public and not for poets and prosodists, could casually refer to the "legitimate" sonnet and be confident of being at once understood: she justifies her use of the Shakespearean form; for the "legitimate sonnet is ill calculated for our language" (*Elegiac Sonnets,* 1786, Preface, p. iii). Such was the case throughout Keats's own day and even afterwards: Tom Hood's *Rhymester* (ed. of 1882), for example, still maintained that the Petrarchan form alone is "regular and constant" (p. 86); and even the tolerant Edwin Guest considered the Shakespearean a "loose form," by the construction of which the legitimate sonnet had been "trifled with" (*History of English Rhythms,* II, 377).

[11] *Book of the Sonnet* (edd. Hunt and Lee, 1867), I, 8–15.

[12] Hunt had hardly used the Shakespearean form; but it is of some interest that in three of the six appearances of it in the *Juvenilia* (1801) the two concluding lines are not allowed to be couplets.

couplet removed from the end and placed after the octave in order to break the flow of the continual alternate-rhyming; and, following these fourteen lines, comes a terminating quatrain.

Now the metrical pattern of this ode is more complicated and irregular than that of the other odes. Yet there was nothing haphazard about its construction. Its stanzaic pattern was a very conscious one, and one with which Keats sought to satisfy a definite intention. "Let us," in attempting to improve the form of the sonnet, he had said in the last of his experimental sonnets, "If by dull rhymes,"—

> Let us find out, if we must be constrained,
> Sandals more interwoven and complete,
> To fit the naked foot of Poesy:
> Let us inspect the Lyre, and weigh the stress
> Of every chord, and see what may be gain'd
> By ear industrious, and attention meet;
> Misers of sound and syllable, no less
> Than Midas of his coinage . . .

He immediately afterwards turned to the writing of the *Ode to Psyche* and, before copying it out, wrote of it:

> The following Poem—the last I have written is the first and only one with which I have taken even moderate pains. I have for the most part dashed off my lines in a hurry. This I have done leisurely—I think it reads the more richly for it.[13]

Yet, despite the care he lavished on the construction of the *Ode to Psyche,* Keats perceived the unneeded complication of its metrical form. He desired a more regular and unified stanza, and devoted himself to developing one which consisted, in the main, of a single Shakespearean quatrain, *abab,* followed by a strictly Petrarchan sestet, *cdecde.* Such is the rhyme-pattern of the odes *To a Nightingale, On Melancholy,* and *On Indolence;*[14] that of the *Ode on a Grecian Urn* differs only in changing the sestets in the first and fifth stanzas to *cdedce* and in the second stanza to *cdeced.*

There is some evidence that, if he indeed developed his ode-stanza from the *disjecta membra* of the two sonnet-forms, Keats may also have had in mind the patterns used in his earlier ode, *Lines on Seeing a Lock of Milton's Hair,* in which he had reverted to rhyme-schemes common

[13] *Letters,* p. 339.

[14] The exceptions are few: the second stanza of the *Ode to a Nightingale* simply continues on with the *a*-rhyme (*abab cad cad*); the last stanza of the *Ode on Melancholy* has *abab cde dce;* the fifth stanza of the *Ode on Indolence* also has *abab cde dce,* and the sixth, *abab cde ced.*

in the odes of the preceding century.[15] This evidence, however, hardly discounts the fact that the ode-stanza which Keats now developed was an answer to his misgivings about the two sonnet-forms. The argument is not advanced here that the ode-stanza was necessarily that specific "better sonnet form" which Keats had said he was intending to devise. It is contended only that—whatever other reasons may have helped to dictate his abandonment of the sonnet for the ode—he was dissatisfied with both the Petrarchan and Shakespearean rhyme-schemes; that he was seeking

> Sandals more *interwoven* and *complete*
> To fit the naked foot of Poesy;

that what he desired to avoid in both sonnet-forms is absent in the ode-stanza as it was finally developed; and that other parts of the Petrarchan and Shakespearean sonnets are present in the stanza.

Keats, then, disliked the "pouncing rhymes" of the Petrarchan octave and of the Shakespearean final couplet because of the forced hurry and almost epigrammatic quickness of their effect. He preferred a more leisurely pace; "I think it reads the more richly for it," he said of the *Ode to Psyche*. He was aware, at the same time, of the tendency of the Shakespearean sonnet to fall into a sharp division of three quatrains and a couplet, with a resulting synthetic effect. He disliked, too, the laxity and "elegiac" languor which characterizes continual alternate-rhyming; his liking for a tightly-unified stanza had contributed largely to his having experimented as much as he did with *ottava rima* and the Spenserian stanza. It was his intention to devise a stanzaic medium which would be at once slow in movement, without the hurried

[15] Mr. N. S. Bushnell, "Notes on Professor Garrod's *Keats,*" *M.L.N.*, XLIV (1929), 287–196, has pointed out that the first stanza of this poem possesses a rhyme-scheme (*ababccdeed*) also found in Gray, Akenside, Smart, and Langhorne; that the rhyme-scheme of its last stanza (*ababcddcee*) is found in an ode—written, I believe, by William Richardson of Sheffield—which is in Pearch's *Collection;* and that these rhyme-schemes rather than those of the two sonnet-forms were very likely in Keats's mind when he turned to the odes of May, 1819. But rhyme-scheme alone is not very important in fixing form unless coupled with similarity of line-length. The *ababccdeed* pattern was indeed a popular eighteenth-century ode-form, and to the names of previous employers one might add those of Swift, Percy, John and Walter Scott, Wordsworth and others. (Indeed, the use of an ode-stanza composed of four alternate-rhyming lines followed by six others which assume a pattern not unlike a Petrarchan sestet has always been common. *Cf.*, for example, *ababcdcdee,* in Browne's *Shepherd's Pipe*, Spenser's *Epigram IV*, Herbert's *Church Rents and Schisms*, Carew's *Deposition from Love*, and, afterwards, used by Young, Chatterton, Hunt, Willis, Moore, and Mrs. Hemans. Tom Moore, again, uses simply *abab cdcdcd* ["From this hour"]; Mrs. Hemans uses *abab cde dec;* and following Herbert (*The Pearl*) both Campbell and Moore employed *abab ccdede.* The pattern Mr. Bushnell cites from Pearch's *Collection* is a very infrequent one, but in accordance with the same principle of ode-construction.) But all of these ode-patterns were extremely irregular in length, as were the forms used in the *Lines on Seeing a Lock of Milton's Hair.* If precedent must be found, more warrant is forthcoming in simply establishing connection with the Augustan ten-line pentameter ode, with its concluding Alexandrine, the rhyme-scheme *abab cdcdee,* and used, for example, by Lowth, Denton, Boyse, Whitehead, Chatterton, and later Mrs. Hemans.

"pouncing rhymes" of the couplet, and at the same time unified, closely-knit, and restraining in effect—a stanza truly "more interwoven and complete," and one of which "the rise, the progress," would be slow and satisfying, by no means leaving "the reader breathless instead of content," and which at last "sets soberly although in magnificence." "I think Poetry," Keats had written to Taylor more than a year before,

> Should surprise by a fine excess and not by Singularity. . . . Its touches of Beauty should never be half way thereby making the reader breathless instead of content: the rise, the progress, the setting of imagery should like the Sun come natural to him—shine over him and set soberly although in magnificence leaving him in the luxury of twilight.[16]

The evolution of this stanza, which restrains the fullness of Keats's lines and strengthens his luxury, is in itself almost the *ne plus ultra* of that striving for a heavily weighted and condensed completeness of presentation which characterizes in so large a measure the entire stylistic development of Keats after *Isabella,* and through which he sought to satisfy his yearning for an almost physically felt intensity of image and sound. But the development of this stanza was only a part of Keats's prosodic attainment in that notable month in the late spring of 1819. For Keats's inherent and even sensuous craving for a ripe and heavily laden completeness led him also, as never before, to employ a rhythm and draw upon a diction the very phonetic qualities of which would heighten the richness of his stanzas and, at the same time, to make use of whatever metrical means would achieve a classical rigor and severity of structure. . . .

[16] Feb. 27, 1818, *Letters,* p. 108.

5510